Post-war Britain, 1945–64

Post-war Britain, 1945–64

Themes and Perspectives

Edited by Anthony Gorst, Lewis Johnman and W. Scott Lucas

Published in Association with
The Institute of Contemporary British History

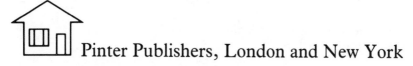 Pinter Publishers, London and New York

© The Institute of Contemporary British History, 1989

First published in Great Britain in 1989 by
Pinter Publishers Limited
25 Floral Street, London WC2E 9DS

British Library Cataloguing in Publication Data

A CIP catalogue record for this book is available from the
British Library

ISBN 0-86187-760-8

Library of Congress Cataloging-in-Publication Data

Postwar Britain, 1945–64 : themes and perspectives / edited by Anthony
    Gorst, Lewis Johnman, and W. Scott Lucas.
      p.   cm.
    Collection of articles delivered in outline at the Institute of
Contemporary British History's first summer school in July 1988.
    Bibliography: p.
    Includes index.
    ISBN 0-86187-760-8
    1. Great Britain—History—George VI, 1936–1952.   2.   Great
Britain—History—Elizabeth II, 1952–   I.   Gorst, Anthony.
II.   Johnman, Lewis.   III.   Lucas, W. Scott.   IV.   Institute of
Contemporary British History.
DA588.P67   1989
941.085—dc20   89-4017
                                                                            CIP

Typeset by Florencetype Ltd, Kewstoke, Avon
Printed and bound in Great Britain by
SRP Limited, Exeter

Contents

List of Contributors

Patrick Bennar was formerly Deputy Secretary at the Department of Health and Social Security.

Peter Catterall is a Research Fellow of the Institute of Contemporary British History.

Dr Justin Davis Smith is currently head of Research at the Volunteer Centre UK.

Anthony Gorst is a modern historian working in London.

Eric Grove is associate Director of the Foundation for International Security.

Dr Sarah Harper is a Lecturer in Geography at Royal Holloway and Bedford New College, University of London.

Dr Lewis Johnman is a Lecturer in Economic History at Thames Polytechnic, London.

W. Scott Lucas is a senior Lecturer in the School of History, University of Leeds.

Professor David Marquand is a Professor in Contemporary History and Politics at the University of Salford.

Dr Roger Middleton is a Lecturer in Economic and Social History at the University of Bristol.

G. Wyn Rees is a Lecturer in the Department of Defence and International Affairs, Royal Military Academy, Sandhurst.

Tillman Remme is a freelance historian and journalist working in London.

Dr Anthony Seldon is Co-Director of the Institute of Contemporary British History.

Dr Simon Stevenson is currently Lecturer in British and European Social History at Griffith University.

Dr A.J. Stockwell is a Senior Lecturer in History at Royal Holloway and Bedford New College, University of London.

Preface

Anthony Seldon

Many of the articles in this collection were delivered in outline at the Institute of Contemporary British History's first summer school at the LSE in July 1988. The summer school attracted a wide audience, and it is hoped that this book will prove of value to those who attended and to the rapidly growing numbers in the UK and abroad who are studying in depth post-war Britain.

The editors chose to include these chapters in the book so as to provide a cross-section of the main interests of the summer school and indeed of the ICBH. Chapters thus cover political themes (the consensus), economic (Keynesian legacy), social (welfare state), colonial (Malaya), defence (naval policy) and international (Suez). The book contains not only articles, but also examples of two features of the summer school, a debate and a contribution from an official who witnessed the evolution of policy from the inside. One of the benefits of contemporary history is the opportunity it affords for historians to learn firsthand from those who helped make history.

The ICBH was founded in October 1986 with the objective of promoting at every level the study of British history since 1945. To that end it publishes books and a quarterly journal, *Contemporary Records*; it organizes seminars and conferences for sixth formers, undergraduates, researchers and teachers of post-war history; and it runs a number of research programmes and other activities.

A central belief of the ICBH's work is that post-war history is too often neglected in schools, institutes of higher education and beyond. The ICBH acknowledges the validity of the arguments against the study of recent history, notably the problems of bias, of overly subjective teaching and writing, and the difficulties of perspective. But it believes that the values of studying post-war history outweigh the drawbacks, and that the health and future of a liberal democracy require that its citizens know more about the most recent past of their country than the limited knowledge possessed by British citizens, young and old, today. Indeed, the ICBH believes that the dangers of political indoctrination are higher where the young are *not* informed of the recent past.

This volume offers an important addition to the scholarly literature on postwar Britain, and it is hoped that it will be one of several such books produced under the auspices of the ICBH.

1 The decline of post-war consensus

David Marquand

(Adapted from a seminar paper given at the Institute of Historical Research, February 1988)

My book, *The Unprincipled Society*,[1] was intended to contribute to a debate about the present state of British politics, as well as to a debate about the recent past. In this article I focus on the parts of the book relating to the recent past and and even the more distant past, rather than on the parts dealing with the present and the possible future. The historical parts of the book addressed two central questions. Why was it that, despite great initial successes, the post-war governing philosophy of this country—'Keynesian social democracy' as I called it—failed to overcome the problems of the 1960s and the 1970s and, as a result, collapsed in humiliation in the closing years of the 1974 Labour government? On a deeper level, why were the economic problems facing the post-war 'Keynesian social democrats' so deep-seated? Why, to put the same question in different words, had the British economy suffered a long period of relative decline even before the problems of the 1960s and 1970s made themselves manifest?

Collapse of consensus

I begin with the first of my two questions: why did the post-war consensus collapse in failure in the late 1960s and 1970s? It can, of course, be argued that there was no such thing as a post-war consensus. After all, the two great parties differed profoundly over the distribution of income and the nature of political authority. How could there be a consensus between them. The answer, I believe, is that their differences were fought out within a framework of common assumptions about the role of the state and the management of the economy. The question, then, is why did that framework break down? Two sets of answers have been dominant in the recent past, one given by the New Right, the other by the New Left. These sets of answers overlap; in many ways, they are mirror images of each other. Both say, in essence, that Keynesian social democracy collapsed because it was bound to collapse. It was a philosophy of the middle way, and there cannot be a middle way. It was a philosophy of the mixed economy, and the mixed economy is doomed by its internal contradictions. The whole attempt to find a synthesis between traditional capitalism and traditional socialism will always, and by definition, fail. More particularly both the New Right and, in a rather different way, the New Left have put at the centre of their answers a series of propositions relating to what came, in the jargon of the 1970s, political science, to be called 'overload'.

The New Right thesis

The New Right, in particular held that Keynesian demand management was inherently inflationary. It worked by buying off the inflationary pressures generated by over-mighty trade unions. For a while, Keynesian demand management could keep up the level of demand, and therefore the level of employment, in the way that Keynes had proposed. Sooner or later, however, the trade unions would grow accustomed to the going rate of inflation, and force real wages even higher, in order to compensate for the inflation produced by the first set of demand-boosting measures. Then the economic managers in Whitehall would have to pump yet more demand into the economy so as to buy off these new pressures, and so on, in an inexorable inflationary spiral. According to this argument the consequence must be unemployment of a more or less catastrophic level. All Keynesian pump priming can do is to postpone the evil day. The longer it is postponed, the more evil it will be when it finally comes. For the real cause of unemployment is not deficient demand at all. It is the distortions in the labour market created by trade union pressure. So the only real solution is to tame the unions.

Secondly, and more interestingly for people studying politics and contemporary history, the New Right hold that another kind of inflationary spiral is at work as well: an inflationary spiral which results from the nature of democratic politics. Democratic politics, according to this argument, should be seen as a peculiar kind of market. The political parties are like entrepreneurs: the policies are like the goods that entrepreneurs try to sell, and the voters are like consumers. But there is an important difference between the vote market and real markets. In a real market the consumer operates within a budget constraint. If he wishes to buy more of one good, he has to buy less of another good. He makes his own judgements in the market place under this discipline. But in the vote market no such discipline operates. If you, the voter, buy an expensive policy, other people will pay the price of your decision. You will have to pay only a very tiny part of it. In the vote market, it is not rational to behave in a prudent way; it is *more* rational to opt for the most expensive policies. The voter is like a member of a party of friends dining in an expensive restaurant who have agreed that they will share the bill equally between them. In such circumstances it will not pay you to opt for the cheapest items on the menu. Others may choose expensive ones, and if they do, you will end up by subsidising them. The most sensible thing to do is to order the caviar and champagne.

According to this argument, voters, in a democratic system of competitive party politics, are driven by the dynamics of the system to demand more and more, while the politicians are driven by the same dynamics to promise more and more. For in the vote market expensive policies sell best. Because of all this, democratic policies have a built-in tendency to economic overload. Governments constantly try to do more than they can, or should. They pay for their exaggerated ambitions by printing money. That leads to inflation, and inflations lead to yet more demands, yet more promises, yet more exaggerated ambitions and yet more inflation.

Another part of the overload thesis says that not only is the vote market, the 'demand side' of the political equation, inherently inflationary but so too is the supply side. The supply side is inherently inflationary because the bureaucrats who actually determine the size of government (the politicians do not really control the bureaucrats in this mode) operate, just like everybody else, to maximize their own interests. 'Bureaucrats', says Gordon Tullock, a theorist of the public-choice school of economists which developed these arguments, 'are like other men'. They pursue their own interests. There is nothing surprising or odd about that; so does everybody else. But, whereas the disciplines of the market ensure that entrepreneurs who pursue their own interests also serve the interests of society at large, this is not true of the bureaucracy. In the bureaucracy, you maximize your profits by maximizing the size of your bureau. So there is an in-built tendency, within the goverment machine itself, for that machine to grow.

Finally, some overload theorists have offered a more complicated cultural argument. This says that, for a variety of reasons, a variety of cultural changes took place throughout the western world in 1960s and 1970s. As a result, traditional attitudes and traditional forms of social control started to crumble. The famous 1975 report on the governability of democracies to the so-called Trilateral Commission put this argument rather powerfully.[2] According to the report, a 'democratic surge' led all kinds of excluded groups—women, blacks and other ethnic minorities—to demand a place in the sun. In doing so, they put strains on the system with which it could not cope. Their demands could be satisfied only through the same sort of inflationary process that the other overload models posit.

That is, of course, a grossly over-simplified account of the New Right's interpretation of the collapse of 'Keynesian social democracy', but I think it is reasonably fair. And that account is not confined to the New Right. Echoes of it can be found in neo-Marxism writings as well. The theory of the fiscal crisis for example, which was first developed by American Marxists and then brought over to Britain, has obvious echoes of the New Right's thesis.

Criticism of the New Right thesis

That thesis has a double significance in contemporary British history. It provided the intellectual basis for the agenda around which British politics have revolved for most of the last decade. Secondly, it provides an ideal starting point for an attempt to offer an alternative interpretation of the recent past, whilst at the same time demonstrating, albeit unintentionally, that such an alternative is badly needed.

For the plain fact is that the New Right thesis does not stand up. It simply is not true. The most authoritative studies of voting behaviour in the 1960s and 1970s suggest that the inflationary vote market did not exist; voters were not voting in an undisciplined fashion for the most inflationary policies on offer. If anything, they were rather sceptical when politicans made inflationary promises to them, and thought the economy was likely to perform rather worse than the politicans said it would do if they gained power. Some of the Butler/Stokes findings about the 1960s, it is true, suggest that the level of unemployment was a very important factor determining the level of support for the government of the day.[3] But that does not support the neo-liberal overload thesis. What the electors were doing was rewarding the governments which they thought had performed well in the past, while punishing governments which they thought had performed badly. It offers no support for the theory that they were falling for promises for the future. And it is crucial to the overload argument that they should have done so.

More importantly, it is not possible to correlate any constructable index of overload with economic performance. To be sure, there are difficulties here. In theory, it might be possible to define overload—and the consequent expansion in the role of the state—in terms of subtle changes in attitudes and values which could not be measured in figures. I must confess, however, that such a definition would seem to me suspect. And what the figures show is that there is no correlation between the absolute share of the gross domestic product (GDP) going to public expenditure, or the rate of increase in the share, on the one hand, and the performance of the economy on the other. Some economies which devote higher proportions of GDP than Britain to public expenditure have performed better than the British. Japan devotes a much lower proportion; and, of course, also does a lot better than Britain. Yet, if overload cannot be measured either by the absolute share of GDP going to public expenditure or by the rate of increase in the share, it is difficult to see what the notion can mean.

Much the same applies to the Hayekian argument about the economically dysfunctional role of organized labour. According to that argument, trade unions, by distorting the Labour market, misallocating resources and thus causing inflation, make the economy perform less well than it otherwise would. Yet some countries where the proportion of the eligible population enrolled in trade unions is higher than in Britain, for example Austria and Sweden, enjoyed a markedly better economic performance than Britain. Similarly, some economies where the proportion is lower also performed markedly better. Nor is there any correlation between trade union strength and the rate of inflation. Germany has powerful trade unions and has, on the whole, enjoyed a much lower rate of inflation than Britain, right through the post-war period.

As for the cultural explanation, Britain's culture was rather conservative by comparison with others in the 1960s and 1970s, and was rather slow to change. If by this cultural change what is meant is growth of 'post-materialism' — the placing of new non-materialistic demands on the political agenda (the demand for greater participation, stronger environmental protection, women's rights, and so forth) — then Britain had less of it than most other developed countries, at least in Europe.

Institutional crisis and the failure of corporatism

For all these reasons, the New Right's interpretation of the crisis which destroyed the Keynesian social democratic consensus of the post-war period seems to me to fail. Where should we look for an alternative? I believe we should look at two interconnected developments. Firstly, it seems to me that in the 1960s and 1970s this country suffered a genuine institutional crisis, in the sense that it became progressively more difficult for governments to mobilize consent for the policies they thought necessary to manage the economy by and through the institutions of the British state. Britain did not, as some observers imagined, become ungovernable. She did, however, become a great deal more difficult to govern. Governability was visibly ebbing in the winter of 1973–4 when the Heath government fell, having failed to secure compliance with its incomes policy. It ebbed again during the spring and summer of 1975, when inflation and wage claims were roaring ahead and a weak and insecure Labour government looked on. It ebbed most obviously in the notorious 'winter of discontent' of 1978–9, which brought that government to its knees. The institutions of the British state buckled in the face of the tasks they were trying to perform.

This leads on to the second set of developments. I do not believe that close relationships between government and the organized employers and organized labour are inherently likely to damage the economy. In many countries with such relationships economic performance has been a great deal better than in Britain. It can hardly be disputed, however, that the attempts made by the British governments of the 1960s and 1970s to achieve such relationships, and to manage the economy through them, were not successful. Despite all sorts of experiments in tripartism, government could not get the organized producer groups to do what it wanted. As the failure of successive attempts to raise the level of investment makes clear, this was as true of organized capital as organized labour. And, as everyone knows, the trade unions, despite protestations of goodwill at the beginning of successive incomes policies, usually broke away in the end, leaving those policies in ruins.

At this point, the first of my two opening questions—why did post-war Keynesian social democracy collapse?—intersects with the second, why did Britain suffer a long period of relative economic decline *before* the post-war period began? It is clear that the economic problems facing British governments in the 1960s and 1970s were, in a host of ways, more obdurate than those facing their continental and Japanese counterparts; that the British economy was more vulnerable to the shocks which disturbed the entire industrial world in the 1970s than were most competing economies. It is clear too that this special British vulnerability goes a long way to explain the economic and political failures which brought the Keynesian social democratic era to a close.

Why, then, was Britain so vulnerable? The key, I believe, lies in the long period of relative economic decline which began in the last quarter of the nineteenth century. The two gravediggers of post-war Keynesian social democracy—the failure of the British version of neo-corporatist tripartism and the institutional crisis to which that failure gave rise—were the products of a deeper malaise of the political economy, the roots of which can be traced back for nearly 100 years. It follows that, if we are to understand why Keynesian social democracy collapsed, we must try to understand the origins and nature of that malaise.

The role of the state

I believe that the task should be approached in the following way. Everywhere in the developed world, the state has played a crucial part in helping the economy to adjust to changes in the world market. Even early in the industrial revolution in Britain, the state played a crucial facilitating role. In virtually all other industrial countries, it played a much larger one. Ronald Dore has drawn a contrast between the 'developmental' and 'regulatory' state. According to him all modern states, at least in the developed world, are 'regulatory' in the sense that they regulate economic activities in order to protect the vulnerable from abuses of market power. Some are also 'developmental', in the sense that they try to develop the capacity of the national economy to compete in a cut-throat world economy.

The 'developmental state' has to do two things above all. It has to establish close relations with economic actors, in order to steer market forces in the direction that it wants them to take. Secondly, it has to answer, more or less explicitly, a crucial distributional question, which is central to the process of development. Economic development will always produce losers as well as gainers. Somebody has to allocate those gains and losses. In a pure market system this is done by the market. Under a 'developmental state', it is done through politics. Voters—or some of them, at any rate—are bought off; losses are, so to speak, socialized. From a narrowly economic point of view, resources will probably be allocated less efficiently than they otherwise would have been. But, provided the state is vigilant in pursuit of its developmental goals and does not allow itself to be deflected from them into a nostalgic defence of the economic status quo, the economic benefits of social peace outweigh the costs in allocative efficiency.

Against that background, Britain's long decline becomes easier to understand. If market-led adjustment is to take place, two things have to happen: the losers, or potential losers, have to be denied political leverage; and the ideology of market liberalism has to be generally accepted, so that the outcomes which the market produces are regarded as fair. If neither of these two things happens, then market-led adjustment will not take place. If the losers have political leverage they will use it to resist adjustment; if the ideology of market liberalism is not accepted, market outcomes will not be regarded as just, and the process will not be seen as legitimate.

Early-nineteenth-century Britain was the classic example of market-led adjustment. She was not a democracy. Losers were, by and large, excluded from the political process. The ideology of market liberalism carried all before it, despite occasional voices in the wings complaining about its consequences. As time went on, however, Britain slowly became a democracy, and the ideology of market liberalism slowly lost its hold. The preconditions for market-led adjustment thus disappeared. Elsewhere, notably in Imperial Germany and to some extent even in the professedly market-liberal United States, a 'developmental' state tried deliberately to modernize the economy in the interests of national power and autonomy. But in Britain the demise of market-led adjustment was not followed by the emergence of a 'developmental' state. Though the state intervened in the economy, it did so to protect the existing pattern of economic activity, not to change it. The question is, why? Why, after abandoning market-led adjustment, did Britain not become a 'developmental' state on the pattern of her more successful competitors?

Failure of a developmental state to evolve

It is a more complex question than may appear at first sight. On repeated occasions in the last century or so, political leaders have tried to move towards the 'developmental' model. The first was perhaps Joseph Chamberlain. It is true, of course, that many of his assumptions pointed in a rather different direction. There was a conservative, defensive aspect to his campaign for tariff reform, which is alien to the notion of a developmental state. Imperial preference was intended to keep foreign competition out of Britain's existing markets, not to equip her to capture new markets or to develop new products and processes. Other aspects, however, did coincide with the developmental model. He sought, quite explicitly, to use the power of the state to strengthen the economy. He also tried to construct a cross-class coalition of social forces, capable of settling the distributional question which lies at the heart of the politics of economic change in a way which would command majority support. And, of course, he failed.

Similar attempts were made in the late 1920s and early 1930s by David Lloyd George and Oswald Mosley. Both of them groped for a version of the developmental state; both also tried to construct cross-class political coalitions for economic change. Both of them failed too. The pattern was repeated in more recent times. In the early 1960s, Harold Wilson attempted to mobilize new social groups under Labour's banner, in the name of the 'white hot heat' of technological change; in the early 1970s, Edward Heath also tried, in some respects at any rate, to tread where Lloyd George and Mosley had sought to tread 40 years before. As everyone knows, Wilson and Heath failed as well.

Why this succession of failures? It is fashionable to assume that the roots of Britain's economic decline must, by definition, lie in the abandonment of the market-led model of economic development. That assumption underpins both Corelli Barnett's belief that Britain's post-war economic troubles can be attributed to the welfare consensus developed under the wartime coalition[4] and Martin Wiener's suggestion that their roots lie in a 'counter-revolution of values' in the middle and late nineteenth century, which unmanned Britain's political and economic élites and turned the children of the hard-driving, profit-maximizing early Victorian entrepreneurs into genteel, classics-imbued humanitarians or pseudo-squires.[5] The trouble with that assumption, however, is that, as suggested above, most of Britain's more successful competitors had never adopted the market-led model in the first place. If we are to find a satisfactory explanation, then, we must dig deeper.

The true explanation, I believe, is that the ethos of market liberalism survived even after the doctrines were abandoned: that attitudes and values which had provided the foundation for, and had, in turn, been enormously fortified by, the triumphs of market liberalism in the early nineteenth century lingered on into a time when the circumstances which had made those triumphs possible had vanished. In the age of the chemical plant, and even of the computer, Britain's industrial, economic and political cultures were still suffused with assumptions born of the age of steam.

Cultural conservatism

Three aspects of this strange paradox of cultural conservatism deserve particular attention. In the first place, one reason why a succession of British political leaders failed to construct a 'developmental' state is that—in striking contrast to those of Japan and most of continental Europe—Britain's political culture has been inimical to the growth of a state tradition. The very notion of the state, of a public power standing apart from private interests and pursuing the collective purposes of the whole society, is alien to the British political tradition. It is true, of course, that the odd intellectual has sometimes flirted with it. The Hegelian idealists of the late nineteenth century provide the most obvious cases in point. But these flirtations have never resonated in the wider society. Hegelian idealism was intellectually fashionable for a while, but British attitudes to, and assumptions about, the state were affected only marginally, if at all.

The second aspect of Britain's cultural conservatism is more complex. As I tried to show above, one of the chief reasons why the post-war Keynesian social democrats failed to cope with the economic problems confronting them was that they could not establish satisfactory relationships with the organized producer groups. One reason for that failure is that British producer groups have been too fragmented, too undisciplined and too narrowly concerned with the immediate interests of their own clienteles to sustain the sorts of relationship which have characterized the political economies of Scandinavia and central Europe. One of the reasons why British producer groups have been narrow, fragmented and undisciplined is that they, too, have been shaped by the market-liberal ethos of the early nineteenth century: by the attitudes and values of the same 'possessive individualism' which was inhibited the growth of a state tradition.

That leads on to the third aspect of our cultural conservatism. One reason why successive British politicians failed to construct a cross-class coalition for economic change lies in the curious nature of Britain's class relations. On one level, of course, these relations have been comparatively peaceful. The Marxist notion of the class war has never appealed to more than a fraction of the British working class; by the same token, the British upper classes have never been as intransigent in the defence of their privileges as some of their continental equivalents have been. But although we have not experienced an open, Marxist-style hot war between labour and capital, we have undoubtedly experienced a strange, sometimes almost subterranean, cold war, and it is at least arguable that the economic costs of the latter have been much greater than those of the former. I suspect that the roots of this subterranean cold war are to be found in the late-nineteenth-century switch from 'active' to 'passive' property which Harold Perkin has described so well in *The Origins of Modern English Society*.[6] And, as Perkin himself suggests, that too is intimately related to the 'possessive individualism' which runs through our whole culture.

Notes

1. Marquand, D. (1988) *The Unprincipled Society: New Demands and Old Politics*, Jonathan Cape.
2. Crozier, M. *et al.* (1987) *The Crisis of Democracy: Report on the Governability of Democracies to the Trilateral Commission*, New York University Press.
3. Butler, D. and Stokes, D. (1969) *Political Change in Britain*, Macmillan.
4. Barnett, C. (1986) *The Audit of War. The Illusion and Reality of Britain as a Great Nation*, Macmillan.
5. Wiener, Martin J. (1981) *English Culture and the Decline of the Industrial Spirit*, Cambridge University Press.
6. Perkin, H. (1972) *The Origins of Modern English Society 1780–1880*, paperback edn. Routledge and Kegan Paul.

COMMENTARY ONE

Andrew Gamble

The Unprincipled Society is an important book, the most sophisticated and illuminating analysis of Britain's problems from a social democratic perspective to have appeared in the last twenty years. Social democrats have often been on the defensive in the recent past, obliged to defend the mixed economy and the institutions and policies of the 1940s settlement from the criticisms of the New Right and the New Left. Many questions which were thought to have been settled by Anthony Crosland in *The Future of Socialism* in 1956 have been reopened.

Marquand acknowledges that the post-war consensus collapsed in the 1970s and that many of the policies and doctrines associated with it, such as Keynesianism, were discredited. But he rejects the idea that the causes of this failure can be attributed to the social democratic regime itself. Rather he ascribes its failure to its incompleteness. The structure and ethos of the political institutions which had been created during the nineteenth century undermined and ultimately destroyed the social democratic project.

Marquand, like Perry Anderson and Martin Wiener, seeks the origins of Britain's relative economic decline in the structures and legacies bequeathed from earlier historical development. In contrast to the emphasis which Anderson places on class and Wiener on culture, Marquand focuses on politics and the nature of the British state. It is the absence of a state tradition in Britain, he believes, which prevented the conversion of the nineteenth-century regulative state into a developmental state capable of reversing Britain's relative economic decline.

The notion of a developmental state is crucial to Marquand's argument. Social democracy required a strong executive democratic state. Instead the attempt was made to implement the social democratic programme through the mechanisms of the existing state. The ethos of market liberalism which had become so strong in the nineteenth century was never successfully challenged. Britain needed a cultural revolution comparable to the revolution which accompanied the industrial revolution, but never achieved it.

Marquand concedes that market-led adjustment and a regulatory state were very successful in the nineteenth century. But he argues that Martin Wiener and Corelli Barnett are quite wrong to think that the roots of economic decline lie in the abandonment of the market-led model of economic development: the market-led model has never been abandoned. In a crucial passage in his book, he states that in Britain 'the reaction against full-blooded market liberalism took place under the same philosophical aegis as the movement towards it' (p. 223). The contrast between collectivism and individualism is a contrast within a single tradition of thought and practice.

Implicit in this account is the belief that market liberalism must be buttressed either by authoritarian government, to deny the losers from market exchange political leverage, or by social consensus on the fairness of market outcomes. Neither of those two conditions could be maintained once organized capitalism and mass democracy developed. An active interventionist state to promote economic growth and to create a consensus on distribution of income and life-changes was increasingly needed.

For Marquand there is no way back to the society of market liberalism. To the extent that the project of the New Right succeeds, it will reintroduce the kinds of problem that created the crisis of market liberalism after 1880. The socialist solution is equally unreal. There is no alternative to trying to make the mixed economy work and developing a style of active intervention and co-operation between public and private agencies.

Marquand makes his case forcefully and eloquently. But some questions remain. He is right to point out that some of the popular versions of New Right criticisms of social democracy are easily exploded. But it is not easy to dispose of the insights of the New Right into the problems of modern government, such as their analysis of the pressures for more and more areas of decision-making to become subject to political negotiation and the influence of well-organized lobbies, and the tendency for the benefits of state spending to go disproportionately to middle- and upper-income groups.

The shortcomings of the British version of social democracy make plausible the attempt to return to market-led adjustment, restricting the scope of state activity and responsibility in the economy and encouraging a greater role for enterprise and independence. The protagonists of popular capitalism have their own ideals of participation and citizenship to set against those of social democracy. They have their own vision of One Nation. They are engaged, rather successfully at present, in building their own cross-class coalition. After the disappointing results of British collectivism, a return to the individualist strand of the tradition may seem overdue.

Marquand is right to argue that British individualism and British collectivism remain part of the liberal ethos and will never regenerate an effective developmental state. It is difficult to see, however, the means by which this developmental state is to be brought into existence. If Joseph Chamberlain, David Lloyd George, Oswald Mosley, Harold Wilson and Edward Heath all failed to make headway against the traditions and institutions of the existing state, why should this change? What new circumstances will make it change?

Many early critics of the revival of market liberalism in Britain believed it could only be temporary: the tensions and conflicts created would threaten the stability of the social order and lead at last to the radical transformation of institutions, structures and culture for which reformers in Britain have been waiting so long.

In one sense Marquand is plainly right. It is not hard to see the outlines of a new agenda for the 1990s that relegates the cruder forms of market liberalism to the sidelines and puts much greater emphasis on state action in guiding development and creating consensus. There are post-Thatcherite spokesmen in all parties proclaiming such ideas. But there is nothing inevitable about their triumph, and they are likely in their turn to prove just as ineffective as the modernizers of the 1960s if they are unable to change the character of the British state.

There are also other possibilities. Marquand's prognosis may belong too much to the era of organized capitalism and national economies. With the growing pace of internationalization, the behaviour of world markets supplies ever tighter constraints for national policy making, with important consequences for domestic political structures and parties. Is it perhaps possible that we are moving into a new era where regulative rather than developmental state forms will work better in promoting the next stage of capitalist development?

The evidence is contradictory. It is possible that the European Community will evolve public agencies with some of the capacities of a developmental state which will give to Britain some of the things its own state has failed to provide. At the same time the unmistakable emergence of an underclass and the increasing erosion of the social rights associated with the social democratic ideal of citizenship have so far proved compatible with the maintenance of order and political consent. There may be more ways than one to ensure the legitimacy and reproduction of the contemporary capitalist order. The ideal of a developmental state was immensely important in its time, but that time may now have passed.

COMMENTARY TWO

Peter Clarke

David Marquand is surely right to argue that consensus does not imply perfect harmony or the absence of serious political disagreement, but provides a framework within which other important arguments can take place. It is arguable that *some* kind of consensus always exists to prevent the disintegration of civil society. But the consensus of the 1950s and 1960s had a peculiarly large social and economic content. As Anthony Crosland put it at the time: 'Many liberal-minded people . . . have now concluded that "Keynes-plus-modified-capitalism-plus-Welfare-State" works perfectly well' —though he himself was not endorsing this as a sufficient political creed (Crosland, 1964: 79). There will be little disagreement about what Marquand conveniently identifies as the four planks of the consensus which has now broken down: (1) full employment, (2) the welfare state, (3) the mixed economy and (4) interventionist micro-economic policies. But their relative importance and degree of mutual coherence can be appraised by considering the historical pedigree of each in turn.

The commitment to 'a high and stable level of employment after the war' in the famous White Paper of 1944, issued by Churchill's Coalition Government, was fundamental. Not only was it significant in itself, but it also interlocked, tongue and groove, with the second plank. Sir William Beveridge, rightly considered as the major architect of the welfare state, well understood this from the outset, as can be seen from his eponymous report back in 1942. The Beveridge Plan for social security explicitly assumed that it would be buttressed through children's allowances and a comprehensive health service (including rehabilitation). His third assumption, that full employment would be maintained, was in many ways more far-reaching—indeed some would now say far-fetched. It should, however, be noted that the actuarial assumption made here was for an overall level of unemployment of 8.5 per cent (though Beveridge himself soon became converted to a target of 3 per cent). What it required, the report explained, was 'not the abolition of all unemployment, but the abolition of mass unemployment and of unemployment prolonged year after year for the same individual' (Beveridge, 1942, par. 441).

Beveridge adduced five reasons for this contention. One was that cash payments, while suitable for tiding workers over, would, in the longer term, have a demoralizing effect. Another was that it became impossible to test unemployment by an offer of work if there were no work to offer. The availability of work, moreover, actively drew in people who would otherwise lapse into debility. These three reasons were concerned with the working of a social insurance scheme, 'Fourth, and most important,' Beveridge continued, 'income security which is all that can be given by social insurance is so inadequate a provision for human happiness that to put it forward by itself as a sole or principal measure of reconstruction hardly seems worth doing.' Participation in productive employment, he suggested, was a great end in itself—reinforcing the theme that mere cash subsistence support on a dole could never be regarded as a psychologically adequate or morally civilized substitute. Finally, Beveridge pointed to the heavy cost of his plan warning that 'if to the necessary cost waste is added, it may become insupportable'. For unemployment simultaneously increased claims while depleting available resources (Beveridge, 1942, par. 440). Beveridge had his mind upon the problems of the 1930s; but there is a cogency to this argument which is by no means lost in the 1980s.

The welfare state can thus be seen as a predestined victim of the failure to maintain full employment. This line of causation, of course, has often been inverted in recent years, in suggesting that the guarantee of social security has itself undermined the incentive to work and thereby created an escalating economic problem of which unemployment is but a symptom. Be that as it may, an association between these two concepts, both in their hopeful ascendancy in the 1940s and in their sorry decline from the 1970s, can hardly be denied. In fact this strengthens the argument for the social and economic coherence of the consensus framework.

The significance of the third plank, however, is arguably rather different. The notion of a mixed economy implies that Labour in practice was unwilling or unable to make a significant extension of nationalization after 1950 and that the Conservatives in practice accepted a stable frontier between public and private enterprises—until Thatcher came to power. In retrospect, the issue may appear somewhat inflated by both parties. Labour had pointed to public ownership as the path to socialism: but the implementation of Morrisonian nationalization notoriously struck some workers as just meaning that they had 'the same bosses'. Likewise, when privatization acquired its own momentum in the 1980s, its effects fell short of the prospective claims on behalf of competition and improved service. One might say that the promises Labour made to the producers in the 1940s, and those the Conservatives made to the consumers in the 1980s, turned out to be equally insubstantial.

Now that the rise and fall of public ownership in Britain can be seen as an historical episode which has almost turned full circle, its economic impact seems to have been negligible but its political impact piquant. It was a process whereby, under Labour, the government painfully accumulated capital assets which were, a generation later, turned into ready money by the Conservatives —the proceeds being split between a hard-up government and those voters who purchased shares at knock-down prices. On a cynical view, all that socialism achieved was to build up a war chest which could be raided at will by its own political enemies and used to suborn many of its erstwhile supporters.

Finally, it should be observed that the fourth plank in the consensus which collapsed in the 1970s had not, unlike the others, been nailed down during the 1940s but was of more recent timber. For the steps which both Labour and Conservative governments took in the 1960s and 1970s to animate the economy through direct intervention can surely be seen as a *response* to a perceived *breakdown* of the post-war settlement. It was the attempt to cut loose from the cycle of 'stop–go' policies at the Treasury which led first Macmillan, then Wilson, and later Heath, to seek more *dirigiste* alternatives. In this sense they were already rejecting the adequacy of existing policy. Whether a 'Butskellite' continuity at the Treasury in the early 1950s should be seen as a consensus within a consensus—or whether Butler, as Conservative Chancellor of the Exchequer, substantially modified the policies of his Labour predecessor Gaitskell—are in turn unsettled questions which will only be illuminated by further primary research.

One immediate conclusion, however, stands out. David Marquand's insight that 'Keynesian social democratic policies were frustrated by Keynesian social democratic politics' seems particularly apt (Marquand, 1988: 58). For the version of 'Keynesianism' which had become current by the 1950s was a way of trying to manage the economy at arm's length. Politically, it simply took the line of least resistance rather than mobilize consent to tackle more deep-seated problems. It relied almost wholly upon manipulating overall demand by means of fiscal policy and—from Butler's time onward—bank rate adjustments. It is ironical that Keynes, who had spent long tracts of his active life campaigning for the direct control of public investment, should have been commemorated after his death by the appropriation of his name for a system relying on the indirect regulation of private consumption.

It was only when this phase of Keynesian demand management failed to solve the problems of the British economy, or was perceived to have failed, in the early 1960s, that governments (both Conservative and Labour) turned their attention to the supply side. In doing so, they in fact turned back to many of the problems concerning structural rigidities within the economy which had bedevilled the interwar years. By the 1980s, indeed, the landmarks of the 1930s were reappearing in politics too, as a government of the right proceeded to blow down the now tottering house of cards which, for good or ill, had stood since the Beveridge Report. The shopworn shibboleths of consensus were now known as 'the policies that failed before'.

References

Beveridge, Sir W. (1942) *Social Insurance and Allied Services*, Cmd 6494.
Crosland, A. (1964) *The Future of Socialism*, first published 1956.
Marquand, D. (1988) *The Unprincipled Society*.

COMMENTARY THREE

John Turner

Economic history is too important to be left to the economic historians, but I think Marquand is too ready to give a political scientist's explanation for long-term economic phenomena which are themselves highly problematic. Moreover I think that the really difficult questions which future historians will ask about the post-war consensus is not why it broke down but what it was. In that sense both the questions he addresses need further thought before they are answered.

The supposed origins of Britain's long-term economic 'decline'—actually a relative retardation which became a genuine contraction only in the early 1980s—have attracted a large and controversial literature (see references appended). Historians have stressed not only comparison between Britain and other industrial economies but also the interaction between Britain and the international economy, from the 1890s to the present day. Neither this literature nor the economic history of Britain's industrial competitors offers much support to Marquand's explanations of economic decline: that Britain was failing because it had maintained the ethos of market liberalism after abandoning its doctrines, that British governments failed to establish fruitful relationships with organized producers, and that Britain's competitors 'never adopted the market-led model in the first place'.

The best recent work suggests that by the end of the nineteenth century the British economy was locked into an industrial structure which was incapable of fast growth. This was for two reasons: early industrialization had entrenched those sectors which were to face the most acute competition from newly industrializing countries, and the capital market discouraged the shift of domestic investment into fast-growing industries because 'the London stock exchange offered perhaps the best choice of essentially *safe* securities [i.e. foreign fixed-interest securities] available anywhere in the world' (Kennedy, 1978: 145)

While it can be argued that Britain's early industrial competitors were less disadvantaged in these respects, this was not because these countries were busily rejecting the 'market-led model' and climbing into bed with organized producer groups. Instead the governments of Germany, Japan and the United States went about the sort of 'defensive, conservative' tariff practices which Marquand criticizes when he finds them in Joseph Chamberlain: the United States government undertook a flamboyant if ineffectual campaign against 'trusts': and the record of any of those governments before 1914 in dealing with organized labour, as a main producer group, was far more confrontational and indeed repressive than anything attempted in the United Kingdom. The constraints on British growth—industrial structure and the capital market— were outside the operating range of any known government before 1945.

Other countries were more resilient in the face of world economic developments after 1918, but it can be argued that closer relations between governments and organized economic interests were the consequence, not the cause, of differential economic development (e.g. Tolliday, 1984: 52–3). Cohesive relationships, such as the *Zentralarbeitsgemeinschaft*, which yoked government, business and labour into a policy-making unit in Germany between 1918 and 1924, broke down when the economic going got rough (Feldman, 1977). Indeed the disputes between governments, vested interests and other social elements over modernization sometimes became quite robust in modernizing states: in 1932 Baron Dan Takuma, a leading Japanese industrialist, was assassinated by traditionalists – a fate which British businessmen had no reason to fear (Hirschmeier and Yui, 1981: 120–3; cited and discussed by Davenport-Hines, 1988: 223).

In any case, the interwar British economy, warts and all, grew faster than it had done before 1914 and recovered better from the Great Crash than almost any other industrialized country except Japan, whose growth in this period depended upon building up a regional dominance in the Pacific basin, and Germany, which achieved a fast but brittle recovery by preparing for a world war. Before explaining the relative failure of Britain and the success of other countries in terms of their political structures, it is as well to make sure what those relativities were and what the political structures did actually deliver. Where economic developments have comprehensible, if rather complex, economic explanations, it is more parsimonious to consider those explanations before speculating about the links between political structures and economic outcomes.

The fate of the post-war consensus is another fascinating minefield. Marquand defines that consensus as a 'framework of assumptions about the role of the state and the management of the economy', but this is a more controversial point than he allows. Did the two major parties agree about the proper role of the state, or did they just share a common assumption about what the voters would wear and grit their teeth at the differences between that and their own ideological preferences? After all, 'Butskellism' is named after two men, one of whom never led the Conservative Party at all and the other of whom had a very rough ride leading Labour in opposition from 1955 to 1963. Did their party colleagues share their apparently covergent instincts? What of the years in which others dominated the Conservative and Labour parties? This is more than a debating point, because if the post-war 'consensus' was actually no more than a compromise there is room for different explanations of its eventual demise.

Although some of Marquand's article looks like a bonfire of straw men, one must agree that the various 'overload' theories are distinctly weak and tendentious. The crudest New Right variants, which hold that politics in an interventionist state is devoted to inflationary outbidding of the competing party, fall down because historical evidence points against them. The more complex Huntingdon position, that for some reason the social conventions which maintained 'social control' until the late 1960s have collapsed, is more difficult to refute only because it is so vague. But Marquand's own position would be greatly strengthened if he were to recognize the importance of economic change in making the British economy, as much as British society, unmanageable in the 1970s. He is right to observe that the origins of Britain's vulnerability in the 1970s stretched back to the 1890s rather than the 1940s, but even so some more recent decisions—for instance the policy of maintaining a fixed and rather high parity for sterling in the 1950s—are part of an important economic explanation for the failure of demand management, and more specifically credit management, to work successfully in the 1960s, without creating balance of payments crises.

Marquand's ultimate explanation for the demise of the post-war consensus is contained in three political propositions: the absence of a statist tradition, the failure of the state to establish satisfactory working relations with the organized producer groups, and the persistence of class antagonism. These are good points, well taken, but they call into question the very notion of a consensus. The post-war dispensation should surely be read as a temporary and vulnerable phenomenon, remarkable for its power to convince the unwary that it was permanent—ironically this was Keynes's own view of the golden age before 1914 (Keynes, 1919: 1). It was a compromise between hostile groups, not a consensus. This is what the New Right and the New Left have been saying, but it also seems to be the logical outcome of Marquand's argument. He begins with a new Whig interpretation of history, contrasting 'modernisers' with 'cultural conservatives'. At the end of his paper I am not convinced that he has shown that the cultural conservatives could have lost in any conceivable circumstances.

References and select bibliography

Crafts, N.F.R. (1979) 'Victorian Britain did fail', *Economic History Review*, 2s, **32**, pp. 533–7.

Davenport-Hines, R. (1988) 'Trade associations and the modernisation crisis of British industry' in H. Yamazaki and M. Miyamoto (eds), *Trade Association in Business History*.

Hirschmeier S. and Yui, T. (1981) *The Development of Japanese Business 1600–1980*.

Kennedy, W.P. (1987) *Industrial Structure, Capital Markets and the Origins of British Economic Decline*.

Landes, D.S. (1969) *The Unbound Prometheus*.

Lazonick, W. (1981) 'Competition, specialization and industrial decline', *Journal of Economic History*, **41**, pp. 31–8.

Levine, A.L. (1967) *Industrial Retardation*.

McCloskey, D.N. (1970) 'Did Victorian Britain fail?', *Economic History Review*, **23**, pp. 446–59.

McCloskey, D.N. (1973) *Economic Maturity and Entrepreneurial Decline*.

McCloskey, D.N. (1979) 'No it did not: a reply to Crafts', *Economic History Review*, **32**, pp. 538–41.

Matthews, R.C.O., Feinstein, C.H. and Odling-Smee, J.C. (1982) *British Economic Growth, 1856–1973*.

Saul, S.B. (ed.) (1972) *Technical Change: The United States and Britain in the Nineteenth Century*.

Tolliday, S. (1984) 'Tariffs and steel, 1916–1934: the politics of industrial decline' in J. Turner (ed.), *Businessmen and Politics*, pp. 50–75.

Wiener, M. (1981) *English Culture and the Decline of the Industrial Spirit*.

COMMENTARY FOUR

Keith Middlemas

Perverse though it may be, I prefer to comment more widely on the book than Marquand's truncated and over-compressed paper allows, but will restrict my comments to the questions of where and why Britain went wrong, rather than considering the prescriptive one of what is to be done. Marquand's book, after all, displays a richness of understanding in its survey of recent history and a breadth of knowledge to which no summary—even his own—can do justice.

Three general points of caution need to be made. The first has to do with the limitations set by a project that requires recent history to have lessons and teach morals. That these are called conclusions does not deflect the point. The prescriptive section of the book follows, but also determines, his major deductions: first, that the common understanding of national priorities and acceptance of agreed means to achieve them broke down in Britain in the late 1960s and 1970s; second, that surviving fictions about the parliamentary political process, sovereignty and nationhood grew to be too remote from the reality of Britain's geo-strategic and economic international position; and third, that no adequate moral–political vision has arisen to fill the gap left by what he calls 'Keynesian social democracy'.

Despite the range of sources, at heart here lies a modern Whig interpretation, a historical orthodoxy which ignores much intractable details (for example evidence contrary to Mancur Olsen's argument that producer groups must act purely in their members' self-interest, as if that were a simple matter for them to define) and excludes contrary views emphasizing, as does Jonathan Clarke, the sheer longevity and power of ancient institutions, church or monarchy, or like Tom Nairn, the intractable quantities of nationalism.

It is secondly a politician's book, preoccupied, for all its concern with community and intermediate institutions, with the primordial relations of government and citizens. It assumes that politicians encapsulate the public will, that they lead in the process of education and execution. Past politicians must therefore carry the can in order that future ones may bring about the millennium. Yet how the political class could metamorphose itself in order to create the desired communitarian political morality is nowhere described. The sheer muddle of post-war weak corporatism, the many layers of institutions' and producer groups' competition which undermined Keynesian social democracy, is blamed on politicians, parties and public, rather than on changes in the nature, say, of trade unionism, to which the TUC had to react in the 1970s, or in the constitution, size and relative importance of the different manufacturing sectors of industry—both, like the transformation of the financial world, far beyond the control of any national government.

The third point follows. This is an intellectual's view of change, highlighting the significance of ideas in politics, critical of their incoherence when things go wrong and saying little about how ideas were transmuted into managerial practice whether in government service or the micropolitics of shopfloor and boardroom. 'Lacking a theory of the political economy, Keynesian social democratic politicians and officials could not come to terms, either with the political implications of their economic policies, or with the economic implications of their political assumptions' (page 58) is a good phrase, but the more one looks at it, the more it seems to skim like a surfboard over the actual troughs and waves of policy implementation.

It is an excellent endeavour to try to write the politics back into economic history and show how far that dimension is from being the economist's 'residual' quantity. But in spite of many disclaimers, the focus on government means that intermediate layers, their interactions, the profusion of possibilities and choices which at any given point not only determined options for the public but may have suffocated the singlemindedeness Marquand sees as necessary to action by government, are given low causal priority. The prime mover has to be (in the past as well as in the 1980s) a new 'guiding principle' or 'doctrine' (page 2) corresponding to reality as perceived from above.

That said, the historical survey, going back to the triumph of social liberalism in the late 1900s, is fresh and stimulating. What is said about the nineteenth century is more selective, couched generally in the guarded optimism of William Morris, and ignoring for example the statist aspect of Benthamism. Highly schematic though the argument is, it provides a convincing analysis of why the post World War II political settlement failed to deliver either adjustment or sustained economic growth compared with other nations blessed with a more development-oriented state apparatus.

It follows logically that Britain has lacked not so much the entrepreneurial culture beloved of New Right prophets, but the benign guiding hand of a developmental state capable both of leading and winning consent to adjustment. Parts of this argument are unexceptionable: for example that choices made at certain crucial points in the last 70 years constrained subsequent British governments to a pervasive, weak corporatism in which the only way to obtain consensus in peacetime was by negotiation with the central institutions representing producer groups; and that while this could work in boom years, in conditions of decline postulating a zero sum outcome it had to fail for lack of agreed criteria about distributing losses rather than gains.

It seems clear also that the agencies and institutions which served adequately in the era of British economic dominion became less and less appropriate to a political system based on the brokerage of demand management. Because of their members' 'possessive individualism', producer groups' corporatism did not develop to fill the gap, as it did at least in the field of wage determination in Austria, Scandinavia and West Germany. Yet they retained enough negative power as peak organizations to ensure British governments could not struggle out of the slough which Marquand calls 'negotiated inertia rather than negotiated adjustment'.

I certainly would not quarrel with the conclusion that the Westminster model (traditional club government compounded with Diceyean concepts of sovereignty and then haphazardly modernized) has been unable to create either a developmental state or the sort of consensus necessary to offset the public's 'lost trust', its high level of protest and resentment, and the long erosion of respect for custom and convention. But this does require one to believe that the Westminster model is congruent with what the politicans do, the question that Baldwin once put as 'Does pig make stye, or t'other way round?'; and a deduction that both neo-liberal and neo-socialist solutions have failed to match contemporary reality implies that both are (to use Norman Tebbit's phrase) 'brain-dead', a tall order, given the recent revisionism of both.

More seriously, in terms of the general historical argument, Marquand's mode of analysis seems to confuse the processes of party government with what the state was and now actually is. The two are by no means the same. Whereas the former certainly failed to inspire a developmental state on French or Japanese lines, it is not certain that the latter would have failed had initiatives like the 1974 industrial strategy (captured, in terms of publicity, and then distorted by Harold Wilson's goverment) been allowed to mature. The traditions of the state, and even more of state departments, have longer lives and perhaps more durable influence than those of five-year administrations.

If the enviable model prescribed by Marquand, of a less individualistic, more community-based political morality, able to foster a process of mutual education between politician–pastors and citizen–pupils, were in fact transported back as a vehicle for interpreting the past, many of the aspects elided here would stand out, not perhaps as mountains but as ridges, and even ridges bend and deflect the winds blowing over them.

2 Keynes's legacy for postwar economic management[1]

Roger Middleton
University of Bristol

Introduction

Keynes's first official biographer and close friend, the late Roy Harrod, observed in 1969 that

> Keynes's place in the history of fundamental economic theory is quite secure . . . I would suppose that his influence in ten or twenty years from now will be *greater* than it is at present.
>
> (Harrod, 1969: 808)

Clearly, this was not one of the profession's better predictions so far as the influence of Keynesian policy is concerned, for ten years later, another of Keynes's friends, Thomas Balogh (1979: 67), was to bemoan the fact that anti-Keynesianism was now 'among the fastest growth industries in the world.'[2]

It was during that intervening decade that there developed the reaction against Keynes and Keynesianism. Without undue characterization, we can say that in Britain, the United States and certain other OECD countries, Keynes and his followers were blamed for the appearance of stagflation, the excessive growth of the public sector and related enervation of the market economy. Indeed, it was on the crest of this wave of concern about the continuance of the free market order in Britain that the Thatcher Government was brought to power.

Keynes's legacy for postwar economic management can best be approached from the perspective of this critique of Keynes and Keynesian system. While it might be thought that so much has already been written about Keynes that there is no further need for this mode of analysis, in fact the critique that has developed lacks historical perspective and textual integrity. Thus a prerequisite for establishing Keynes's legacy for postwar economic management is a knowledge of what Keynes's really said on certain key issues about the capitalist economy and the role of public policy, rather than later interpretations of his message.

The belief in the essentials of the Keynesian system began to lose their hold in the late 1960s, and had evolved into a fully developed critique by the late 1970s (see Bleaney, 1985; Keagan, 1985; and Smith, 1987). This is popularly associated with the term monetarism, a label applied rather inaccurately to describe the mix of policies pursued in Britain since 1979. In reality, there was also the revival of Austrian economics, the rational expectations revolution, the development of public choice economics and the clarion call of the supply-siders.

A full analysis would need to consider all the various components of the critique of the Keynesian system. However, time must limit the current exercise to a more selective investigation. Thus we shall focus upon two themes central to Keynes's thought, and about which there has been much misunderstanding: Keynes's critique of the free market order, and his views on economic management and deficit-finance. Finally, in the concluding section of this chapter, we make some observations about the extent to which Keynes can be held responsible for the way in which his ideas were interpreted and implemented.

Keynes and the market

The late 1970s witnessed the revival of an articulate and self-confident liberal political economy which purported to explain the British disease in terms of the free market order having been fettered by the social democratic consensus which had prevailed since the 1940s (Gamble, 1985: 26). The centrepiece of this liberal political economy was that political developments in the form of the social democratic state had generated major economic changes: notably a far-reaching extension of government intervention and regulation with an inevitable impairment of the free market order and consequent erosion of the natural mechanisms ensuring equilibrium and economic efficiency.

Since Keynes was, in his *General Theory*, accredited with the theoretical rationale for the managed economy, and, in his public policy activities, as having contributed towards the creation of the social democratic state which made the managed economy possible, it was natural that he should be blamed when it all appeared to go wrong in the 1970s. This seemed particularly poignant when one of the key actors in the developments of the 1970s, Hayek, had warned at an early point in *The Road to Serfdom* (1944) that there was no sustainable middle way between collectivization and the liberal market order.

All of this raises questions about the nature of Keynes's critique of the liberal market order and of his perception of the legitimate and sustainable domains of the private and public sectors. Thus we need to investigate

Keynes's underlying socio-political philosophy and the extent of his critique of classical and neo-classical economics.[3] We are aided in this task by the large volume of Keynes's writings on such issues (Keynes, 1925a; 1925b; 1926a; 1926b; 1927; 1932; 1934; 1936: chap. 24; 1938; 1939), though it must be said that Keynes never brought his thoughts together and published them in a complete form. No doubt this was because of his heart attack in 1937 and the coming of the Second World War, circumstances which also 'mean that Keynes never fully participated in the hammering out of a polished version of Keynesian doctrine from the rough statement contained in *The General Theory*' (Minsky 1976: 14). In addition, while there has been little systematic work in this area, there have been useful contributions by Cairncross (1978), Johnson and Johnson (1978) and Skidelsky (1979; 1988).

Keynes believed that 'The outstanding faults of the economic society in which we live are its failure to provide for full employment and its arbitrary and inequitable distribution of wealth and incomes.' Thus, his starting point in *The General Theory* was that classical economics could not 'solve the economic problems of the actual world', though once full employment was achieved, its propositions would again become relevant (Keynes, 1936: 372, 378).

Keynes's purpose was never to reject the whole of the classical system. For example, in his last published paper he felt compelled to note:

> I find myself moved, not for the first time, to remind contemporary economists that the classical teaching embodied some permanent truths of great significance, which we are liable to-day to overlook because we associate them with other doctrines which we cannot now accept without much qualification. There are in these matters deep undercurrents at work, natural forces, one can call them, or even the invisible hand, which are operating towards equilibrium. If it were not so, we could not have got on even so well as we have for many decades past.
> . . . if we reject the [classical] medicine from our systems altogether, we may just drift on from expedient to expedient and never get really fit again.
>
> (Keynes, 1946: 185–6)

What were these aspects of the classical case that he thought valid and that transcended his critique of the classical theory of employment? First, private profit and property, the foundations of the capitalist system. Here Keynes's views resembled those of many other progressive liberals; that there had to be incentives, though these should be tempered by social justice (Keynes, 1936: 374).

Secondly, competition and individualism, which again were secure within Keynes's conception of the managed economy. Writing within the context of the expanded economic functions of the state that he envisaged as a precondition for securing full employment, he saw them as follows:

> They are partly advantages of efficiency — the advantages of decentralisation and of the play of self-interest. The advantage to efficiency of the decentralisation of

decisions and of individual responsibility is even greater, perhaps, than the nineteenth century supposed; and the reaction against the appeal to self-interest may have gone too far. But, above all, individualism, if it can be purged of its defects and its abuses, is the best safeguard of personal liberty in the sense that, compared with any other system, it greatly widens the field of personal choice. It is also the best safeguard of the variety of life, which emerges precisely from this extended field of personal choice, and the loss of which is the greatest of all the losses of the homogenous or totalitarian state.

(Keynes, 1936: 380)

From these two standpoints, and that of his macroeconomic insight that the route to full employment lay through measures to raise both the average propensity to consume and the marginal efficiency of capital, Keynes (136: 380–1) claimed that the managed economy was the salvation of both individualism and capitalism:

Whilst . . . the enlargement of the functions of government, involved in the task of adjusting to one another the propensity to consume and the inducement to invest, would seem to a nineteenth-century publicist or to a contemporary American financier to be a terrific encroachment on individualism, I defend it, on the contrary, both as the only practicable means of avoiding the destruction of existing economic forms in their entirety and as the condition of the successful functioning of individual initiative.

For if effective demand is deficient, not only is the public scandal of wasted resources intolerable, but the individual enterpriser who seeks to bring these resources into action is operating with the odds loaded against him . . .

The authoritarian state systems of to-day seem to solve the problem of unemployment at the expense of efficiency and of freedom. It is certain that the world will not much longer tolerate the unemployment which, apart from brief moments of excitement, is associated—and, in my opinion, inevitably associated—with present-day capitalistic individualism. But it may be possible by a right analysis of the problem to cure the disease whilst preserving efficiency and freedom.

Nor did Keynes's views change on this essential. Thus, in 1943 he wrote:

I have not abandoned the view that something like free enterprise can be made to work. I think we ought to have a good try at it. And that try ought to be based on the assumption that the underlying conditions are not such as to make it impossible.

(Keynes, 1943d: 354)

Similarly, as we have seen above, in his last published paper (Keynes, 1946) he made a plea that the wisdom of the classical economists should not be lost amid the welter of enthusiasm for planning and the 'new' economics.

It is also clear from Keynes's published writings that he valued individual freedoms highly; and that he wanted no truck with Marxism, 'a doctrine so illogical and so dull' (Keynes, 1926b: 285), or the sort of mass appeal to radical social planning sought by sections of the interwar Labour Party—'the *class* war will find me on the side of the educated *bourgeoisie*' (Keynes, 1925b: 297). As Minsky (1976: 147) puts it: Keynes believed that 'his theory made the traditional radical analysis and programs both obsolete and unnecessary; his new theory rendered obsolete the muddle that he felt Marxist economics to be.[4]

Other respects in which Keynes questioned the classical agenda of government and created mistrust and possible misinterpretation of his views include the issues of investment control and savings. Keynes never favoured the control of private industrial investment, though he had no such inhibitions about regulating overseas investment to meet balance of payments objectives. Similarly, Keynes sought greater control and co-ordination of public investment. In *The General Theory*, Keynes had called for a somewhat greater 'socialisation of investment' (Keynes, 1936: 378), and 'the growth and recognition of semi-autonomous bodies within the State—bodies whose criterion of action within their own field is solely the public good as they understand it' (Keynes, 1926b: 288). However, he was also careful to qualify his prescriptions:

> beyond this no obvious case is made out for a system of State Socialism which would embrace most of the economic life of the Community. It is not the ownership of the instruments of production which it is important for the State to assume. If the State is able to determine the aggregate amount of resources devoted to augmenting the instruments and the basic rate of reward to those who own them, it will have accomplished all that is necessary.
>
> . . .
>
> Thus, apart from the necessity of central controls to bring about an adjustment between the propensity to consume and the inducement to invest, there is no more reason to socialise economic life than there was before.
>
> (Keynes, 1936: 378–9)

Keynes's views on savings must have deeply upset ingrained Victorian notions of financial probity (Skidelsky, 1977a: 2), as must his colourful language when he wrote of his aspiration to see the 'euthanasia of the rentier, and, consequently, the euthanasia of the cumulative oppressive power of the capitalist to exploit the scarcity-value of capital' (Keynes, 1936: 376). Keynes's purpose, of course, was to show that thrift was not virtuous if it prevented the achievement of full employment. However, it could be seen as an attack upon an essential element of the free market order if Keynes's views about the long-term satisfaction of human wants are disregarded or rejected.

Keynes's critique of the free market system concerned both forms of market failure; that is in the technical sense of economic efficiency, and in the sense that efficient economic markets may produce outcomes which are politically unacceptable in prevailing conditions. It was the lack of social acceptance of this which prompted Keynes's plea for government intervention; an argument which, of course, has become more general in the postwar period (see Lehner and Widmaier, 1983: 240–1).

What appears surprising in retrospect is the limited nature of his critique of the free market. For example, *The General Theory* assumes competitive goods markets; this at a time when there was much work being undertaken on imperfect competition, some of it within Cambridge itself (see Chamberlain, 1933 and J. Robinson, 1933). Indeed, Joan Robinson (1969: xi) later wrote that 'Keynes was not much interested in the theory of imperfect competition, though he had given my book on that subject a vague blessing.'[5] That Keynes limited his critique of the classical theory by avoiding issues of market imperfections says much about the limited purpose that guided the critique that did develop. It may be that Keynes wanted to demonstrate that involuntary unemployment was not dependent upon imperfections in the goods market so as to limit the political implications of his analysis.[6] Whatever the reason, towards the end of *The General Theory*, Keynes was quite explicit that:

> If we suppose the volume of output to be given, i.e. to be determined by forces outside the classical scheme of thought, then there is no objection to be raised against the classical analysis of the manner in which private self-interest will determine what in particular is produced, in what proportion the factors of production will be combined to produce it, and how the value of the final product will be distributed between them.
>
> (Keynes, 1936: 378–9)

As we turn from the issue of Keynes's views on the market to those on economic management and deficit-finance, we can introduce our next theme by noting that an important reason why he thought the market could be overridden at certain points was his belief in the efficacy of intelligent public policy relative to uncoordinated private market interests. Against this backcloth we are now in a position to examine Keynes's views on economic management and the ways in which these may have left an inheritance which was to be perceived as causing problems in the postwar period.

Keynes and deficit-finance

Study of the interwar economic policy debate reveals one overriding and consistent strand in Keynes's thought which runs from *A Tract on Monetary Reform* (Keynes, 1923), through *A Treatise on Money* (Keynes, 1930b), to *The General Theory* and beyond. This was Keynes's belief that internal balance should not be sacrificed for external objectives, such as the exchange rate or the current account balance of payments. From this followed Keynes's stance on full employment and the policy innovations necessary to stabilize demand.[7]

It has become fashionable in certain quarters, particularly those associated with the revival of belief in the free market, to argue that Keynes's legacy was a government commitment to a full employment target below the 'natural' rate of unemployment with consequent implications for inflation (see, for example, Brittan, 1975; Institute of Economic Affairs, 1986; and Friedman, 1968, for the theoretical basis of this argument). Of course, in the specialist literature of Keynes studies (Kahn, 1974; 1976; 1984), it is equally well-known that this is a gross misrepresentation.

Keynes was far less optimistic about what might be achieved in terms of the full employment level of unemployment than his more dirigistic contemporaries. For example, Beveridge (1944: 21) had argued for a 3 per cent target rate. Keynes had responded to this with the comment that there was 'No harm in aiming at 3 per cent unemployment, but I shall be surprised if we succeed', and himself thought 5 per cent a more realizable target (Kahn, 1976: 30).[8] In any case, whether as a consequence of Keynesian demand management or not (Matthews, 1968), the record over the first quarter century of the postwar period exceeded all expectations, with an average rate of only 1.7 per cent over 1948–70 as against 10.0 per cent for 1921–38 (Middleton, 1985: 12).

Nor can Keynes be accused fairly of being blind to the potential inflationary consequences of full employment. Again, his consistent stand on this and the general problem of inflation has been well documented in Keynes studies. To this end (Keynes, 1943e: 187) is normally cited:

> Some people argue that a capitalist country is doomed to failure because it will be found impossible in conditions of full employment to prevent a progressive increase of wages. According to this view severe slumps and recurrent periods of unemployment have been hitherto the only effective means of holding efficiency wages within a reasonably stable range. Whether this is so remains to be seen. The more conscious we are of this problem, the likelier shall we be to surmount it.

Moreover, it was not simply the technical economic problem of excess demand and a tight labour market that concerned Keynes. He was also very conscious of the potential for trade unions to abuse their power, writing as early as 1926: 'the *Trade Unionists*, once the oppressed, [are] now the tyrants, whose selfish and sectional pretensions need to be bravely opposed' (Keynes, 1926a: 309). In the modern literature, the full employment commitment is criticized in some quarters because it lessened the penalty function for wage-setters. Whilst we cannot know 'exactly what his personal "trade-off" would have been between high employment, inflation and [the] curtailment of economic liberties' (E.A.G. Robinson, 1977a: 59), we do have the following in a letter of late 1943:

> Some people over here are accustomed to argue that the fear of unemployment and the recurrent experience of it are the only means by which, in past practice, trade

unions have been prevented from over-doing their wage-raising pressure. I hope this is not true . . . the more aware we were of this risk, the more likely we should be to find a way round other than totalitarianism. But I recognise the reality of the risk.

. . . The task of keeping efficiency wages reasonably stable (I am sure they will creep up steadily in spite of our best efforts) is a political rather than an economic problem.

(Keynes, 1943f: 37–8)

With the benefit of hindsight, this might be viewed as less than satisfactory. But, was it invalid for Keynes, and in effect for later Keynesians, to assume that inflation was a political problem? So far as Keynes is concerned, two factors are relevant. First, his writings on this, as with the broad stance of most of his work, concerned the short- to medium-term. The long-term did not interest him relative to the challenge and urgency of the immediate policy problem.[9] Secondly, we should ask to what extent a person is responsible for later developments in which their ideas (or some version of them) help to shape the future—a theme we return to in our concluding section (pp. 33–6).

We can apply the same logic to another criticism of recent years, namely that one consequence of Keynes's legacy was 'that "full employment" [became] an exclusive definition of social well-being, . . . to be pursued at virtually any cost' with the effect that it became 'a dangerously inflationary and growth-inhibiting misdirection of policy in the context of the contemporary welfare state'. The key here is the 'contemporary welfare state', for it is presumed that 'social security [was] an alternative to full employment as a means of shielding people against economic distresses and disasters' (Johnson and Johnson, 1978: 224).

Surely a much more important question is not the extent to which Keynes was personally culpable, or indeed Beveridge for that matter, since he also held in common many of Keynes's assumptions about the social value of full employment (see Harris, 1977), but why the belief in full employment proved so durable in the postwar period. Moreover, there are problems even with this question, for since it is commonplace that full employment was frequently sacrificed for balance of payments stability in the postwar period, it is at least arguable that an essential element of the Keynesian revolution never operated in practice (Tomlinson, 1981; 1985). If this be the case, we have a further reason for why subsequent developments cannot be lain at Keynes's door.

Before proceeding to discuss Keynes's support for deficit-finance and stabilization policies, we ought to briefly mention monetary policy in passing. Despite the best efforts of Leijonhufvud (1968), Moggridge and Howson (1974) and others the myth persists that Keynes denigrated the importance of monetary policy to the extent that it should have little role in stabilization as compared with fiscal policy. In reality, Keynes was primarily a monetary economist whose views on monetary policy evolved dramatically during his lifetime, but who at no time ever expounded the extreme position imputed to him by many current critics. This misrepresentation, it might be said, is no worse than Keynes's treatment of Pigou (1933) in *The General Theory*. This rather misses the point, for the policy implications are far more significant.

Turning now to Keynes's espousal of deficit-finance, we need to consider the recent public choice critique of the instrument (budget deficits) that Keynes bequeathed to policy-makers. This is founded upon a critique of Keynes's political philosophy, which is well-expressed in the following:

> In his economic writings he was concerned with the extent to which the pursuit of self-interest in the market place did or did not promote the general interest. But it never occurred to him to see the political process as a market place, governed by the self-interest of politicians, officials and voters. He took it for granted that decisions would ultimately be made by a small group of the educated bourgeoisie, who were inspired by a disinterested concern for the public good. He assumed that wrong decisions were taken out of intellectual error or, at worst, narrowness of vision; and that if the correct ideas were promulgated with sufficient clarity and vigour they would eventually win the day.
>
> (Brittan, 1977: 41–2)

From this the case has been developed by Buchanan, Wagner and others to the effect that once the nineteenth-century fiscal constitution of balanced budgets was overthrown in favour of functional finance there would arise scope for political manipulation of the economy and thus the enlargement of the state and political business cycles.[10] We can address this at a number of levels.

First, the policy innovation of functional finance is neither a necessary nor a sufficient condition for political manipulation of the economy and the consequent impairment of economic performance. Studies abound of the practical adverse consequences of government on economic performance, and there is now a large literature on institutional sclerosis (Whiteley, 1986). For example, we have Hughes's (1977) long-term study of the US, which pays particular attention to tariffs; and Olson's (1982) broader study of the role and consequences of distributional coalitions.

Secondly, while there is no doubt that functional finance does provide scope for political manipulation, indeed it was fear of this which informed much of the interwar Treasury's opposition to Keynes's call for deficit-financing (Middleton, 1985: 87–9), this in itself tells us little. This question, like that of the role of the Keynesian revolution in the postwar growth of the public sector, must be related to independent political forces: the impact of the Second World War, the growth of democracy and the changed nature of party competition, changes in market structure and the growth of corporatism, and broader economic and technical developments which implied changed responsibilities for government.

Thirdly, there is no unambiguous evidence to support the case of the existence of political business cycles in Britain. Clearly, postwar governments have had an 'economic' reaction function; the 'political' reaction function, however, is much more tendentious (see Whiteley, 1986: 82–3). Moreover, the growth of the public sector in Britain, at least as conventionally measured, has not been excessive relative to our competitors. Indeed, over 1960–83 the rise in the public expenditure/GDP ratio was lower in the UK than in any other European Community country (Hadjimatheou, 1987: 18). Since it is in Britain, rather than in other countries, that Keynes's message was most fully absorbed, the Buchanan and Wagner thesis looks increasingly suspect.

Finally, recent research into the Public Record Office records on postwar economic management is gradually revealing a rather different picture of the emergence of Keynesian demand management than had been thought hitherto. The works of Peden (1988), Rollings (1988) and Tomlinson (1987) clearly suggest that until at least the middle 1950s it was the control of inflation, within the context of excess demand, rather than the fear of unemployment, which determined the incorporation of Keynesian budgetary managment.

It is also becoming clear that an important underlying motive for the Treasury in this process was that the Keynesian system allowed the Treasury to employ the need for a budget surplus as a means of controlling public expenditure growth,[11] one of its traditional concerns. Thus, a target budget surplus rule replaced the interwar balanced budget rule; which leads us to the hypothesis that for a full decade at least after the Second World War in effect there was an inverse Buchanan/Wagner rule: that far from Keynes overturning the traditional constraints on expenditure by discrediting the intellectual foundations of the balanced budget rule, functional finance actually provided an additional buttress for the Treasury's traditional concern of expenditure control.

If we combine this hypothesis with the broad stance of Matthews (1968), that it was private not government spending propensities which generated full employment until the later 1960s, we arrive at a rather different interpretation of the outcome of the Keynesian revolution for say pre-OPEC I British budgetary policies. At this point different economic and induced political forces came into play in circumstances which Keynes or the early Keynesians could not have been expected to anticipate.

We cannot, however, evade the general point of the public choice literature that Keynes's subscribed to a highly idealized conception of the role of ideas and policy makers in modern pluralistic democracies. Here indeed there appears to be something of a paradox, for how do we balance Keynes's belief in the possibilities of state intervention with his personal views about the limited capabilities of the political agents of such intervention, which in themselves appear to conflict with his 'presuppositions of Harvey Road'. We have much material on these themes in the Keynes Collected Writings and in memoirs by his colleagues and friends (see, for example, E.A.G. Robinson

1947; S.E. Harris 1947; M. Keynes 1975 and Clark 1977). Thus, for example, we have Keynes oft-quoted remark to Duncan Grant:

> You have not, I suppose, ever mixed with politicians at close quarters. They are *awful* . . . I have discovered, what previously I didn't believe possible, that politicians behave in private life and say exactly the same things as they do in public. Their stupidity is inhuman.
>
> (cited in Harrod, 1951: 157)

This was made early in his career, but the impression is given that it endured. Thus de Cecco (1977: 18–19) has written that Keynes:

> remained convinced till the last that only the dismal mediocrity of politicians, the short-sightedness of entrepreneurs, the imbecility of the rentier and incompetence and greed of bankers prevented Britain from reaching an age of plenty, a new and lasting renaissance.

Finally, to this we should add Harrod's (1951: 193) observation:

> If, owing to the needs of planning, the functions of government became very far-reaching and multifarious, would it be possible for the intellectual aristocracy to remain in essential control? Keynes tended till the end to think of the really important decisions being reached by a small group of intelligent people, like the group that fashioned the Bretton Woods plan. But would not a democratic government having a wide multiplicity of duties tend to get out of control and act in a way of which the intelligent would not approve? This is another dilemma— how to reconcile the functioning of a planning and interfering democracy with the requirement that in the last resort the best considered judgement should prevail. It may be that the presuppositions of Harvey Road were so much of a second nature to Keynes that he did not give this dilemma the full considerations which it deserves.

Further research is needed here, but meanwhile it would seem that Cairncross (1978: 47–8) comes closer to the practical truth:

> He trusted to human intelligence. He hated enslavement by rules. He wanted governments to have discretion and he wanted economists to come to their assistance in the exercise of that discretion. But he certainly held no exalted view of the wisdom of governments or the virtues of economic science . . ..
>
> The unwisdom of governments and the errors of their advisers weighed less heavily with Keynes than the need to hold open the door to better management of our affairs. More damage would be done in the end by blind trust in some man-made institution that excluded all discretion than by considered policies which could improve through time as experience accummulated.

Thus, Keynes did little more than follow the tide of other advanced opinion in correctly anticipating that more government intervention was inevitable; for him the real issue was whether reason and intelligence would guide this trend. There is a further consideration that needs to be introduced at this point. In the interwar period Keynes had conveyed the impression that he would countenance long-term budget deficits and had sought to demonstrate in *The General Theory* 'how "wasteful" loan expenditure may nevertheless enrich the community on balance' (Keynes, 1936: 128–9). However, during the Second World War, when Keynes was once more within Whitehall, he shifted his ground considerably and moderated the presentation of his proposals.

From Keynes's involvement in the discussions leading up to the 1944 employment policy White Paper (HMSO, 1944), we can see that he now stressed the need for immediate action in the advent of a downturn, because stabilization would be far more difficult if a full scale depression was allowed to develop (Keynes, 1943a: 316; 1943c: 323); emphasized the role of the capital budget in stabilization, rather than the current budget where deficit-financing 'would be a last resort, only to come into play if the machinery of capital budgetting had broken down' (Keynes, 1943d: 352); and came to view 'budget deficits as the direct result of *failure to achieve stable full employment* national income growth rather than as an efficient remedy for unemployment' (Kregel, 1985: 32).

In short, this was Keynes the statesman, rather than the pamphleteer; 'the croakings of a Cassandra who could never influence the course of events in time' (Keynes, 1972: xvii) and had now moved on to the realm of what was considered possible and advisable within the prevailing political and administrative system. As he said of Lerner's (1943) paper on functional finance, where the argument is couched in terms of a chronic not intermittent deficiency of demand, 'His argument is impeccable. But, heaven help anyone who tries to put it across the plain man at this stage of the evolution of our ideas' (Keynes, 1943b: 320). Thus it is not even historically correct to say that Keynes bequeathed unqualified approval for deficit-finance; if that ever did develop, itself a doubtful proposition, it derived from other forces.

Conclusions

During the long postwar boom, from the late 1940s to OPEC I, there was a broad consensus in Britain about the economic role of the state. Both Labour and Conservative administrations, with differing degrees of emphasis, shared the assumptions of the mixed economy. The breakdown of this consensus, and the revival of belief in the free market, is usually attributed to the deterioration of Britain's economic performance in the 1970s. However, such is the way that this debate developed in Britain, that it became a critique of the whole of postwar economic performance with much of the blame being laid at Keynes's door. Yet, as Okun (1975: 50–1) has observed:

Many of those who view capitalism as a rotten system blame John Maynard Keynes and Franklin Delano Roosevelt for saving it; but those who view it as a magnificent system rarely credit them with saving it.

There is no paradox here, at least according to the critics of Keynes and Keynesianism, for his system—albeit unconsciously—far from establishing the preconditions for capitalism's viability in Britain in fact achieved the obverse. Whilst Harris (1955: ix) is undoubtedly right that 'Keynes's mission in life was to save capitalism, not destroy it', in effect it has been the Austrian critique, rather than that of monetarism or the new classical macroeconomics, which has proved the most potent and most adaptable in its application to the British case. Keynes was far more the architect of the mixed economy, with his emphasis upon the potentialities of intelligent public policy, than of long-term budget deficits; and it is the Austrian critique which is the most relevant here. For example, we have von Mises (1963: 744) accusation that:

> At the bottom of interventionist argument there is always the idea that the government or the state is an entity outside and above the social process of production, that it owns something which is not derived from taxing its subjects, and that it can spend this mythical something for definite purposes. This is the Santa Claus fable raised by Lord Keynes to the dignity of an economic doctrine and enthusiastically endorsed by all those who expect personal advantage from government spending.

It is clear from this that Keynes never really engaged with the Austrian critique. Indeed, he had been extremely critical of Hayek's *Prices and Production* (1931), describing it as 'one of the most frightful muddles I have ever read . . . an extraordinary example of how, starting with a mistake, a remorseless logician can end up in Bedlam' (Keynes, 1931: 394). Later, however, according to Harrod (1951: 436) they 'achieved a happy relation of friendship'; indeed, he makes reference to Keynes's qualified support for Hayek's *The Road to Serfdom* (1944). His support was indeed qualified; the first passage of this source giving a quite false impression:

> In my opinion it is a grand book. We all have the greatest reason to be grateful to you for saying so well what needs so much to be said. You will not expect me to accept quite all the economic dicta in it. But morally and philosophically I find myself in agreement with virtually the whole of it; and not only in agreement with it, but in a deeply moved agreement.

The letter then continued:

> The line of argument you yourself take depends on the very doubtful assumption that planning is not more efficient. Quite likely from the purely economic point of view it is efficient.
>
> . . .

I should therefore conclude your theme rather differently. I should say that what we want is not no planning, or even less planning, indeed I should say that we almost certainly want more. But the planning should take place in a community in which as many people as possible, both leaders and followers, wholly share your own moral position. Moderate planning will be safe if those carrying it out are rightly orientated in their own minds and hearts to the moral issue . . . .

. . . Dangerous acts can be done safely in a community which thinks and feels rightly, which would be the way to hell if they were executed by those who think and feel wrongly.

(Keynes, 1944b: 385–8)

There is no historical sense to the way in which the Austrian critique has been absorbed into the contemporary policy discourse. Whilst Keynes may have been one of the most articulate exponents of the mixed economy, the notion of economic management long predates him. For example, consider the following written by three progressive Conservatives in 1927:

we have seen the end of 'laissez-faire'. Somewhere between the two extremes, between Marxian Socialism and complete 'laissez-faire', must lie the land in which exploration is not only profitable but essential.

(Boothby *et al.*, 1927: 19–20)

The authors are that old interwar trio, Boothby, Macmillan and Stanley who were so important in the planning movement of the 1930s (See Marwick, 1964; Winch, 1972: 223–9). In reality, it is politicians such as Macmillan, author of *The Middle Way* (1938), a future Conservative prime minister no less, who are equally responsible for later developments, if, indeed, responsibility is an appropriate concept in these circumstances.

It is this notion of responsibility which brings us to the heart of the matter. Is it meaningful to talk of Keynes's responsibility in respect of the evolution of postwar British economic management? To what extent is an intellectual and political propagandist responsible for the way in which their ideas are absorbed and implemented in their name?[12] This raises interesting questions about intellectual property rights. In truth, the crass anti-Keynesian industry resembles, for example, those who seek to blame Jesus for the persecution of the Jews. Perhaps Keynes (1945: 384) was overly optimistic when he believed that 'Insufficiency of cleverness, not of goodness, is the main trouble' in human action. As E.A.G. Robinson (1947: 40) aptly put it: 'From beneath a Georgian skin there peeped out from time to time an almost Victorian sense of moral purpose and obligation'.

And, finally, what of the Keynesian revolution? Keynes had expressed the aspiration that 'If economists could manage to get themselves thought of as humble, competent people, on a level with dentists, that would be splendid!' (Keynes, 1930a: 332). Clearly, this did not transpire.

Indeed, such is the low public esteem and self-image of economists that they have almost retreated from public debate, at least in the way we would recognize from the interwar period and the heyday of the Keynesian consensus. Is it not remarkable that British economists have been almost silent since the March 1981 letter signed by 364 economists in protest against the monetarist policy experiment? In such circumstances what becomes of Keynes's legacy? Little can be said here with any confidence until economic historians begin to conceive of the Keynesian revolution in rather different ways from those hitherto. Current work, in particular that of Peden, Rollings and Tomlinson has concentrated far too much on the instruments of economic management (in particular the search for the holy grail of deficit-financing), rather than the underlying philosophy of economic intervention and whether governmental objectives would have been recognizable to Keynes. There has to be a return to basics, to Keynes's essential message: that capitalist economies are not self-stabilizing, and thus there is a role for government beyond the classical agenda of creating a framework of laws and institutions within which the free market could operate optimally.

Clearly, something is amiss with the current perception of Keynes in certain quarters. His legacy is not secure when the current prime minister can go on record and unquestioned to the effect 'that I really am the true Keynesian, when I'm taken as a whole' (*Sunday Times*, 27 February 1983).

Notes

1. This paper is a preliminary report on work in progress, and is drawn from a larger project on economic management and the market order to be published by Edward Elgar in 1992. I should like to thank the University of Bristol research fund for financial assistance; and Alan Booth, George Peden and participants in research seminars at the Universities of Bristol and Leeds for their many helpful comments on earlier version of this paper. Any remaining errors of fact, analysis or interpretation are, of course, entirely my own. Unfortunately, this paper went to press before I was able to read Fitzgibbons (1988) which, to judge from the reviews, contains much of interest on Keynes's political philosophy.

2. Nor were they fortunate with their other predictions. Thus Harrod (1969: 809) said of Friedman's revived quantity theory, 'It is not likely that it will have a long life'; while Balogh (1979: 67) noted more generally, 'I firmly believe that the destructive wave of monetarism and the deification of market economics is on the wane, shattered on the rocks of practical experience.'

3. We should note here that Keynes (1936: 3) did not acknowledge the distinction in *The General Theory*, and instead subsumed neo-classical writers within the classical tradition.

4. Keynes's impact on socialist thinking has been much neglected in Britain. For an early study of his appeal to the Labour Party, see Rowse (1936); and for later influence, see Jay (1946; 1980), Jenkins (1953), Crosland (1956), Williams (1982), Bryan (1985) and Durbin (1985; 1988).

5. Kaldor (1983: 47) records that 'Joan often told him that she had tried to interest Keynes in imperfect competition for many years, and its relevance to the problem of the insufficiency of demand—but she never succeeded. However, later Kalecki succeeded, as is shown in the article which Keynes published in the March 1939 issue of the *Economic Journal*, where Keynes spoke about "our prevailing *quasi*-competitive system".' See also E.A.G. Robinson (1977b: 79).
6. This route, of course, was followed by Kalecki (1935; 1843).
7. See Keynes (1944a: esp. 16) for a full statement of Keynes's objectives for postwar economic management: 'We are determined that, in future, the external value of sterling shall conform to its internal value as set by our own domestic policies, and not the other way round. Secondly, we intend to retain control of our domestic rate of interest, so that we can keep it as low as suits our own purposes, without interference from the ebb and flow of international capital movements or flights of hot money. Thirdly, whilst we intend to prevent inflation at home, we will not accept deflation at the dictate of influences from outside. In other words, we adjure the instrument of Bank rate and credit contraction operating through the increase of unemployment as a means of forcing our domestic economy into line with external factors.'
8. E.A.G. Robinson (1977a: 59): 'my own belief is that his doubts had nothing directly to do with effects on inflation; they were primarily concerned with structural change and structural unemployment and with difficulties of making very high employment consistent with a balance of payments.'
9. See Skidelsky (1988: 4) for a possible explanation.
10. The literature on this is now vast, and includes Buchanan and Wagner (1977; 1978), Buchanan, Burton and Wagner (1978); and Buchanan, Rowley and Tollison (1987).
11. It should be noted that the term budget surplus does not equate with a negative PSBR at this time, but to a rather special definition of the budget balance which had little economic meaning (see Rollings, 1988: 292–5).
12. We know little of Keynes's views on the absorption of his ideas by economists and politicians, though we do know that in 1944 he commented in a letter to a friend that he had recently been at a dinner with a group of US Keynesian economists and been the only non-Keynesian present.

References

Balogh, T. (1979), 'Post-Keynesian international economics', *Challenge*, 22(4), 67–8.

Beveridge, W.H. (1944), *Full Employment in a Free Society*, London, George Allen & Unwin.

Bleaney, M. (1985), *The Rise and Fall of Keynesian Economics: An investigation of its contribution to capitalist development*, London, Macmillan.

Boothby, R., Macmillan, H., Loder, J. de V. and Stanley, O. (1927), *Industry and the State: A Conservative view*, London, Macmillan.

Brittan, S. (1975), *Second Thoughts on Full Employment Policy*, London, Centre for Policy Studies.

Brittan, S. (1977), 'Can democracy manage an economy', in Skidelsky (ed) (1977b), 41–9.

Bryan, D.E.M. (1985), 'The development of revisionist thought amongst British labour intellectuals and politicians (1911–64', University of Oxford, unpublished DPhil thesis.

Buchanan, J.M., Burton, J. and Wagner, R.E. (1978), *The Consequences of Mr Keynes: An analysis of the misuse of economic theory for political profiteering, with proposals for constitutional disciplines*, London, Institute of Economic Affairs.

Buchanan, J.M., Rowley, C.K. and Tollison, R.D. (eds) (1987), *Deficits*, Oxford, Basil Blackwell.

Buchanan, J.M. and Wagner, R.E. (1977), *Democracy in Deficit: The political legacy of Lord Keynes*, New York, Academic Press.

Buchanan, J.M. and Wagner, R.E. (eds) (1978), *Fiscal Responsibility in Constitutional Democracy*, Leiden and Boston, Martinus Nihoff.

Cairncross, A. (1978), 'Keynes and the planned economy', in A.P. Thirlwall (ed) (1978) *Keynes and Laissez-Faire*, 36–58, London, Macmillan.

Cecco, M. de (1977), 'The last of the romans', in Skidelsky (ed) (1977b), 18–24.

Chamberlain, E.H. (1933), *The Theory of Monopolistic Competition: A re-orientation of the theory of value*, Cambridge, Mass, Harvard University Press.

Clark, C.G. (1977), 'The "golden" age of the economists: Keynes, Robbins et al. in 1930', *Encounter*, **48**(6), 80–90.

Crosland, C.A.R. (1956), *The Future of Socialism*, rev edn. (1964), London, Jonathan Cape.

Durbin, E.F. (1985), *New Jerusalems: The Labour Party and the economics of democratic socialism*, London, Routledge & Kegan Paul.

Durbin, E.F. (1988), 'Keynes, the British Labour Party and the economics of democratic socialism', in Hamouda and Smithin (eds) (1988), 29–42.

Fitzgibbons, A. (1988), *Keynes's Vision: A new political economy*, Oxford University Press.

Friedman, M. (1968), 'The role of monetary policy', *American Economic Review*, **58**(1), 1–17.

Gamble, A. (1985), *Britain in Decline: Economic policy, political strategy and the British state*, 2nd edn, London, Macmillan.

Hadjimatheou, G. (1987), 'Is public expenditure growth a problem?', *Royal Bank of Scotland Review*, **153**(1), 17–24.

Harris, J. (1977), *William Beveridge: A biography*, Oxford, Clarendon Press.

Harris, S.E. (ed) (1947), *The New Economics: Keynes' influence on theory and public policy*, London, Dennis Dobson.

Harris, S.E. (1955), *John Maynard Keynes: Economist and policy maker*, New York and London, Charles Scribner.

Harrod, R. (1951), *The Life of John Maynard Keynes*, London, Macmillan.

Harrod, R. (1969), 'The arrested revolution', *New Statesman*, 5 December, 808–10.

Hayek, F.A. (1931), *Prices and Production*, London, Routledge.

Hayek, F.A. (1944), *The Road to Serfdom*, London, Routledge & Kegan Paul.

HMSO (1944), Ministry of Reconstruction, *Employment Policy*, BPP 1943–4 (6527), viii, 119.

Hughes, J.R.T. (1977), *The Governmental Habit: Economic controls from colonial times to the present*, New York, Basic Books.

Institute of Economic Affairs (1986), *Keynes's General Theory: Fifty years on. Its relevance and irrelevance to modern times*, London, Institute of Economic Affairs.

Jay, D. (1946), *The Socialist Case*, London, Socialist Book Club.

Jay. D. (1980), *Change and Fortune: A political record*, London, Hutchinson.

Jenkins, R. (1953), *Pursuit of Progress: A critical analysis of the achievement and prospect of the Labour Party*, London, William Heinemann.

Johnson, E.S. and Johnson H.G. (1978), *The Shadow of Keynes: Understanding Keynes, Cambridge and Keynesian economics*, Oxford, Basil Blackwell.

Kahn, R.F. (1974), *On Re-reading Keynes*, Fourth Keynes Lecture in Economics, London, Oxford University Press.

Kahn, R.F. (1976), 'Unemployment as seen by the Keynesians', in G.D.N. Worswick (ed) *The Concept and Measurement of Involuntary Unemployment*, 19–34, London, George Allen & Unwin.

Kahn, R.F. (1984), *The Making of Keynes's General Theory*, Cambridge University Press.

Kaldor, N. (1983), 'Keynesian economics after fifty years', in G.D.N. Worswick and J. Trevithick (eds) *Keynes and the Modern World*, 1–28, 46–8, Cambridge University Press.

Kalecki, M. (1935), 'A macrodynamic theory of business cycles', *Econometrica*, 3(3), 327–44.

Kalecki, M. (1943), 'Political aspects of full employment', *Political Quarterly*, 14(4), 322–31.

Keagan, W. (1985), *Mrs Thatcher's Economic Experiment*, rev edn, Harmondsworth, Penguin.

Keynes, J.M. (1923), *A Tract on Monetary Reform*, Collected Writings of John Maynard Keynes, Vol. IV (1971), London, Macmillan.

Keynes, J.M. (1925a), 'Am I a Liberal?', in Keynes (1972), 295–306.

Keynes, J.M. (1925b), 'A short view of Russia', in Keynes (1972), 253–71.

Keynes, J.M. (1926a), 'Liberalism and Labour', in Keynes (1972), 307–11.

Keynes, J.M. (1926b), 'The end of laissez-faire', in Keynes (1972), 272–94.

Keynes, J.M. (1927), 'Liberalism and industry', in H.L. Nathan and H. Heathcote Williams (eds) *Liberal Points of View*, London, Benn.

Keynes, J.M. (1930a), 'Economic possibilities for our grandchildren', in Keynes (1972), 321–332.

Keynes, J.M. (1930b), *A Treatise on Money*. Collected Writings of John Maynard Keynes, Vols. V–VI (1971), London, Macmillan.

Keynes, J.M. (1931), 'The pure theory of money. A reply to Dr. Hayek', *Economica*, 11(4), 387–97.

Keynes, J.M. (1932), 'The dilemma of modern socialism', *Political Quarterly*, 3(2), 155–61.

Keynes, J.M. (1934), 'Is the economic system self-adjusting?' *The Listener*, 21 November 1934.

Keynes, J.M. (1936), *The General Theory of Employment, Interest and Money*. Collected Writings of John Maynard Keynes, Vol. VII (1973), London, Macmillan.

Keynes, J.M. (1938), 'My early beliefs', in Keynes, *Essays in Biography*. Collected Writings of John Maynard Keynes, Vol. X (1972), 433–50, London, Macmillan.

Keynes, J.M. (1939), 'Democracy and efficiency', *New Statesman and Nation*, 28 January 1939.

Keynes, J.M. (1943a), Letter to L.C. Robbins, 29 March, in Keynes (1980b), 316–17.

Keynes, J.M. (1943b), Letter to J.E. Meade, 25 April, in Keynes (1980b), 319–20.

Keynes, J.M. (1943c), 'The long-term problem of full employment', 25 May, in Keynes (1980b), 320–5.

Keynes, J.M. (1943d), J.M. Keynes to Sir. W. Eady, 'Maintenance of Employment: The draft note for the Chancellor of the Exchequer', 10 June, in Keynes (1980b), 325–7.

Keynes, J.M. (1943e), 'Objective of international price stability', *Economic Journal*, 53(2), 185–7.

Keynes, J.M. (1943f), Letter to B. Graham, 31 December, in Keynes (1980a), 36–8.

Keynes, J.M. (1944a), House of Lords speech, 23 May, in Keynes (1980a), 9–21.

Keynes, J.M. (1944b), Letter to F.A Hayek, 28 June, in Keynes (1980b), 385–8.

Keynes, J.M. (1945), Letter to T.S. Eliot, 5 April, in Keynes (1980b), 383–4.

Keynes, J.M. (1946), 'The balance of payments of the United States', *Economic Journal*, 56(2), 172–87.

Keynes, J.M. (1972), *Essays in Persuasion*. Collected Writings of John Maynard Keynes, Vol. IX, London, Macmillan.

Keynes, J.M. (1980a), *Activities 1941–1946: Shaping the post-war world: Bretton Woods and reparations*. D.E. Moggridge (ed). Collected Writings of John Maynard Keynes, Vol. XXVI, London, Macmillan.

Keynes, J.M. (1980b), *Activities 1940–1946: Shaping the post-war world: Employment and commodities*. D.E. Moggridge (ed). Collected Writings of

John Maynard Keynes, Vol. XXVII, London, Macmillan.

Keynes, M. (ed) (1975), *Essays on John Maynard Keynes*, Cambridge University Press.

Kregel, J.A. (1985), 'Budget deficits, stabilisation policy and liquidity preference: Keynes's post-war policy proposals', in F. Vicarelli (ed) (1985) *Keynes's Relevance Today*, 28–50, London, Macmillan.

Lehner, F. and Widmaier, U. (1983), 'Market failure and growth of government: A sociological explanation', in C.L. Taylor (ed) *Why Governments Grow: Measuring public sector size*, 240–60, London, Sage.

Leijonhufvud, A. (1968), *On Keynesian Economics and the Economics of Keynes: A study in monetary theory*, London, Oxford University Press.

Lekachman, R. (1967), *The Age of Keynes: A biographical study*, London, Allen Lane.

Lerner, A.P. (1943), 'Functional finance and the federal debt', *Social Research*, 10(1), 38–51.

Macmillan, H. (1938), *The Middle Way: A study of the problems of economic and social progress in a free and democratic society*, London, Macmillan.

Marwick, A. (1964), 'Middle opinion in the thirties: Planning, progress and political "agreement"', *English Historical Review*, 79(1), 285–98.

Matthews, R.C.O. (1968), 'Why has Britain had full employment since the war?', *Economic Journal*, 78(3), 555–69.

Middleton, R. (1985), *Towards the Managed Economy: Keynes, the Treasury and the fiscal policy debate of the 1930s*, London, Methuen.

Minsky, H.P. (1976), *John Maynard Keynes*, London, Macmillan.

Mises, L. von (1963), *Human Action: A treatise on economics*, 3rd edn, Chicago, Henry Regnery.

Moggridge, D.E. and Howson, S. (1974), 'Keynes on monetary policy 1910–1946', *Oxford Economic Papers* (new series), 26(2), 226–47.

Okun, A.M. (1975), *Equality and Efficiency: The Big Tradeoff*, Washington, DC, Brookings Institution.

Olson, M. (1982), *The Rise and Decline of Nations: Economic growth, stagflation and social rigidities*, New Haven, Yale University Press.

Peden, G.C. (1988), 'Old dogs and new tricks: The British Treasury and Keynesian economics in the 1940s and '50s', conference paper, 'The state and the growth of economic knowledge', Wilson Centre, Washington, DC, 14–16 September 1988.

Pigou, A.C. (1933), *Theory of Unemployment*, London, Macmillan.

Robinson, E.A.G. (1947), 'John Maynard Keynes, 1883–1946', *Economic Journal*, 57(1), 1–68. Rep. in R. Lekachman, (ed) (1964) *Keynes's General Theory: Reports of three decades*, 13–86, London, Macmillan.

Robinson, E.A.G. (1977a), 'A comment', in T.W. Hutchison (1977) *Keynes versus the Keynesians? An essay in the thinking of J.M. Keynes and the accuracy of its interpretation by his followers*, 58–60, London, Institute of Economic Affairs.

Robinson, E.A.G. (1977b), Contributions to discussion, in D. Patinkin and J.C. Leith (eds) *Keynes, Cambridge and the General Theory: The process of criticism and discussion connected with the development of the General Theory*, 79–80, London, Macmillan.

Robinson, J. (1933), *The Economics of Imperfect Competition*, London, Macmillan.

Robinson, J. (1969), *Introduction to the Theory of Employment*, 2nd edn, London, Macmillan.

Rollings, N. (1988), 'British budgetary policy 1945–54: A "Keynesian revolution" ', *Economic History Review*, 2nd ser, **41**(2), 283–98.

Rowse, A.L. (1936), *Mr Keynes and the Labour Movement*, London, Macmillan.

Skidelsky, R. (1977a), 'The revolt against the Victorians', in Skidelsky (ed) (1977b), 1–9.

Skidelsky, R. (ed) (1977b), *The End of the Keynesian Era: Essays on the disintegration of the Keynesian political economy*, London, Macmillan.

Skidelsky, R. (1979), 'The decline of Keynesian politics', in C. Crouch (ed) *State and Economy in Contemporary Capitalism*, 55–87, London, Croom-Helm.

Skidelsky, R. (1988), 'Keynes political legacy', in Hamouda and Smithin (eds) (1988), 3–28.

Smith, D. (1987), *The Rise and Fall of Monetarism*, Harmondsworth, Penguin.

Tomlinson, J. (1981), 'Why was there never a "Keynesian revolution" in economic policy?, *Economy and Society*, **10**(1), 72–87.

Tomlinson, J. (1987), *Employment Policy: The crucial years 1939–1955*, Oxford, Clarendon Press.

Whiteley, P. (1986), *Political Control of the Macroeconomy: The political economy of public policy making*, London, Sage.

Williams, P.A. (1982), *Hugh Gaitskell*, rev edn, London, Jonathan Cape.

Winch, D. (1972), *Economics and Policy: A historical survey*, rev edn, London, Fontana/Collins.

3 The early years of the National Health Service – an insider's view

Patrick Benner

Note. This article was written some months before the publication in January 1989 of the Government's proposals for changes in the running of the National Health Service.

Dr Webster's excellent book in the Peacetime History series about the inception and early years of the National Health Service (Webster, 1988) has appeared opportunely. Change is again in the air, and it may be interesting to set down some thoughts about trends and events in the early years of the service which, with hindsight, seem to be of particular significance, and then to speculate whether any lessons can be drawn or predictions made from the experience of forty years ago. In doing this, my perspective is that of someone who entered the old Ministry of Health (then still in the form established by the 1919 Act) in 1949, necessarily in a junior capacity, and moved into the reconstituted Ministry at the beginning of 1951; so I personally saw, though rather from the underside, some of the events of those years, while others were still green in the memory of colleagues.

It is often said, with truth, that the National Health Service Act of 1946, far from representing a revolution, was simply an important step in a long evolutionary process; and Dr Webster demonstrates convincingly how far back some of its roots lie (Webster, 1988: 1–24). To me as a new arrival, however, it seemed at the time that the process must have been revolutionary rather than evolutionary, and that there had been a great cataclysm in 1946/8 as a result of which an entirely new service had been brought to birth. Its form seemed to have been fashioned in concrete at the time of its creation, and was intended to endure unchanging. Evolution did not seem to come into the picture. And the man who had brought these great events to pass was Aneurin Bevan, the author and only begetter, who would see to it that no one meddled with the structure he had created. Bevan did indeed have a very high reputation in the Ministry, and for many years afterwards colleagues would look back and say he was the finest Minister we had ever had. I am sure that this awareness of the crucial role of a 'great man' or 'hero' served at the time to obscure the existence of evolutionary forces and to foster the idea of a once for all 'big bang'.

The fact is, of course, that the true picture had been obscured by the bitter controversy which had attended the launching of the NHS; for the consensus which quickly gave the new service so firm a basis in popular and political esteem did not exist initially. Bevan's difficulties were indeed very great; and their nature conveys some lessons for the present. Contrary to what might be expected, they were not primarily political in the narrow sense of that word. He had little trouble with the Parliamentary Opposition and, although his Cabinet colleagues expressed uneasiness about some aspects of his proposals, he did not have serious difficulty in persuading them to let him have his way. Rather, his problem lay in reconciling, on terms which he found tolerable and which commanded a sufficiently wide measure of acceptance, the conflicting interests of the various powerful organizations in the health field. These included in particular the local authorities, the voluntary hospitals, and above all the medical profession—and there one must distinguish sharply between the consultants and the general practitioners, whose attitudes and aspirations, then as now, differed widely and sometimes conflicted. Some other health professions, notably the dentists, also caused difficulties, but these were generally rather more peripheral.

Bevan's problem was that he was not faced with a simple 'them against us' conflict, but with something much more complex; for while some of his own objectives were directly contrary to the wishes of some of the interests concerned, the wishes of the various interests were not infrequently in headlong collision with one another. The most striking example of the latter is the conflict between the local authorities and the voluntary hospitals about who should be responsible for running the new service, which was immensely complicated by the emotional revulsion of the consultants against entering a service in which they would become the employees of the local authorities and of the general practitioners against becoming the direct employees of anyone. Less complex, though not easier to handle, was the problem presented by private practice: the doctors were deeply attached to it, while Bevan regarded it with profound political distaste.

This type of conflict with and between the various interests is likely to face anyone who wishes to make changes in the organization of health services, as much now as in 1946. But whereas Bevan's main difficulties on the professional front were with the doctors, the position now is that the health professions generally have become increasingly self-conscious and powerfully organized—the growth in the strength and influence of the nursing profession is especially striking—and have strongly held and sometimes differing views about health service matters. NHS management has likewise become self-conscious and organized, and is also liable to have firm views about the form and structure of the service. There is thus still ample opportunity for a government which meditates fundamental change to find itself embroiled in serious conflict; and, as Bevan quickly discovered, there are practical limits to how far a Minister can safely go in overriding the wishes of those providing or managing the health services, for their co-operation—willing rather than grudging—is necessary if the services are to function satisfactorily and the Minister is to avoid the political opprobrium likely to arise from any serious breakdown for which responsibility can colourably be laid at his door.

Against this background, it is no wonder that Bevan had to compromise in several important respects and to abandon some cherished objectives. His main achievement—and it was a substantial one, for which he deserves much credit—was that he managed to get the service launched in a form which, if not ideal, was viable and at least tolerable to the interested parties: in other words, that he succeeded in getting something done where others, notably the Coalition Government, had failed.

There were two areas in particular where his inability to secure all he had originally hoped for had serious long term implications. First, the service established by the 1946 Act was not unitary, but tripartite; and the local authorities which, as the main respositories of managerial skills in running and co-ordinating health services generally and hospitals in particular, had expected that the new service would be entrusted to them, found themselves relegated to a subordinate position. The loss of the local authorities' managerial skills, patchy though they admittedly had been, appreciably increased the initial difficulties of the NHS, since the new hospital authorities had to start entirely from scratch. Even more damaging in the long run was Bevan's inability to achieve the benefits which would in principle have been obtainable from the scope which a unitary service would have secured to plan health services as a whole, with the hospital, community and general practice sectors brought together into a rational structure all the parts of which were developed so as to give one another mutual support. This had long been the goal of reformers; but the failure to achieve it in 1946 is perhaps not surprising given that, forty years later, complete unification still eludes us.

In addition, the unexpected defeat of the local authorities led to a collapse of morale in the public health field, which was the only sector for which they retained responsibility. The result was that the public health function, as personified by the Medical Officer of Health, entered into a long period of decline. The supply of new, able entrants into this area of medicine diminished, levels of skill and confidence declined correspondingly, and the situation became so bad that a major rescue operation had to be launched in the 1970s. It is doubtful whether the ground lost in the decades after the inception of the NHS has even now been entirely regained. This is a serious matter, for we are coming to realise that a sound public health service (to use the old terminology) is as badly needed now as it was forty years ago.

Secondly, Bevan was unable to persuade the medical profession to accept a service in which all hospital doctors worked full time, and had to concede the principle of part time contracts for hospital consultants and an entrenched position for private practice. Only a very small number of private hospitals providing acute service survived nationalization, but the provision made in section 5 of the 1946 Act for the designation of private pay beds in NHS hospitals ensured the continuation of private practice on a significant scale. Despite that, however, private practice was at that time (and for a good many years to come) looked on within government with deep reserve. In the case of the Labour government, it was a reserve amounting to hostility; but Conservative governments were also conspicuously reluctant to commit themselves to anything in the nature of open public support for private practice. There was indeed for some years an expectation—which seemed to be borne out as the number of pay beds slowly diminished—that private practice would gradually wither away until it ceased to be of major significance. This did not in fact happen; and the structure which Bevan accepted in 1946 left open the way to change in response to later modifications in public and political attitudes towards private practice.

There are three strands in the history of the early years of the service which, with hindsight, seem of particular relevance. The first is the financial troubles which arose at the very outset, largely because of failure on the part of both the Coalition and the Labour governments to arrive at a realistic estimate of the likely annual cost of the NHS. Sufficient allowance was not made for the quantitative inadequacy of the health services, nor for the antiquated and decayed state of much of the capital stock. This is a surprising failure, because the shortcomings of the services as they stood had been well documented, in particular through the survey of hospital resources carried out during the war under the auspices of the Nuffield Provincial Hospitals Trust, with the support of the Coalition government. Perhaps more understandably, there was also a failure to allow for the financial effect, in a free comprehensive service, of the pent-up demand for some forms of care, especially optical and dental, and to realise that the pay of most health services staff was unacceptably low and that the new Whitley Council machinery, once it had come into action, was likely to produce an expensive catching up operation.

As a result of this unrealistic financial forecasting, the expenditure estimates were very substantially exceeded in each of the first two years of the NHS. At that point, however, the total net cost of the service stabilized, though at a much higher level than had originally been expected, so that, as Dr Webster points out (Webster, 1988: 257–62), after 1950/51 the annual increases in hospital expenditure—which is where the big money was—were modest in real terms (and certainly less than was objectively desirable). Expenditure does in fact seem to have been fairly well under control; but the damage had been done, for the political effect of those two early years was disastrous—largely, no doubt, because the unexpected extra cost was highly embarrassing to the Labour government against the background of the economic and other difficulties with which it was faced. In addition, Bevan's unwillingness to give any ground in response to the anxieties of his colleagues, and indeed even to concede that a serious problem existed, seems to have done considerable harm both to his own position and, more seriously, to the way in which the NHS was perceived. The overall result was that within government—though not in the public mind—the NHS came to be seen as a nuisance and a major financial liability and acquired a firmly established reputation for extravagance, waste and inefficiency which, though largely unjustified, dogged it almost continuously thereafter, and still does to some extent even to this day. Political attention was therefore diverted from the inherited deficiencies of the service and the need to correct them, and concentrated instead on the supposedly urgent task of securing financial savings and correcting inefficiency, so as to avoid throwing good money after bad.

The fact is, no doubt, that in some respects the NHS was launched at a peculiarly unfavourable time. The main reason for its existence was that the old patchwork of health services was no longer adequate, and required fundamental modernization and expansion. This necessarily implied extra expenditure above all else. But the post-war period, beset as it was with economic difficulties, a general need for reconstruction at home and the appearance of unexpected defence requirements, was a time when demands for new expenditure were bound to be unwelcome, especially when they were unforeseen. So although the creation of the NHS was a political necessity, it came into being at the precise time when the scope for bringing about the developments the securing of which was one of its main *raisons d'être* was exceptionally limited. It is therefore not to be wondered at that the Ministry of Health became increasingly involved in the defensive and essentially negative task of fighting off demands for cuts and economies and the imposition of charges additional to those which were introduced in 1951/2. And the Ministry's difficulties were compounded by the enfeeblement, in terms both of reduced actual political influence and of damage to internal morale, which was brought about when it was split up early in 1951 and the Minister of Health ceased to be of Cabinet rank. Thus it seems fair to say that the establishment within government circles of unfavourable attitudes towards the NHS—in particular, a persistent and very damaging belief in its extravagance and inefficiency—was one of the most harmful legacies of the Bevan era.

Secondly, there were a number of forces which, in the early years of the NHS, were working for immobility and an inward-looking conservatism. One sprang from the financial difficulties just referred to; for Ministers of Health and their Department were obliged to adopt a firmly defensive posture and to concentrate on repelling attacks from within Whitehall to the exclusion of imaginative new thinking. Moreover, the new service did not have an easy start internally. It took some long while to establish with precision what the NHS actually consisted of—as late as 1952, arguments were still going on about whether certain institutions were part of the service or had remained outside it. Moreover, hospitals which were incontrovertibly within the NHS were sometimes reluctant to be there, and relations between the Ministry and the new hospital authorities were often uncomfortable. There was a strong sense of 'them and us', a fair amount of actual or implicit resentment and hostility towards the Ministry, and the odd instance of downright bloody-mindedness. Nowhere was the resentment and hostility greater than in the London teaching hospitals. Inevitably, therefore, the administrative wheels were full of grit, and effort which would ideally have been devoted to improving the service was diverted into internal politicking. It is no wonder that, during the middle and late 1950s, Ministers were anxious for the NHS to be allowed a period of peace and quiet.

Another cause of immobility originated in the fact, well brought out by Dr Webster (Webster, 1988: 393), that the NHS as it emerged in 1948 merely represented the best deal that could be done between the various contestants after long and exhausting battles—as he says, it was a sort of 'line of truce'. No one was prepared to contemplate changes which might threaten the stability of a compromise which, even if imperfect, had been achieved at the cost of so much pain and strife. In particular, the Ministry and the medical profession, much as they might (and in many respects undoubtedly did) dislike and fear one another, both had a vested interest in stability; and the result was the development of a sort of partnership between them—unoffficial, unavowed and occasionally broken by active hostilities (especially over pay), but usually strong enough to outbalance distrust and dislike—which worked strongly in favour of the maintenance of the status quo and against any change save of the most cautious nature.

This support for the status quo was buttressed by a firm general belief in this view that an absolute distinction could and should be drawn between clinical and administrative matters, and that doctors must be seen as carrying full responsibility for the conduct of clinical affairs. In those early days, the Ministry, as a matter of principle, took a largely (though not wholly) laisser faire attitude towards clinical planning, clinical methods and the longer term planning of clinical services. The medical staff of the Ministry certainly interested themselves in these matters; but the medical profession was generally seen as being in the driving seat, and was handled with kid gloves. It would in the circumstances of the time have been very difficult for the Ministry to play a positive part in what is now regarded as one of the most important elements of health service planning; and this had a good deal to do with the prevailing appearance of immobility. Of course, many important advances occurred in medical knowledge and skills; but the influence exercised by the Ministry was largely informal, and most of the drive came from elsewhere.

Still another factor militating against change was the public popularity which the NHS rapidly achieved as people came to appreciate the benefits of a service which was universal and in the main free (entirely so until 1951). A political consensus quickly developed as all parties rallied behind the NHS and claimed to be, if not its progenitors, then at least its guardians. Within a very few years, the NHS had become a sacred cow with which no sensible politician would venture to meddle; and the result was that many aspects of it—especially structure, financing and coverage—became political no-go areas. Thoughts about substantial changes thus became unprofitable. It should be noted, however, that this political consensus did not overcome Whitehall's distrust of the NHS. Its political benefits were appreciated, but not to the extent that early priority was given to making good its inherited deficiencies; and capital allocations continued to be minute, particularly when compared with the substantial resources which were devoted to, for example, housing.

With so many influences favouring maintenance of the status quo, it is no wonder that the decade after 1948 was a 'mark time' period, during which little headway could be made with developing and improving the service or planning ways of making good the less satisfactory features of the 1946 settlement. The stodgy and over-complacent Guillebaud Report (1956) was a suitable monument to it.

The third significant influence during the early years of the NHS sprang from Bevan's unexpected decision to nationalize the hospital service. This seems to have been essentially a tactical manoeuvre to deal with the mutual antagonism of the local authorities and the voluntary hospitals and the refusal of the hospital doctors to accept a service run by local government. Seen in this light, Bevan's action was successful; but what he appears to have left out of account was that, by nationalizing the hospitals, he had placed the Ministry of Health in a position which logically required it to assume a central managerial role for which, as an old-style regulatory Whitehall department, it was neither prepared nor equipped. It took the Ministry a long time to realize what had happened, let alone to take remedial action; and for many years it continued to regard its main task simply as the formulation of policies which were then promulgated in circulars. Virtually no consideration was given to the administrative feasibility or financial consequences of the policies which were recommended to health and hospital authorities, nor was there any machinery for systematically monitoring the performance of authorities and observing how effectively the Ministry's policies were being carried out. Concepts such as financial and manpower planning, the establishment of priorities and the preparation of long term development plans gained a foothold only slowly—an effective start on long term national hospital planning, for example, was not made until the 1960s. And the word 'monitor' was in those early years unknown as a verb—it was understood only as a noun denoting either a pupil invested with authority over a class or a shallow draught ironclad used for bombarding shore installations.

It seems unlikely that Bevan realized that he had established the NHS in a form which logically required the existence of a managerial, as well as a regulatory and policy-making, body at the centre. And not only logically, but politically as well; for there was continuing difficulty in reconciling the doctrine of local managerial responsibility, which was always strongly emphasized, with the Minister's unlimited statutory responsibility for the hospital service and all that went on in it. Significantly, Ministers always provided substantive answers to queries and complaints from Members of Parliament about the detailed working of the hospitals, because it was regarded as politically unacceptable to take refuge behind the managerial responsibility of the hospital authorities. This contradiction was underlined by the accusations of managerial incompetence which were persistently levelled against the NHS within Whitehall. Happily, the performance of the hospital authorities was in the main reasonably good—administratively, the NHS has always given good value for money, better probably than any other method of organizing health care; but the managerial gap at the centre represented a missing link in the chain, and undoubtedly rendered more intractable the difficulties which the NHS encountered during its early years.

In conclusion, I will attempt to move from examination of the past to speculation about the future; and this is perhaps best done by considering what changes there have been in the conditions which shaped events in 1946 and the immediately succeeding years.

The options for change which now present themselves to government are broadly what they have always been—structural reform (tried twice since 1946, and found of uncertain outcome and anyway slow to produce effects); improved management of the NHS so as to improve economy and efficiency; abandonment of some parts of the service; imposition of new and/or increased charges; introduction of some form of contributory insurance scheme in the public and/or the private sector; imposition of a special tax or of a specific contribution under the National Insurance scheme; or strengthening of the private health sector to a greater or lesser extent so that some demand can be diverted towards it. If, then, the options are essentially unchanged, have there been changes in circumstances which make some of them relatively more or less attractive?

The public's attitude towards the NHS seems to have been much as it has always been—a high degree of attachment and support, which renders politically unattractive changes which can be represented as a substantial contraction or undermining of the service. There has likewise been little reduction in the influence of the health professions—if anything, the reverse is the case—and it would be as difficult now as it was in 1946 to make changes to which they were strongly opposed. One difference now as compared with 1946 is that whereas then the medical profession was hostile to many of Bevan's ideas, now it is strongly supportive of the continuation of the NHS in broadly its present form, though better financed; and broadly the same is true of the nursing profession. The professions and the public are thus on the same side, which was not the case in 1946. It still seems likely, therefore, that only a very determined government with strong ideological commitments would be prepared to contemplate any substantial dismantling of the NHS or the replacement of evolutionary by revolutionary change.

There are, however, two areas where substantial alterations have taken place since 1946. The first is the development of managerial skills. The Department of Health has done a good deal towards filling the managerial void at the centre which was created in 1946 and persisted for many years thereafter. At the same time, managerial capability in the NHS, though never so serious a weakness as received opinion in Whitehall used to make out, has markedly improved (in effect keeping pace with the advance in managerial skills which has taken place in nearly every area of national life); and availability of the factual information needed for effective management has developed and will continue to do so. Perhaps the most important of all, there are significant signs that the medical profession is increasingly coming to accept that it has managerial duties, and that it is proper for consultants to be responsible for the management of the resources placed at their disposal and to concern themselves with managerial as well as clinical matters. The clinical field is thus now coming to be seen as firmly within the proper scope of rational service planning. These changes have probably gone some way towards weakening belief in the cruder forms of the old myth that the NHS is inherently extravagant and inefficient; and there seems a fair prospect that continuing improvement in NHS management and in its ability to ensure economy and efficiency will, almost for the first time, inspire confidence within government that the NHS is capable of making effective use of the resources allocated to it and of providing good value for money.

The second area of change lies not in the NHS itself but in the private sector. Private health has now become respectable, and has greatly expanded. The political cloud which hung over it for so many years seems to have been dispelled, so much so that expansion of private acute care (sometimes in partnership with the NHS) and of private health insurance schemes is now widely seen as a positively desirable development to the extent that it can potentially shift some of the burden of health care from the shoulders of the NHS and bring into the health care arena financial and manpower resources which would not otherwise have been available. Relative to the NHS, the private sector is comparatively small and, in absence of major policy changes which do not seem very likely, will probably remain so for some time to come; but the elbow-room and the hope of extra resources which it provides make a significant change from the circumstances of 1946.

These lines of thought seem to suggest that, if change is on the way, it is on the whole unlikely to be of a radical nature, revolutionary rather than evolutionary, but instead may be concentrated in the areas of improved management within the NHS—where there is surely still considerable scope for further development—and of continuing modest expansion of the private health sector combined with an improved partnership between it and the NHS.

References

Webster, C. (1988), *The Health Services since the War, Volume 1. Problems of Health Care. The National Health Service before 1957.* HMSO

Report of the Committee of Enquiry into the cost of the National Health Service (Cmd. 9663, 1956)

4 The struggle for control of the airwaves: the Attlee governments, the BBC and industrial unrest, 1945–51

Justin Davis Smith

The Attlee governments of 1945–51 accepted in principle an independent BBC free from government control. Herbert Morrison, who as Lord President was answerable in Parliament for broadcasting, assured Parliament in December 1946, during a debate on the renewal of the Charter and Licence, that the Government intended to '. . . preserve the independent status of the BBC . . ..' It would, he said, 'be bad for the liberty of our country if the Government had the direct day-to-day management of the BBC'.[1] Lord Simon, Chairman of the Corporation after the war, was of the opinion that the Labour Governments did give 'steady support to the independence of the BBC'. (Simon, 1953: 32). The evidence, however, suggests otherwise.

During several unofficial industrial disputes after the war representation was made to top officials at the BBC to keep unofficial strikers off the air and to allow leading trade union officials, opponents of the strike, to broadcast appeals for a return to work, without any right to reply from those on strike. Attempts were also made to persuade the BBC to 'structure' the news bulletins in such a way as to encourage a swift resumption of work. The BBC, led by the fiercely independent Director-General Sir William Haley,[2] resisted these attempts by governments to influence broadcasting policy. Paradoxically, therefore, the BBC, so often accused by the British Left of an anti-Labour bias, can be seen during this period to have acted in support of minority interests and the right of unofficial strikers to equal treatment, against powerful Labour governments anxious to restrict access to the air-waves to 'legitimate' trade union representation.[3]

In comparison to the period immediately following the end of the First World War the period after 1945 was remarkably strike free. From VE Day on 8 May 1945 to September 1949, ten and a quarter million days were lost as a result of industrial disputes, compared with 170 million days lost during the corresponding period after 1918. The situation after 1945 was also in contrast to the Second World War which had witnessed a sharp rise in industrial disputes, the vast majority of which were unofficial due to the legal restrictions which had been imposed on strike action in 1940. The ban on strikes, contained in Order 1305, was maintained by the Attlee administrations with the result that there was an almost total absence of official strikes between 1945–51. There was, nevertheless, a rash of unofficial strikes after the War, especially in the docks and the mines, which caused grave concern to the Labour administrations, faced with the daunting task of rebuilding a shattered and bankrupt nation after six years of total war. To break these disputes the governments turned to the pre-war expedients of the armed force and emergency regulations available under the Emergency Powers Act of 1920. Troops were, in fact, introduced no fewer than 11 separate industrial disputes during the lifetime of the Attlee administrations and a state of emergency was declared during two dock strikes in 1948 and 1949. Preparations were also made for the introduction of civilian volunteers to replace unofficial strikers. The Governments saw the BBC as a vital addition to their strike breaking weaponry.

The Second World War had given rise to state intervention in all aspects of national life and the BBC was no exception. Both at home and in its overseas broadcasts the Corporation was subject to strict government controls, though from 1943 these controls were slackened to some extent. Government influence was very much in evidence in the coverage of industrial disputes. For the first four years of the war the BBC steered clear of strikes. In November 1943 the Chief Industrial Commissioner of the Ministry of Labour, Harold Emmerson, approached the Corporation with the request that better treatment of strikes should in future be given. It had been brought to the Government's attention that the BBC news bulletins were widely quoted by factory workers (more so than the daily newspapers) and it was felt that they should be used to counter attempts to stir up industrial unrest. Guidelines were issued to the BBC. 'The strike', Emmerson explained, 'should be put in its proper context, the issues should be outlined clearly, the scope of the stoppage should be brought out and the usual newspaper "flan" should be eschewed.' To ensure close consultation between the Government and the BBC the industrial relations department of the Ministry of Labour was placed at the disposal of the Corporation, to provide 'unlimited help' on the strike situation.[4]

With the end of the war senior officials at the BBC emphasized the need to free the Corporation from wartime restrictions and controls. Formal control was removed in 1946 with the dissolution of the Ministry of Information and its replacement with a Central Office of Information. Parliament was given the assurance 'that the independence of the BBC will be in no ways altered' under the new organization.[5] Nevertheless, it was the opinion of at least one official at the BBC that state control remained strong throughout the post-war years. In 1951, he wrote that the BBC 'by a process of inevitable development, is now in the position of a quasi-governmental institution which is steadily approaching in outlook, in organization and in ultimate control the position of an ordinary government department'. (Coatman, 1951: 287).

It is my contention that this analysis is, at least in part, incorrect. Certainly 'ultimate control' remained in the hands of the government: Under Clause 4 (3) and (4) of the Licence and Agreement under which the BBC operated, the Corporation was required to broadcast any announcement or to refrain from sending any broadcast material which the Postmaster-General by notice might require. As a last resort Clause 21 of the Licence empowered the Postmaster-General, in an emergency, to take over the running of the Corporation's premises and stations. Government control over all material broadcast by the BBC was thus, in theory, absolute. In practice, however, successive governments had steered clear of invoking such direct powers of control and the Attlee administrations were to prove no exception. The emergency regulations introduced to break the dock strikes in 1948 and 1949, as with those introduced to break the general strike in 1926, did not deal specifically with the BBC. Although state influence over some aspects of broadcasting policy, in particular international affairs, remained important, over the coverage of industrial disputes the BBC showed a marked degree of independence which, on occasions, brought it into open conflict with the Labour Goverments.

Labour's attempts to influence the coverage of industrial disputes took a variety of forms. In the first instance it was held essential that the news bulletins presented the 'facts' of the strikes in a manner most likely to bring about a return to work. Of course, as Herbert Morrison admitted to William Haley, the BBC could not suppress news. But often the presentation of news was all important.[6]

In December 1945 an official from the Ministry of Labour accused the BBC of behaving 'rather like the popular and less responsible papers', in emphasizing in the news headlines the rejection by the Central London Strike Committee of the Evershed Committee's report on the port transport industry, rather than giving prominence to the fact that union officials were to recommend its acceptance.[7] In June 1948 criticism was levelled against the BBC for reporting in the news the number of dockers on strike rather than placing the emphasis on those who had refused to stop work.[8] Similarly, in February 1951, Cabinet heard a complaint 'that the BBC in its news bulletins had tended to exaggerate the extent of the dock strike and had failed to draw attention to the numbers of men who had remained at work'.[9]

The Government was also anxious that the fullest possible coverage be given to ministerial statements on strikes. In May 1947, the Minister of Labour, George Isaacs, speaking in St Albans, charged the BBC with deleting 'the most important part' of his recent broadcast statement, thereby delaying settlement of the dispute by several days. In subsequent correspondence with the Director-General Isaacs stressed 'the immense importance of the BBC' in any emergency affecting the welfare of the community, in bringing before the public 'the salient facts on the authority of the Government'.[10] There could have been no clearer statement of the importance the Government attached to a sympathetic broadcasting service in helping to defeat unofficial strikes.

The presentation of news by the BBC, however, was governed by strict guidelines. The Beveridge Committee of 1949–50, set up to look into the future of broadcasting, was told that the role of the corporation was to 'state the news of the day accurately, fairly, soberly and impersonally' (Briggs, 1979: 570). An internal BBC memorandum setting out the Corporation's policy on the treatment of strikes, stressed that it should not withhold news about an industrial dispute merely because it might be of inconvenience to the Government.[11] From these guidelines the BBC was not willing to depart. Haley told Isaacs in May 1947 that, although the BBC was always willing to give careful attention to the views of the Ministry of Labour, 'the full responsibility for the contents of the bulletins, must remain with the Corporation'.[12] Nevertheless, as Kenneth Morgan (1984: 324) has pointed out, many news headlines were slanted in an anti-Labour direction.

It was not simply in the presentation of news that the governments sought to influence the BBC in its coverage of industrial affairs. During several disputes representation was made to the BBC to secure broadcasting facilities for union leaders to appeal for a return to work, without a right of reply for the men on strike. These demands were resisted by the Corporation.

Controversy arose during an unofficial dock strike in October 1945 when the BBC refused to allow the secretary of the dockers' section of the Transport and General Workers' Union (TGWU), Mr Donovan, to broadcast an appeal to return to work. The strike had begun in Birkenhead over the rate of pay for handling pit props and had spread rapidly to the ports of Liverpool, Manchester and London. The Government was determined to end the strike and introduced troops into the Liverpool docks to unload cargoes of perishable food. At 8.00 p.m. on 12 October Attlee contacted Haley on the telephone and requested that in the national interest Donovan be put on. Although he had not seen the message himself, Attlee said he understood it was purely factual and entirely non-controversial and would help bring about an end to the strike. Haley disagreed. The purpose of the broadcast, he argued, would clearly be to influence the strike 'and however wrong the strike might be it would be wrong of the BBC to take sides in it'. If the strike leaders wished to reply to Mr Donovan the BBC 'under its trust of impartiality, would be bound to allow one of them to broadcast'. As this was likely to bring more men out it was not in the public interest that the broadcast take place. The BBC, he said, would of course report any statement by Donovan in the news but this was very different matter from a broadcast by him in person. For Haley the situation was comparable to the General Strike when the BBC had 'allowed itself to be used by the Government, a course for which it had been strongly criticised in later years'. He was anxious that this should not happen again. In May 1926, the

General Manager of the BBC, John Reith, had refused to allow the leader of the Opposition, Ramsay MacDonald, to broadcast during the strike, although access to the air-waves had been freely granted to the Prime Minister, Stanley Baldwin. For Attlee the General Strike was a different matter entirely. The present dispute was unofficial and the strike leaders were, in his opinion, only 'odds and ends'. Haley, however, was insistent that the Corporation's independence and impartiality should not be compromised. He had determined, he told the Prime Minister, on becoming Director-General, to 'remove from no body of citizens, not even strikers, the right to impartial treatment by the BBC'.[13] Attlee was forced to back down and the statement by Donovan was subsequently reported in the news. The Director-General's stand was later fully endorsed by the Board of Governors.

In June 1948 the BBC again fell foul of the Government over its refusal to allow the General Secretary of the TGWU, Arthur Deakin, to broadcast without the right of reply on the situation in the London docks. The strike had begun as a protest against the disciplinary action taken by the local dock labour board against 11 men who had refused to unload a cargo of 'dirty' zinc oxide. By 18 June there was an almost complete stoppage in the London docks which posed a serious threat to food supplies. On 23 June 300 troops moved in to Poplar docks to unload perishable foodstuffs. The strike was unofficial and did not have the backing of the Transport Workers' Union. As in October 1945 the Government intervened directly to try to persuade the BBC to reverse its decision. Once again the Corporation held firm. On 25 June 1948 Morrison met Haley and impressed on him the importance of bringing the strike to a swift conclusion. In addition to the damage being inflicted on the nation's economic recovery the Government, he said, feared that a prolongation of the dispute might lead to a wave of unofficial, politically fomented strikes as had recently occurred in France. It was therefore vital that Deakin be allowed to broadcast an appeal to return to work. 'There should, of course', Morrison stressed, 'be no right of reply from the other side.' Haley reiterated the view that to allow only one side in a dispute to speak would compromise the BBC's impartiality but that the same objection would not be raised to a ministerial broadcast as the government of the day had a clear duty to carry on the affairs of the nation. The Cabinet, however, had already rejected this course of action on the grounds that only a broadcast from a union leader could re-establish the authority of the TGWU and Morrison now made it clear that the Government might invoke the powers contained in the Charter and Licence and instruct the BBC to put Deakin on the air.[14]

The threat was an empty one. The Government had clearly misunderstood the clause of the Licence and Agreement covering the powers of direction which, although carrying an obligation on the BBC to broadcast any material handed to it, specifically refrained from requiring the BBC to direct a particular person to broadcast. Moreover, the BBC retained the right to announce that any particular broadcast had gone out under instruction from the government. The revelation that the BBC had been directed to allow Deakin to broadcast an appeal to return to work would have greatly embarrassed Labour, which throughout the dispute had stressed its unwillingness to become involved. On the same day the Board of Governors met and reaffirmed the position taken by Haley. On 28 June the Director-General informed Morrison that the BBC, although not prepared to put Deakin on the air, would 'provide immediate facilities' for a ministerial broadcast. At 9.00 p.m. the Prime Minister broadcast an appeal to the dockers to return to work. It was an immediate success, the dockers returning to work within 48 hours.[15]

In his broadcast Attlee stressed the importance of the system of collective bargaining, 'which is without parallel in the world', in maintaining industrial peace and the damage that would be caused to this system if the government ever agreed to deal with unofficial elements. The Government, however, did have a duty to the public. The present dispute not only threatened to deprive the public of essential services but was inflicting severe damage on the nation's economic recovery. For these reasons the Government had deemed it necessary to proclaim a state of emergency. Attlee then turned his attention to the past horrors of casual labour and issued a veiled threat to the dockers on strike. The huge gains made by the dock workers under the Labour government, he demanded, required a measure of responsibility and discipline in return. The broadcast ended with an attack on the part played by communists in fomenting the trouble.[16] The newspapers praised the broadcast for 'its simplicity and directness, a masterpiece of composition'. (Harris, 1982: 422–3). One Labour backbencher congratulated Attlee on a speech which 'was urgent and moving, . . . so human and full of commonsense, it was absolutely right'.[17] Attlee, not renowned for his rhetorical skills, had by all accounts scored a notable success. It was later divulged, however, that the speech had been drafted by Ernest Bevin.[18]

The success of the broadcast convinced the government of the importance of the BBC in helping to bring disputes to a swift and satisfactory conclusion. But to achieve this end it was deemed essential that the right of reply be withheld from unofficial strikers. This issue came to a head in April 1949 during a strike in the London docks over the dismissal by the London Dock Labour Board of 32 'ineffective workers'. On 13 April Isaacs broadcast to the nation on the dispute, describing it 'as an excuse for reckless action, intended to cause trouble and to upset the economic life of our country'. William Haley informed the Government that the BBC was prepared to consider any requests from the 'other side' for the right of reply. The Government's response was to again threaten to invoke the powers of censorship contained in the Licence and Agreement. A member of the Prime Minister's staff warned Haley on 13 April that, although the Government was not anxious to 'wield a big stick, . . . they had certain powers and might wish to consider using them'.[19] The right of reply, it was claimed, had been forfeited because the strike was illegal. However, no request for a reply was made and the matter was quietly dropped.

In June 1949 the Minister of Labour once again broadcast to the nation on the occasion of a dispute in the docks. Again it appeared to do the trick. By what Jeffery and Hennessy (1983: 202) have termed 'The magic of the wireless', the men returned to work. Inevitably, calls were made for the Government to make greater use of the BBC during industrial disputes. In July 1949, when the unrest spread to the London docks, Mr W.J. Brown demanded in the House that use be made of all the resources available, in particular the BBC, 'to a very much greater extent than has been done so far to get the facts of this case over to the men'.[20] Isaacs did broadcast again on 13 July. This time it had little perceptible influence on the resolve of the dockers to remain out. The Government had overplayed its hand. Major Robert Neville (whose troops had been drafted into the docks during the strike) informed Attlee, after talking to strikers, that the men now wanted to hear the Government's argument on the spot. 'They do not', he said, 'regard the less direct medium of a broadcast as meeting the case any longer.'[21]

Not only was Labour anxious to deny unofficial strikers the opportunity to reply to ministerial broadcasts or broadcasts from trade union officials. It was determined to keep them off the air altogether. At the beginning of May 1949, with the outbreak of unrest in the Bristol docks in support of the Canadian Seamen's Union, BBC West Region planned a programme of recorded statements with the aid of the TGWU, the Port Authority and the Port Employers' Association, under the title of the 'Gulfside Incident', designed to help explain the dispute to the public. From the first it was intended to include the voice of one of the dockers on strike. The programme was due to go out at 9.15 p.m. on 5 May. On the afternoon of the 5th representation from the National Dock Labour Board was made to the Government to persuade the BBC to cancel the programme.[22] That evening the Prime Minister contacted the Director-General. The proposed broadcast, Attlee argued, was 'inflammatory' and might well inflame feelings at a delicate stage of the dispute. Moreover, the strike was illegal and the BBC should be wary about giving the microphone to a person who was committing an illegal act. Haley informed the Prime Minister that the broadcast had already been cancelled by West Region as a result of difficulties raised by the local Dock Labour Board.[23] This was the first time the BBC had bowed to outside pressure. Interestingly, in Cabinet on 26 May, it was agreed that the Minister of Labour should arrange for a broadcast to be made on the West Regional programme explaining the 'true' facts and significance of the dock strike, with particular emphasis on communist involvement. The unofficial strikers, of course, were to take no part in the programme.[24]

The question of whether the BBC was open to prosecution for supporting or inciting an illegal strike was raised in the aftermath of this incident. The

Corporation's legal advisers confirmed that it would in fact be committing an offence if it allowed a broadcast which, either expressly or by implication, incited employees to take part in an illegal strike. Under Order 1305, first introduced in 1940, but continued after the War by the Labour Governments, strikes and lockouts were illegal unless a dispute had been reported to the Minister of Labour and had not been referred by him for settlement within 21 days. Haley, however, remained sceptical. 'I still do not believe any government would dare to prosecute a newspaper which ran an article by a striker on "why we have stopped work", he wrote on 23 May. 'If however the newspaper went on to appeal to other workers to do the same thing that would be another matter.' Haley could see no reason why the BBC should be treated any differently.[25] The Controller of West Region stressed the serious consequence of this legal judgement for the independence of the BBC. 'We strain every nerve to give facilities to all parties', he wrote, 'but if it is a criminal offence to give facilities for strikers, we are cut off from an essential element in impartiality.'[26]

The threat of legal action inevitably made the BBC less willing to risk open confrontation with the Government. Regional Controllers were notified that in future they would be required to consult with Head Office in advance of any broadcast on industrial disputes. Legal sanctions, moreover, were not confined to the criminal law. In October 1951 the BBC was advised that even with the repeal of Order 1305, which removed the threat of criminal prosecution, the Corporation was still vulnerable to civil proceedings for damages at the suit of employers if it allowed a broadcast which, either explicitly or by implication, invited employees to break their contract of employment.[27] Excessive caution in the broadcasting of controversial matters was the result of such legal strictures, though this did not always take the form the Government desired. In February 1951, for example, the Cabinet heard of the failure of the BBC to publish certain parts of a speech made by the Attorney-General at Buckingham, in which he claimed that the arrested men were not dockers on strike but agitators. It was suggested that this might in some measure be due to bias shown by the press agencies from where the BBC drew the news, and that it might be necessary to try to build up a direct contact between the Dock Labour Board and the BBC. It later came to light that the BBC had steered clear of publicizing the speech while the seven arrested dockers were appearing in court so as not to be held in contempt of court.[28]

The repeated failure of the Government to persuade the BBC to accept direction over the coverage of strikes, inevitably led to moves to strengthen state control over the Corporation. In December 1950 the ministerial Emergencies Committee met to discuss the question of broadcasting in a civil emergency. Much of the discussion centred around the 'technical' problems of maintaining a broadcasting service in an emergency. The maintenance of a skeleton service was not held to be a serious problem as most important installations of the BBC were equipped with emergency power plant. The major problem was public reception of the service during a power strike and plans were drawn up for the transmission of news and government statements, 'either by means of loud-speakers installed in the streets at central points, or by mobile loud-speaker sets'. But consideration was also given to the question of government control over broadcasting. Too often, ministers complained, the Corporation 'had interpreted their obligation to be neutral in political affairs as requiring them to give facilities not only to the Government but to unofficial strikers'. It was essential that the Government be able to rely on the BBC to broadcast in the 'national interest'. Whilst the powers of direction could be used as a last resort, much more, it was felt, would be gained by voluntary co-operation. The Government in fact had shown a marked reluctance to invoke direct powers of control. Any attempt to direct the BBC outside of a war-time emergency would have caused a major political storm. The Committee agreed that talks 'at an appropriate level' might induce the BBC to be more co-operative in the future.[29]

The matter was taken up in January 1951 at a meeting between officials from the Home Office and representatives from the BBC and the General Post Office. The importance of keeping secret the discussions were stressed from the outset. For the Government Sir Frank Newsam argued that, in times of industrial unrest, 'the BBC should be ready to listen to views as to what was or was not in the national interest'. Haley disagreed, arguing that the Corporation had a duty to maintain impartiality and not to become the mouthpiece of government propaganda. He was not prepared, he said, 'to give any blank cheque on behalf of the Governors'. However, a recommendation that in a civil emergency an 'informal and confidential' meeting between the Director-General and the Home Office be held to bring to the attention of the BBC the Government's view as to where the national interest lay, was accepted by Haley.[30] Morrison later informed Newsam that whilst he did not depart from the conclusions reached at this meeting, there must be all possible discretion in seeking to influence the way in which the BBC handled the news. 'Care must . . . be taken', he said, 'to avoid doing anything which would be represented as Government censorship of news.'[31]

Harold Laski once wrote that 'strikes almost invariably fail when moral and financial support is withheld from the strikers by the public, while demands which the community as a whole believe to be justified are not generally resisted to the bitter end'. (Knowles, 1954: 294). Certainly the Attlee adminstrations of 1945–51 saw broadcasting as an important addition to their strike-breaking armoury. Ministerial broadcasts were put out at times of severe industrial unrest and were structured, not only to appeal for a return to work, but also to sway public opinion against those on strike. Emphasis was placed on the damage being caused to the economy, on the threat to essential supplies and services and to the role of communists in fomenting the unrest. The Governments were not alone in their claim that communists were responsible for much of the industrial unrest after the war. In June 1948 Arthur Deakin claimed that 37 out of 48 members of the unofficial strike committee were communists,[32] and the dispute in the docks in the summer of 1949 was described by the Chairman of the Labour Party, Sam Watson, as the work of foreign agencies whose job was 'to throw a spanner in the works of British recovery'.[33] One historian of the period has argued that 'there is no doubt that this trouble was fomented and in several cases directly instigated by the Party or by communists from overseas'. (Pelling, 1975: 158). The available evidence, however, does not support these claims. What is more the governments were fully aware of the tenuous nature of the allegations. In June 1948 Scotland Yard advised ministers that the dock strike was not being organized by communists although 'there was some indication that the CP was beginning to take an interest in it for "political reasons" '[34], while an investigation by the Ministry of Labour concluded that 'the organisation is a very mixed bag indeed and includes . . . people who are not extremists'.[35] The same was true of the 1949 dispute. In June 1949 Harold Wilson informed Isaacs that 'the Liverpool strike was not communist in origin and only a very small minority of the strike committee were communists'.[36] The Chief Constable of Liverpool reported that, although the strike committee included men 'who held communistic views', it was widely recognized that 'the views of these members . . . were not acceptable to the majority of the workers'.[37]

In the post-war economic climate any dispute which interrupted production and dislocated trade was seen by the government as the work of subversives. Herbert Morrison told delegates at the Labour Party Conference in 1947 that 'Today any avoidable strike—whether caused by employers or workers—is sabotage. And an unofficial strike is sabotage with violence to the body of the Labour Movement itself.'[38] The BBC was one important way of conveying this message to the public and undermining strike action. But ministerial broadcasts in themselves were not deemed sufficient. The Governments were also intent on removing all dissident opinion from the air. In this they were largely unsuccessful. The refusal of the BBC to compromise its independence in the coverage of industrial disputes must be applauded. Much of the credit for the stand taken by the Corporation must go to the Director-General, Sir William Haley. Francis Williams, public relations adviser to Attlee in 1946 and a Governor of the BBC from 1951–2, was not alone in stressing the good job Haley did at the BBC 'especially in defence of its independence against erosion by government interference' (Williams, 1970: 270).

We must be careful, however, not to overstate the degree of independence, nor assume that the BBC was sympathetic to the airing of minority views. The Corporation was always likely to be sympathetic to the Government's case. 'The Governors', Haley told Newsam in 1951, 'are a respectable and patriotic body, possessed of discretion', and would 'always be ready to listen to the point of view of the Government'.[39] Ministerial statements, despite the complaints from the Government, were fully covered in the news bulletins. There was certainly no desire within the BBC to allow unofficial strikers to broadcast. Thus, although it was felt impossible to allow only one side of a dispute to broadcast without a right of reply, the Corporation chose to withdraw access to the BBC from all rather than risk giving a 'propaganda platform' to unofficial strikers. The notion of the BBC as a forum for open and informed debate did not find favour with the Corporation. A memorandum prepared by the News Information section of the BBC in July 1956 on the treatment of strikes, explained that the Corporation was to endeavour at all times not to do anything that might make a settlement more difficult. Thus it was not to broadcast 'anything that might prejudice negotiations' and was to arrange elucidatory broadcasts 'only if a deadlock had been reached'.[40] The lack of open debate on the BBC was a major failing. On the few occasions it was allowed it was roundly applauded. For example, a broadcast during an unofficial strike of transport workers in January 1947 elicited the following response from Lady Megan Lloyd George: 'It was a discussion between a trade union official and a strike leader. It was vigorous and topical and, of course, extremely interesting.'[41] Those on strike, moreover, constantly accused the BBC of unfair treatment. In February 1951, at a mass meeting of striking dockers in Manchester, the men who were exhorted to listen to 'Radio Athlone' to hear 'the truth which was distorted by newspapers and the BBC'.[42]

Broadcasting in many ways continued to be largely conformist or conservative in character. The Beveridge Inquiry in 1949–50 heard complaints by the Labour Party of a built-in anti-Labour bias. 'The selection of speakers; subjects and news items', it was held, was 'too narrowly restricted'. (Briggs, 1979: 355). The popular discussion programme 'Any Questions' set in rural, Conservative England, with its over-representation of Tory speakers, was just one programme singled out for criticism. At the 1946 Trades Union Congress a resolution reflecting this concern was moved calling for the direct representation of particular interests upon the governing body of the BBC.[43] Criticism was not confined to the Left. Mr Waldron Smithers opposed the granting of the Corporation's Licence in December 1948, on the grounds of left-wing bias and similar complaints were received by the Listeners' Association.[44] Perhaps the most pertinent criticism that can be levelled against the BBC during this period was that it tended towards moderation, which worked against the airing of radical views either of the left or right. Mr Brendan Bracken, in dismissing in Parliament the charge of bias against the Corporation, asserted that 'moderation has always been the limit of the Governors of the BBC'.[45] This was certainly the case in the coverage of industrial disputes after the War.

The efforts of the Labour Governments to influence the broadcasting policy of the BBC did not break new ground. Neither did the evident lack of success deter future administrations from following a similar course. The new Conservative administration of 1951 paid lip service to the importance of an independent BBC free from government control. In May 1953 the Prime Minister, Winston Churchill, wrote to the new Director-General of the BBC, Ian Jacob, stressing 'that the BBC should not only be impartial, but be seen to be impartial in its political attitude'.[46] As with the previous labour administration, however, strikes were deemed an exception to the rule.

During a dock strike in October 1954, which arose out of rivalry between two major unions organizing in the docks, the Transport and General Workers' Union and the National Assocation of Stevedores and Dockers (NASD), the Government sought to curb the independence of the BBC. The incident arose out of an invitation to Arthur Deakin by the Talks Department at the Corporation to take part in the series 'Harding Interviews'. Despite the fact that the producer gave an assurance that all references to the strike would be avoided, the Government requested that the programme be cancelled. The fear was that if Deakin was allowed to broadcast then the General Secretary of NASD, Mr Barrett, a figure widely associated in official circles with industrial militancy, might demand the right to reply. On this occasion the BBC bowed to pressure and postponed the broadcast, which took place instead on 1 November after the strike had ended.[47]

The BBC was not so accommodating the following year during a stoppage by the National Union of Seamen. On 5 June 1955 the Minister of Transport, Mr Boyd-Carpenter, wrote to the BBC requesting that a statement should be included in the news bulletins to the effect that, although five liners were strikebound (as had already been reported by the BBC), all others were sailing normally and that the strike was 'confined to Liverpool and Southampton'. The Corporation's response was that the Ministry should issue a statement which would then be included in the News. This the Ministry refused to do. It was clearly felt that an official statement which suggested that the strike was having little success was likely to be treated with scepticism by the strikers, whereas an 'objective' account on the News might help bring about a return to work. The BBC stood firm. According to the Editor of the News Department the Ministry's statement 'would have given a misleading impression of the strike', as only six liners got away normally as against the five which were strikebound. In the event a statement along the lines proposed by the Ministry of Transport was issued by the National Maritime Board and was included in the 9.00 p.m. News bulletin.[48]

In the event of a civil emergency the post-war Conservative administrations, as with their Labour predecessors, could rely on the co-operation of the BBC. On 29 May 1955, during a strike on the railways, the government declared a state of emergency under the Emergency Powers Act of 1920. The following day the Prime Minister, Anthony Eden, broadcast a message live from Chequers. Significantly, the BBC did not offer the right of reply to the men on strike. The following Sunday Eden broadcast for a second time on the strike. He pointed to the success of the emergency planning and praised the public for facing the difficulties 'with good humour and good sense'. Access to the air-waves was withheld from the railwaymen on strike.[49]

The BBC, in the immediate post-war years, cannot be seen as the mere mouthpiece of the governmental machine, at least over the coverage of industrial disputes. Nevertheless, in times of civil emergency, the government of the day could certainly rely on the BBC to conduct its affairs in the 'national interest'.

On 4 August 1954, under section 1.3 of the Television Act of 1954, the BBC's monopoly was finally broken and the Independent Television Authority was set up, to run initially for a period of ten years. The first independent television programmes were broadcast on 22 September 1955. With the onset of paid advertising on television (later extended to radio) the issue of the independence and political neutrality of the broadcasting service entered a new phase, although it was government's relationship with the state-owned British Broadcasting Corporation which continued to cause most concern during the following decades. It is an issue which is still causing concern today.

Notes

1. *Hansard* (December 1946), vol. 431, col. 1282.
2. Sir William Haley was Director-General of the BBC between 1944–52.
3. Similarly the Labour and Tory hierarchy put pressure on the BBC in 1950 to remove A.J.P. Taylor, Michael Foot, W.J. Brown and Robert Boothby from the hugely popular discussion programme 'In the News', on the ground that they were unrepresentative of mainstream party opinion. The team were limited to one appearance a month. See Wrigley, C.J. (1980), *A.J.P. Taylor, A Complete Annotated Bibliography and Guide to his Historical and Other Writings*, Sussex, The Harvester Press.
4. Memorandum by Mr George Darling, industrial correspondent at the BBC, 22 November 1943, BBC Written Archives Centre, Caversham, R34/881/2.
5. *Hansard* (March 1946), vol. 420, cols. 520–3.
6. Note of a meeting between Morrison and Haley, 25 June 1948, BBC Written Archives Centre, Caversham, R34/881/3.
7. Letter from Mr L.H. Hornsby (Ministry of Labour) to Mr A.P. Ryan (BBC), 12 December 1945, BBC Written Archives Centre, Caversham, R28/123.
8. BBC Written Archives Centre, Caversham, R34/881/3.
9. Minutes of Cabinet Meeting 12 February 1951, Public Records Office, Kew, Cabinet 13 (51).
10. Letter from Isaacs to Haley, 21 May 1947, Ministry of Labour Files, Public Record Office, Kew, LAB 43/8.
11. Note by News Information on 'The treatment of strikes in BBC programmes', July 1956, BBC Written Archives Centre, Caversham, R34/881/4.
12. Letter from Haley to Isaacs, 27 May 1947, Ministry of Labour Files, Public Record Office, Kew, LAB 43/8.

13. BBC Written Archives Centre, Caversham, R34/881/2.
14. Note of a meeting between Morrison and Haley, 25 June 1948, BBC Written Archives Centre, Caversham, R34/881/3.
15. Minutes of a meeting of the Board of Governors of the BBC, 25 June 1948, BBC Written Archives Centre, Caversham, R34/881/3.
16. Text of Attlee's broadcast, Prime Minister's Private Office Files, Public Record Office, Kew, PREM 8/1086.
17. Letter from David Graham MP to Attlee, 29 June 1948, Attlee Papers, Bodleian Oxford, Dep 71.
18. Note by the Director of Spoken Word at the BBC, George Barnes, 22 September 1949, BBC Written Archives Centre, Caversham, R34/881/3.
19. Letter from Mr Helsby (Prime Minister's Office) to Haley, 13 April 1949, BBC Written Archives Centre, Caversham, R34/881/3.
20. *Hansard* (July 1949), vol. 467, col. 37.
21. Letter from Mr Cass to Mr Sutherland, Ministry of Labour Files, Public Record Office, Kew, LAB 10/904.
22. Files of the National Dock Labour Board, Public Record Office, Kew, BK2/75.
23. BBC Written Archives Centre, Caversham, R34/881/3.
24. Minutes of Cabinet Meeting 26 May 1949, Public Record Office, Kew, Cabinet 38 (49).
25. BBC Written Archives Centre, Caversham, R34/881/3.
26. Letter from Gerald Beadle to George Barney, 2 August 1949, BBC Written Archives Centre, Caversham, R34/881/3.
27. BBC Written Archives Centre, Caversham, R34/881/3.
28. Minutes of Cabinet Meeting 12 February 1951, Public Record Office, Kew, Cabinet 38 (49).
29. Minutes of Emergencies Committee of Ministers, 11 December 1950, Public Record Office, Kew, CAB 134/177.
30. Note of an informal meeting held at the Home Office 19 January 1951, Public Record Office, Kew, CAB 134/177.
31. Note of a meeting between Morrison and Newsam, 1 March 1951, Public Record Office, Kew, CAB 124/984.
32. Reported in *Hansard* (June 1948), vol. 452, cols. 1703–6.
33. *The Times*, 11 July 1949, 2.
34. Minutes of Emergencies Committee of Ministers, 21 June 1948, Public Record Office, Kew, CAB 134/175.
35. Note to Mr Stillwell at Ministry of Labour, 23 June 1948, Public Record Office, Kew, LAB 10/783.
36. Letter from Harold Wilson to George Isaaccs, 13 June 1949, Public Record Office, Kew, LAB 10/832.
37. Report from Chief Constable of Liverpool to Home Office, 25 June 1949, Public Record Office, Kew, LAB 10/832.
38. Report of the Annual Conference of the Labour Party, 1947, 137.
39. Note of Home Office Meeting 19 January 1951, Public Record Office, Kew, CAB 134/177.
40. Note by News Information on 'The treatment of strikes in BBC programmes', July 1956, BBC Written Archives Centre, Caversham, R34/881/4.
41. *Hansard* (February 1947), vol. 433, col. 1261.

42. *The Times*, 8 February 1951, 6.
43. Report of the Annual Trades Union Congress, 1947, 303. For criticisms of 'Any Questions' see Labour Party Archives, Walworth Road GS 23/22.
44. *Hansard* (December 1946), vol. 431, col. 1189.
45. *Hansard* (December 1946), vol. 431, col. 1189.
46. The *Daily Telegraph*, 3 January 1954, 5. Sir William Haley left the BBC to take up the Editorship of *The Times* in July 1952. He was replaced as Director-General by Ian Jacob in December 1952. Between July and December the post had been temporarily filled by Mr B. Nicholls.
47. BBC Written Archives Centre, Caversham, R34/881/3.
48. BBC Written Archives Centre, Caversham, R34/881/3.
49. Text of Eden's broadcasts 29 May and 5 June, BBC Written Archives Centre, Caversham, R34/553/2.

References

Briggs, A. (1961), *The History of Broadcasting in the United Kingdom, Vol. I: The Birth of Broadcasting*, Oxford University Press.

Briggs, A. (1970), *The History of Broadcasting in the United Kingdom, Vol. III: The War of Words*, Oxford University Press.

Briggs, A. (1979), *The History of Broadcasting in the United Kingdom, Vol IV: Sound and Vision*, Oxford University Press.

Coatman, J. (1951), 'The BBC, Government and politics', *The Public Opinion Quarterly*, **XV**, 287–98.

Gorham, J. (1948), *Sound and Fury*, London, Percival Marshall.

Harris, K. (1982), *Attlee*, London, Weidenfeld and Nicolson.

Jeffery, K., and Hennessy, P. (1983), *States of Emergency. British Governments and Strike Breaking Since 1919*, London, Routledge and Keegan Paul.

Knowles, K.G.J.C. (1954), *Strikes. A Study in Industrial Conflict*, Oxford, Blackwell.

Morgan, K.O. (1984), *Labour in Power 1945–51*, Oxford, Clarendon.

Pelling, H. (1975), *The British Communist Party*, London, Adam and Charles Black.

Simon, Lord (1953), *The BBC from Within*, London, Victor Gollancz.

Wrigley, C.J. (1980), *A.J.P. Taylor, A Complete Annotated Bibliography and Guide to his Historial and Other Writings*, Sussex, The Harvester Press.

Wyndham-Goldie, G. 1977, *Facing the Nation. Television and Politics 1936–75*, London, Bodley Head.

Stammers, N. (1983), *Civil Liberties in Britain During the Second World War*, London, Croom Helm.

Usherwood, S. (1972), 'The BBC and the General Strike', *History Today*, **22**, 858–65.

Williams, F. (1970), *Nothing So Strange*, London, Cassell.

5 Some social and political tides affecting the development of juvenile justice 1938–64[1]

Simon Stevenson

Some necessary background, pre-1938

To work backwards from the early 1960s, Figure 5.1, 'The ages at which various court orders could be made', illustrates something of the measures which could be taken against children (under 14s) and young persons (14s– 16s inclusive) throughout the post-war period from 1952 to 1 January 1964 (OP, 1960c: 169). Though one could quite well produce a series of variations upon this design, to illustrate the changes from the Childrens Act 1908 or, alternatively from the turn of the twentieth century, such variations would probably prove superfluous: remarkably little would appear to have changed. Until 1933, when it was raised to eight years, the age of criminal responsibility (i.e. the age at which an individual could be brought before a court charged with specific offences) remained as it had since the medieval church had determined that reasoning and guilt could properly be imputed from seven years of age. English common law had added a theory that those under 14 could only be found guilty subject to a *rebuttable presumption of innocence*, the Latin tag for which was termed *doli incapax*.

1908 marked the major changes of this century.[2] Those under the age of 14 (or 15 as it became in 1933) could not, from 1910, be sent to prison under sentence.[3] Those aged 14 to 16 (15 to 17 from 1933), the age at which a young adulthood effectively began, were now very unlikely to be sent to prison under sentence without the effective intervention of the higher courts of Assize or Quarter Sessions. A certificate of unruliness was required to sentence anyone of these ages to custody in a prison.[4] A new institution, called 'Borstal' (in fact a specially designated prison in Kent) appeared to take the place of indiscriminate imprisonment for certain among that age group 16 to 21 who could not now be sent to prison. From their personal history (specifically their history of criminal habits, tendencies or associations)[5] however, it was now judged politic that a somewhat longer period of indeterminate reformative training (with a maximum of three years) might be

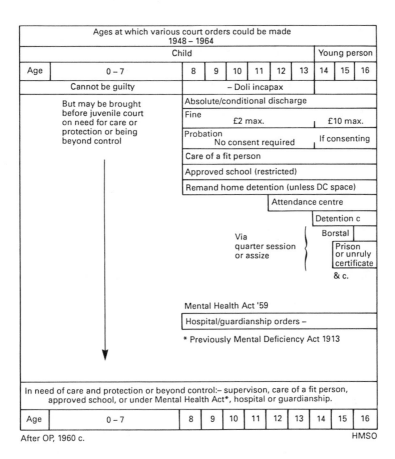

Figure 5.1 Ages at which various court orders could be made.

made available. The Prison Commissioners were also free to transfer juvenile prisoners to Borstal with little formality.[6] (These provisions of Part I of the Prevention of Crimes Act 1908 paralleled for a younger age-group rather similar provisions for indeterminate longer terms of Preventive Detention also made for the older habitual offender housed at Camp Hill, Isle of Wight).[7] As with sentence to imprisonment for the 14s–16s, such orders of Borstal training could not be made without decision of the higher courts — though magistrates' courts could so remand to higher courts by making such recommendation for Borstal training. Few magistrates courts took advantage of this power.

In the background lay more formalization of powers which had been developing since the late 1860s and early 1870s: three types of binding over (two of which did not involve conviction), which were formally-recognized in a Probation of Offenders Act of 1970,[8]—or committal to the 'care of a fit person', (involving conviction, or not, as the case might be). (This term was first coined in a statute called the Youthful Offenders Act 1901.)[9] In practice committal to the care of a fit person was long-recognized not only in the case of Oliver Twist's committal to the care of Mr Brownlow but also in the licensing and apprenticeship provisions included in both the Reformatory and Industrial School Acts. These schools were formally-recognized and encouraged to cater for the under-16s in 1866.[10] (As Section 27 of the Reformatory Schools Act 1866 had also permitted prisons to contract out their children and young offenders to these largely voluntarily-supported schools, there should have been considerable theoretical scope for decarceration of the 8 to 16 age-group before 1908.) By the Children and Young Persons Act of 1933 the names 'Reformatory' and 'Industrial' schools disappeared,[11] the two largely voluntarily-run (but now centrally-funded) systems merging to become known as Home Office 'Approved Schools'— institutions designed to house and train together those whom the courts had either found guilty of some offence or merely in need of care and protection away from their home environment. Reformers of the 1920s had felt these groups had too much in common not to be treated under similar conditions (OP, 1927: 71-2) and we would be right to catch scent of a new post-war penal and child psychology behind the supposedly welfare-oriented Children and Young Persons Act of 1933 (Bailey, 1987: 31-5). A vast literature survives (Child Guidance Council, 1938).

Whatever the welfare-oriented rhetoric of much in the 1933 Act, certain distinctive punitive possibilities (such as whipping and detention in a remand home) still remained to compensate for most courts' loss of the power to imprison after 1st January 1910. (Passage of the Criminal Justice Administration Act 1914 had also implied a wider shift toward the use of fines as the principal means of punishment.) As so often happens, the climate of the times again changed between 1925 (when the Cecil—later Moloney— Committee on the Treatment of Young Offenders had been appointed; OP, 1927) and late 1933 when the consequent Children and Young Persons Act came into force.

When the Children and Young Persons Bill 1932 was actually introduced for Second Reading in the Lords by Viscount Snowden he intimated that the liberalizing measures introduced in 1908 (and now given a further fillip in 1925 by systematic development of probation) were now regarded as having been too successful in diverting children and young offenders away from a proper, due, conviction before the courts:[12]

> A good many cases never come into the courts at all. They are often dealt with by the education authorities, without any reference to the courts, and much too of course, depends upon the attitudes of the police and magistrates. With regard to

the offences with which young children are charged, larceny accounts for more than half. There is a rapidly increasing tendency to deal with these cases by binding over and probation, and less use is made of reformatory and industrial schools. It is to be feared that this is not altogether desirable, and its effect is to be seen in the growth of crime between the ages of sixteen and twenty-one.

Passage of the Act of 1933 marked the beginning of the long, slow increase of juveniles coming before the courts for their own good—something which continues at much increased pace until late 1952—with only short breaks from 1936–39 and 1941–42.

In effect this long introductory summary merely brings me to the opening of the period with which we are concerned—but it is in a sense necessary as indicating to the uninitiated (a), that liberalizing trends were not new, (b) that there was indeed some urge for reversal of this trend in the early 1930s and (c) that appeal to the personal *needs* of the juvenile offender was something that went hand in glove with an increase of cases coming before the court, a necessary increase either of convictions or orders following any such programme, and, therefore, of any further build-up of figures which could be used in a programme of reaction. Constabulary concern at rising figures of juvenile delinquency was half a decade old the day war broke out (OP, 1939: 325). Naturally one should be cautious of the now fashionable view in English historiography that: 'nothing happened in history'—but relative continuity and recurrence of old themes are both important features of all modifications proposed to English juvenile justice from 1908 at least. In part this is because things happen slowly. Given the vicissitudes of politics there is nothing unusual in waiting 15 to 20 years for the recommendations (or non-recommendations) of some Committee or Commission of Inquiry to become law, still less (given the pressures on the revenue) in waiting another five to 15 years after that for some particular Section of an Act finally to be implemented. Sometimes one party will adopt the old clothes of another— even in apparently controversial issues.

1938–48

Among the unfinished business the Labour Government inherited in 1945 from Neville Chamberlain's pre-war National Government was the Criminal Justice Bill first introduced by Samuel Hoare (Viscount Templewood) in 1938. This was finally aborted in its passage by backwoods resistance to abolition of judicial corporation punishment—proposed by the Cadogan *Departmental Committee on* [Abolition of] *Corporal Punishment*, which had reported early in 1938. Although Herbert Morrison had been pressing Churchill for renewed progress on the Bill before the D-Day landings of 1944 he had received short shrift.[13] In place of progress discussions for appointment of a Departmental Advisory Committee on Treatment of Offenders were adopted. Its members discussed the new Bill from 1946 to 1947.[14] In 1937 the Criminal Justice Bill had originally been conceived by Hoare as one to further advance progress in penal reform (and an area which, as he somewhat exaggerated the facts, had 'made little or no advance in 50 years'; Bailey, 1987: 255).

Central to that Bill had been the proposal to permit abolition of imprisonment for the older 17 to 21s. This was to be achieved first of all by strengthening the indeterminate Borstal sentence—so empowering magistrates to commit to it direct instead of having to send these cases to Quarter Sessions for further consideration. Secondly it would strengthen the residence requirements of probation through provision of a series of probation hostels for young offenders, the so-called 'Howard Houses' from which convicted offenders would go out to work as usual on weekdays. Finally, in line both with the proposals of the Cadogan Committee on Corporal Punishment and the Moloney Committee on Treatment of Young Offenders (OP, 1927), there was the further concept of (a) the punitive task or attendance centre for Saturday afternoons (possibly to be run by the police), and (b) the 'short-term' Borstal where offenders might go for a term of less than six months. The latter proposals came from outside the Home Office.

Although the Home Office had proposed abolition of corporal punishment in 1932 (against the majority verdict of the Moloney Committee, reporting in 1927) and had indeed lost this point in Parliament in 1933, the Office view in 1937 remained one that to substitute attendance centres for corporal punishment was undesirable because it associated the police with punishment, it was also administratively unrealistic and congregated troublemakers in one place. Their second ground of objection was that the short-term Borstal was merely to become the Boys' Prison System.

While Morrison's post-war appointment of the Advisory Council on Treatment on Offenders (ACTO) did nothing to relieve the prospects of short-term 'Detention Centres' (as they now became known), the future penal character of such institutions was also something of an unknown quantity. Re-reading the contemporary literature one can scarcely fail to be impressed that if the detention centre (the 'short-term' Borstal) had indeed gained support as a result of the supposed success of the disciplinary measures taken against young soldiers during the War, post-war policy makers both on ACTO and (possibly) within the Home Office still seem to have remained somewhat ignorant of the relatively liberal experiments in detention conducted by the military authorities prior to the invasion of Europe. With hindsight one can see that 1942–3 marked something of a watershed both in military and juvenile punishment. While formally adhering to the principle of 'less eligibility' in a wartime Britain where it was increasingly difficult to become more or less eligible for favourable material treatment, the *Prime Minister's Committee of Enquiry into* **[Discipline in Military]** *Detention*

Barracks, (OP, 1943a) marked a clear break with any idea that a blind eye could be turned to military brutality. By the end of the war, psychologists and psychiatrists were increasingly in evidence in such military detention centres as that run by the Admiralty at Kielder Camp.[15] The army, seeking widespread commitment and motivation to victory through such educational efforts as the Army Bureau on Current Affairs, had also sought familial co-operation in persuading young men out of military detention centres and back to the front line units. This and other non-custodial (therapeutic) alternatives had proved necessary not least because the reality of warfare before and after D-Day caused an acute shortage of technically competent and combat-hardened troups (Penton, 1946: 81–5).

In the case of juvenile offenders, *under 14* (a group for whom corporal punishment was freely available and much more freely used in the early years of the war), enquiry by Rayner Goddard into procedure followed at the Hereford Juvenile Court (OP, 1943b) and which reported in November 1943, carried with it merely as two incidental consequences. First there was an increased reluctance to order birching for children whose parents' right to be present on such occasions was now freshly asserted,[16] and second an increased awareness that any possibility of appeal against sentence must carry with it some further delay in imposition of a form of sentence contemporaries believed best imposed immediately and also one which the Cadogan Committee had already recommended for abolition.

Though figures for whippings later revived, this wartime experience was in effect one in which orders for whipping juveniles had already been temporarily suspended. Under a subsequent Labour Government abolition of corporal punishment by the Criminal Justice Act of 1948 was non-problematic. Far more of a surprise was the presentational aspect of the post-war Bill[17] which, though it still included probation hostels (the old pre-war 'Howard House' concept), now failed to highlight these, focusing instead upon the supposed need for the (dramatically-termed), short-term 'detention centres'.

Additional to this replacement for the earlier 'short-term Borstal' was Viscount Templewood's (partially) successful argument to reintroduce the punitive attendance centre for use at police stations on Saturday afternoons.[18] Given that ACTO had first advanced detention centres in place of the 60-hour attendance centres,[19] the Bill that became law now highlighted two provisions that seemed *potentially* punitive instead of the one proposed in 1937–8. *Potentially* is, I think, the key word here. Neither attendance centres *nor* detention centres affecting the under or over-17s were in fact to make their appearance until the early-1950s. Though reasons of post-war constraint on building expenditure have frequently been cited as hindering this implementation, the truth of the matter remains that post-war priority in building for the law and order sector was rather granted to fulfilment of the much more expensive programme to provide housing for the police. (Outside our terms of reference this may be, but it is indicative of the extent to which priority of investment continued to be directed at measures mentally associated with the prevention of crime rather than its punishment or correction.)

Talk of prevention should now also turn our attention to the post-war Children's Act of 1948. Not only had the dislocations of war further stimulated recorded juvenile delinquency rates — as indeed had been expected in line with the experiences of 1916–17, following introduction of conscription during the First World War (Marwick, 1965: 118–19), but evacuation had also thrust upon many who were unwilling and unprepared various unpleasant experiences of children raised in the slums. In a sense one includes discussion of this background to the Children's Act and appointment of local authority Children's Officers here not so much as an integral part of the evolving story of a criminal justice system for juveniles but to emphasize just how qualitatively different seemed the preoccupations about children and young persons then if we compare the years 1943–4 either with those of 1948–9 or of 1953–4.

Of the first period 1943–4 one can confidently assert that the major preoccupation of the reconstructionists in respect of children was not merely that of establishing machinery to realise the new 'Welfare State' outlined in the *Social Insurance* report (OP, 1942) or endowment of motherhood (Rathbone, 1947) but also to foster a more caring and enlightened attitude towards all children who, as the phrase went, were 'deprived of a normal home life'. As we might realise from re-reading Titmuss, the subject of delinquency scarcely figures in this at all. Why was this? First, though all who were informed well-knew that recorded juvenile delinquency had been increasing dramatically throughout the 1930s and the years of the war, most reformers had merely assumed this to be the product of that extensive depression and dislocation that had occurred from 1929 to 1944. Policies that would be directed to ensure post-war continuance of full employment and universally-available welfare assistance were supposed to undermine such trends while merely remedial measures would remain to assist those whose personalities had already been damaged by a deprived or emotionally-disturbed childhood. Secondly, experience of evacuation demonstrated just how false it would be to give any priority to the issue of delinquency. Occasional depredations on a neighbour's orchard, larder or cashbox naturally featured somewhat lower as a nuisance than the daily and nightly experience of ill manners, lousy heads, ragged clothing, enuresis and coarse language (Titmuss, 1950: 101–13, 110–15, 120–3). Events had temporarily conspired to thrust upon reformers an acute awareness of deficiencies in background home environment.

The delinquency of dislocated urban juveniles from poor homes was then seen as a matter merely symptomatic of the initial background environment (National Council of Social Service *et al*, 1943: 47):

> The modern tendency to dismiss pilfering by children as something they will grow out of needs to be carefully examined in view of the fact that so many of them not

only cause great harm and suffering by their misdeeds but carry their delinquencies into adult life where they may lead to serious crimes.

Respect for other people's property is not innate, but is actually contrary to human instinct; it has to be inculcated. Those in whom it is lacking are often not so much perverted as socially untrained. To leave some things alone is the small child's first lesson in self-denial and social conduct and should be given so early as to become a part of the subconscious. The child born into a family of low social standard has little chance of this education. Since his elders never accept the social code, it is never 'right' to him but merely a vast conspiracy which it is clever to outwit. Life does not make virtue particularly easy for him. His playground is frequently the street and it is there that he spends his holidays, to judge from the fact that two out of three of the 400 children in the same sample had not been away from home for as much as a week in the past twelve months. So he is subject to the constant temptation to steal from shops and stalls; he is in surroundings where all pleasures cost money; money means too much to him from too early an age; delinquent companions are easy to come by; theft offers adventure where no other adventure is; finally, theft and its rewards give him a sense of individual consequence and achievement, the craving for which is inherent in all human creatures, but which may be denied him both in home and school. Honesty is an acquired virtue only skin deep with many of the human race; it is little wonder if he fails to pick up even the veneer.

1948–58

Scarcely had the Children's and Criminal Justice Acts passed on to the Statute Book than a new dissatisfaction broke out in the legislature summed up in the introduction to the Lords of a parliamentary motion on 'The Increase of Crime'—debated on 23 November 1948, a debate instigated by the Archbishop of York, The Most Revd. C.F. Garbett. As with the First War, so with the Second, it had been expected that crime would increase— but should the post-war trend then current have continued so long?[20]

> To say that the present position is due to the war, and the war alone, is an over-simplification of a very complicated matter. . . . the old homely virtues of honesty and truthfulness—because the two go together are vanishing.

Various putative contributory factors were cited: effects of the war on the breakdown in homelife (already discussed);[21] the growing disrespect for law engendered by participation in the Black Market;[22] great inadequacy in the numbers of police[23] (though curiously not of probation officers, the post-war shortage of whom went undiscussed); those government policies which engendered 'a decreasing respect for the rights of the individual'.[24] Against all this the Labour Government's Lord Chancellor, Earl Jowitt's, contention that 'large areas of the country can no longer claim to be Christian'[25] also seemed to purport some future nationalization of private morality. Winding up on his Motion, the Archbishop of York had himself seemed to concur when speaking in these terms:[26]

> Time after time, lately, we have heard of great drives made by the State—drives for economy, drives for greater production, drives for greater safety on the roads. Some of us may be a little sceptical about some of the placards and advertisements and appeals which are made in this connection, although I am sure that these appeals would not continue to be made in this way unless some of them were giving good results. Is it so fantastic to suggest that the State should have a drive for honesty and truthfulness . . .? I would suggest that the appeal be made very largely on social grounds, calling attention to the harm that is done to the nation and to the whole community . . ..

While so many Lords' debates on motions of this kind are indeed fruitless, the good ecclesiastic's appeal for a 'state . . . drive for honesty and truthfulness' was not barren in this instance. The years from 1949 to 1953 did witness collaboration between the Home Office and Ministry of Education in a 'campaign' to reduce juvenile delinquency (as also the purely symbolic appointment in November 1948 of the Franklin Committee to review *Punishments in Prisons, Borstals, Approved Schools and Remand Homes*; OP, 1952). A unique, and unrepeated collaboration, this 'campaign' against juvenile delinquency was partly based upon the assumption that in these matters there was indeed such a thing as the 'public conscience of parents' which Government might hope to educate. Local authorities were stimulated to establish sub-committees to consider local response. To review all the developments of this campaign would not be possible in so short a chapter; most of the details appear in *The Sixth Report of the Work of the Home Office Children's Department* (OP, 1951) and two publications from the Ministry of Education, *Out of School* (OP, 1948) and *Citizens Growing Up* (OP, 1949).

Suffice to say that the programme remains highly suggestive of the importance the Home Office still granted voluntarily-organized, community-based social activity in the combat of juvenile crime. If that sounds too much like looking forward to the later proposals for 'intermediate treatment' in the next Labour Government's White Paper *Children in Trouble* (1968) that is not really the case. First, the suggested programme remained purely preventive; it was not part of the treatment to be ordered by a juvenile court or its agents, the probation officer or childrens officer. Secondly the whole tradition of Home Office exhortation to social work with juveniles had long drawn on just such pre-First World War models of voluntary or novel action with children and young persons as those provided in the activities and writing of such figures as Alexander Paterson, C.E.B. Russell and Margaret MacMillan.[27] Such influential figures of the Second World War and post-war period as Lady Marjory Allen of Hurtwood (initial moving force behind the Children's Act of 1948) or Eva Hubback (contemporaneously advocating causes such as 'The Junk' or as we should call them, 'Adventure-Playgrounds, nursery

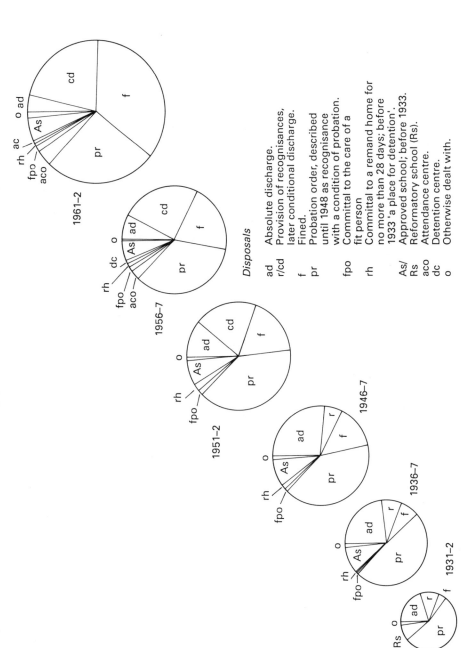

Disposals

ad   Absolute discharge.
r/cd Provision of recognisances, later conditional discharge.
f   Fined.
pr   Probation order, described until 1948 as recognisance with a condition of probation.
fpo Committal to the care of a fit person
rh   Committal to a remand home for no more than 28 days; before 1933 'a place for detention'.
As/ Approved school; before 1933.
Rs   Reformatory school (Rs).
aco Attendance centre.
dc   Detention centre.
o   Otherwise dealt with.

Figure 5.2   How the juvenile courts disposed of all those found guilty of indictable offences, 1931–1962

schools; education in citizenship) all cited as aspects of the 'campaign' against juvenile delinquency from 1949 to 1953—merely followed in directions where pioneers of the years from 1900 to 1920 had already led (Allen and Nicholson, 1975: 165–92). This was the official line of policy.

When asked their opinion by the Home Office in 1952, most local authorities (as the public) took a far more punitive approach to the problem of juvenile delinquency. Their proposals ranged from more detention and attendance centres (none had as yet been opened), to arguments that procedure in the juvenile courts should be given a greater air of formality (for example, that any police attending to give evidence should be in uniform), that press publication of the name and addresses of convicted juvenile offenders should be routine procedure with parents compelled to pay larger fines and damages (or full costs of maintenance in the case of children sent to approved schools). To the right of the (now governing) Conservative party it was not merely backwoodsmen who entered on new discussions as to the possibility of re-introducing the birch. ('Should we flog thugs?' asked an article in *Picture Post* on 22 November 1952. In a double-page spread the still active pre-war Home Secretary, Viscount Templewood, answered 'No', the current Lord Chief Justice of England, Goddard, 'Yes').[28] Of particular concern was the rate at which sexual offences appeared to have increased since the War—the entire period from 1951 to 1953 also being marked by increased anxiety that the secret plans of Government were compromised by the liaison of homosexuals in their midst (Wildeblood, 1955: 45–5; Hyde, 1986: 217–22). Though digression beckons we must move on.

All this loose talk of sterner measures was, of course, just that; many sorts of factors all conspired to prevent its realization. First, there were no detention centres and civil servants only met to devise rules for the future junior detention centre (at Campfield House, Kidlington) in 1952. Second, prior loss of the birch meant that all other 'stern measures' must tend to some custodial or semi-custodial nature; as all such custodial resources were fully stretched by the unprecedented levels of demand experienced in 1952. The reality was that police, courts, local-authority remand homes and approved schools were all looking to some relief from the ever-increasing number of juveniles entering the criminal-justice process.

Ironically, as Figure 5.2 shows, the reality remained one in which—even on conviction of indictable offences—appearance in court was effectively the end of justice process. By far the largest number of those appearing were 'let off' by being absolutely discharged, bound over or fined. Had not the rate of recruitment of probation officers improved in the late 1940s these figures might have looked even more dramatic in 1951–2 or 1956–7 than they had in 1946.

The forms of custodial relief each agency sought took a variety of forms; one was the police-juvenile liaison scheme which cautioned offenders rather than bringing them to court. Though several such schemes existed by the

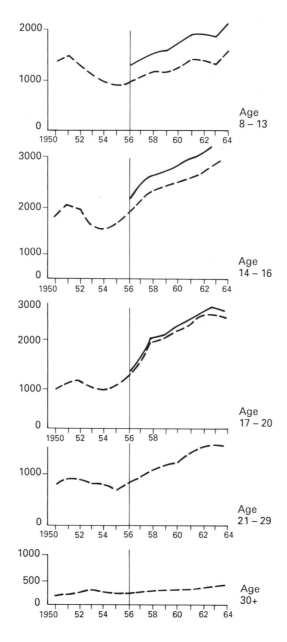

Dotted line: persons found guilty of indictable offences per 100,000 of each age group. Solid line: how many persons were so found guilty if police cautioning figures are included.

Figure 5.3   Trends in Convictions and Cautions: England and Wales, 1949–64

mid-1950s the first of note had been that in Liverpool, a city plagued by higher rates of juvenile delinquency since at least the mid-1930s.[29] From the mid-1950s cautioning of juveniles grew steadily throughout the country— (Figures 5.3 and 5.4) but this was to the dismay of Home Office statisticians, advocates of court-assessed welfare treatments (a group of advocates which always included the Metropolitan Police[30]) and, not least, the many public advocates of 'justice' who always presumed cautioning just another 'let off'. Not just in Liverpool but in many courts of summary jurisdiction in rural areas, particularly Wales, magistrates sought to relieve remand homes and approved schools by imposing fines which were still patently inadequate. Some sought to impose additional, purely notional, costs in more serious cases and although the Home Office deplored this practice they could never find any legal basis upon which to challenge it.[31] Some increase in the maximum-permitted level of fines (set in 1879) was clearly a desirable outcome.[32] In addition to all these measures some magistrates tried increasing experiment with indeterminate 'fit person orders', something which in the short term acted as a form of custody shifting children to the care of local authority children's homes—one additional pressure behind the rate at which local authorities were licensing children to their parents from 1952. Much has been made of the humanitarian and ideological impulse behind this development as Bowlby *et al.*, continued, from 1951–4, to re-stress the importance of the child's relationship with its mother (cf. Winnicott, *et al.*, 1984: 31– 53). Probably the demographic and economic pressures were of exactly equal importance in the steady recourse to use of the Fit Person Order from the early 1950s, (Packman, 1981: 52–74).

What of the role played by the Teddy Boy? His place in the new criminological literature which began to appear in the early 1970s was assured by Paul Rock and Stanley Cohen: his history now automatically goes together with the sociologist's phrase 'moral panic'. But in what sense was he really an influence on post-war policy-making in the field of juvenile justice? The social career of the Teddy Boy was, perhaps of standard attenuation—given the average lifespan of such recognized groups as the 'Mods and Rockers', 'Skinheads' or 'Punks'; the Teddy Boy's life in the public imagination lasted roughly from 24 April 1954 to the racist riots of Notting Hill in December 1958 (Rock and Cohen, 1970: 296–315). The case for any distinct connection with new directions in policy-making for the juvenile justice system is I think thin. Most of the period from mid-1954 to mid-1958 was actually one of more liberalizing tendency. Those many cries for greater parental discipline and example which marked the start of the Church of England's 'Moral Welfare Year' (a campaign to which Home Secretary David Maxwell Fyfe lent his support)[33] in 1953 had all too soon given way to a new emphasis on decriminalization of procedure for the under-14s in the correspondence columns of *The Times* by September and October 1954.[34] The relatively liberal proposals of the (Wolfenden) Report on *Homosexual Offences and*

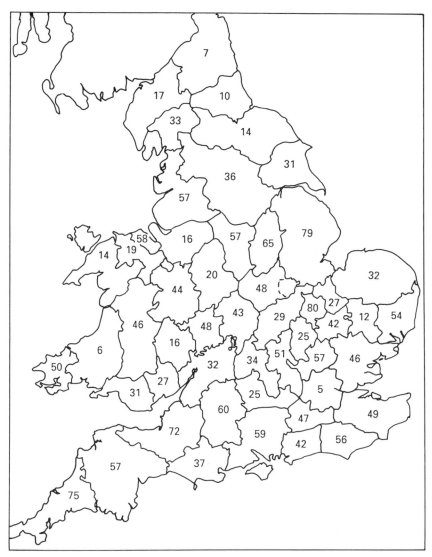

Note:

Use of cautioning in the conurbations outside the Metropolis:
TYNESIDE (i.e. police forces of Gateshead, South Shields, Newcastle,
Sunderland, Tynemouth): 29%; WEST MIDLANDS (Birmingham, Coventry,
Walsall, Wolverhampton): 79%; MERSEYSIDE (Liverpool, Bootle, Wallasey,
Birkenhead): 56%; MANCHESTER & SALFORD: 15%; SOUTH YORKSHIRE
(Sheffield & Rotherham): 43%; WEST RIDING (Leeds, Bradford, Dewsbury,
Halifax, Huddersfield, Wakefield): 115%.

Figure 5.4 Police cautions of those aged 8–14 shown as a percentage of those found guilty in the juvenile court, 1961

Prostitution which reported in 1957 (OP, 1957a: 11–20) yield yet another marker for the more pronounced influence of academic psychology felt from 1954—the year the Wolfenden Committee was appointed. Most important of all numbers of recorded juvenile offenders began to fall from 1952 to 1955. By mid-summer of that latter year more than 20 Home Office approved schools in England and Wales had been closed (much to the dismay of those who had rather hoped to see their conversion to use as schools for the 'maladjusted child').[35] The iceberg of hostility which had existed between potential reformers among magistrates on left and right in the November and December of 1948 had also begun to melt by the mid-1950s.[36] One of those from the reforming Tory wing, J.A.F. Watson (author of *The Child and the Magistrate*, now held conversations with Glanville Williams (Quain Professor of Jurisprudence at London University and editor of essays on *The Reform of the Law* (Gollancz, 1951), concerning abolition either of the knowledge-of-wrong test and/or of all *criminal* jurisdiction for under-14s (Williams, 1954: 498). As this is a complex area I will try to touch on it again later. Suffice to say for the moment that liberal progressives made more progress with the Home Office in this period than Conservative conference-women later made with Ministers at the Party Conferences of October 1958 and 1959 on behalf of those on the right (Macadam and Cleeve, 1959: 53). That the Home Office action in yielding to pressure for appointment of the (Ingleby) Committee on the law relating to Children and Young Persons seems so slow in retrospect is itself perhaps indicative of the new complacence felt concerning juvenile delinquency in this period from 1953 to 1966. As the Report of the Ingleby Committee later described the mood of that time, introducing their report in the rather different atmosphere of October 1960 (OP, 1960c: 3):

> At the time of our appointment [in 1956] the overall picture of the problems covered by our terms of reference was not altogether discouraging. This was true both of juvenile delinquency and of the general problem of children in trouble, including those in need of care and protection and those suffering through neglect in their own homes.

In short, the circumstances in which the Departmental Committee on Children and Young Persons was first convened closely paralleled those in which R.A. Butler, the new Home Secretary had first commissioned *Penal Practice in a Changing Society* (in February 1957)—a study in possible routes to further liberalization and therapeutic regimes in the custodial penal system. From 1956 both the politics of Suez and final passage of the Homicide Act 1957 provided ample distraction for those who might otherwise have been more worried either by the Teddy Boys or any other brand of juvenile delinquent. Perhaps the clearest indication of the Teddy Boy's impact is that seen in passage of the privately-sponsored Metropolitan Police Act 1839 (Amendment) Act 1958:[32] a measure directed principally at the over-paid hooligan element which might be deterred by larger fines; only here was reference to the Teddy Boy explicit (Rock and Cohen, 1970: 313).[38]

1958–64

Other factors than Teddy Boys were also at work by the middle of 1958, certainly by late August of that year when there was the all-too-well-publicized walk-out by boys at the Carlton House senior approved school in Bedfordshire (OP, 1960b). It was a moment when the popular temper again began to move back toward that relative authoritarianism which had already marked the period from late 1949 to late 1953. Pressure for re-introduction of that corporal punishment abolished in 1948 would eventually lead the Home Secretary to comission an ACTO review of the conclusions reached by the Cadogan Committee before the War (OP, 1961).

As one explanation, we might say that figures for juvenile delinquency had also begun to rise; but that was not all. The cries of Conservative conference women against the liberal attitudes of R.A. Butler (Macadam and Cleeve, 1959: 53) might also have formed a natural stalking horse for figures fearful their chance at leadership of the Conservative Party might yet fall prey to the seemingly inevitable succession that would follow Macmillan's departure (Churchill, 1964: 59ff). They were right to think Butler had not the 'common touch' to cater to such popular moods (McKenzie, 1971: 110).

What of such other factors as teen culture, loud American music, the widening 'generation gap'? Fears for the future there certainly were even in Government—but they went far wider than concern with one single manifestation of the problem. First, there was the question what was to be done when the National Service Act of 1940 was finally repealed—in accordance with plans outlined in the preceding Defence Review of 1957 (OP, 1957b)? While many had argued that 'the gap' (the years from 14 to 18 which preceded National Service) was itself crimogenic since it encouraged a sense of purposelessness and drift after leaving school. (A fact possibly contradicted by the relative stability of juvenile delinquency rates in the immediately preceding years.) Some in the Ministry of Education feared a society still more sharply divided between those who would be going on into an expanded system of higher education, sixth form and university, and those now freed from National Service but for whose incidental social life and recreation absolutely no provision was made. The County Colleges proposed in the Education Act of 1944 for all young workers leaving school had not materialized. According to the (Albemarle) Report on *The Youth Service in England and Wales* (OP, 1960a), the danger of anomie was widespread. Perhaps no more anguished statement concerning the state of society's ills had ever appeared in a government publication pleading the expansion of a social-work service (OP, 1960a: 13–14, 75–6):

. . . the crime problem is very much a youth problem, a problem of that age group with which the Youth Service is particularly concerned and towards which the public rightly expects it to make some contribution . . .

we do not think it is easy or wise to speak glibly of a delinquent younger generation and a law abiding older generation. This is only half the story. What to a person of forty or fifty, may show itself as a general malaise, a sense of emptiness, a quiet rejection of social responsibilities or a cautious-controlled cynicism may show itself in an adolescent as an act of wanton violence, a bout of histrionic drunkeness or a grasping at promiscuous sexual experience. There does not seem to be at the heart of society a courageous and exciting struggle for a particular model and spiritual life—only a passive, neutral commitment to things as they are . . .

. . . New and strange faces appear on the doorsteps and congregate in the streets as workers from many lands find a job and a home in Britain. The integration of these families brings problems, and has sometimes created a sense of insecurity and a fear among the established community that housing standards will deteriorate further . . . racial outbursts present a new problem. [(Cf. Hattersley, 1972)] . . .

. . . [In The New Towns] Homes are more attractive, but beyond, all are strangers. The street corners are quiet and uninviting with their searching sodium lamps, and their lack of familiar lights and smells . . . the present generation of teenagers is cut off then from the traditional forms of face-to-face social education in the long established neighbourhoods . . . boredom reigns . . .

For every five young people between the ages of 15 and 20 today there will be, in 1964, six young people . . . [and] In some new towns we expect it [the increase] to be as much as five-fold.
. . .
During the past few years [also] national service has kept roughly 200,000 young men between the ages of 18 and 20 out of civilian life . . . insofar as it is true that national service did provide these young men with challenge and adventure suitable to their age and needs, the Youth Service must accept some of the responsibility for providing in relevant civilian terms, this kind of opportunity.

Though further policy developments towards the delinquent in the period from 1958 to 1964 can scarcely be described as other than complex, I will attempt some simple summary as follows. The outcome of a series of reviews was eventually to prove two pieces of complementary legislation, the Criminal Justice Act 1961[39] and the Childrens and Young Persons Act 1963,[40] elements in both of which stemmed from some four reports. Two of these reports came from ACTO, the first on *The Treatment of Young Offenders* (OP, 1959); the second, on judicial *Corporal Punishment* (OP, 1961) has already been mentioned. To some extent we can think of the second as purely negative: it reaffirmed the policy decisions of 1938 and 1948 and pointed anew to the policy directions set out in the first report. These other available directions were not new in conception of course: *The Treatment of Young Offenders* envisaged merely leaning more heavily upon such devices as senior detention centres and junior attendance centres. Only four of the detention centres provided for under the terms of the Criminal Justice Act of 1948 had as yet been set up. Just as *Corporal Punishment* had pointed to the inter-national embarrassment that might result from trying to re-introduce such measures, so ACTO's strategy in *The Treatment of Young Offenders* had also appealed to internationally-agreed humanitarian standards—standards which British representatives had long helped to promote (OP, 1959: 2):

> . . . the fundamental principle . . . [is] that the penal treatment of young offenders should be primarily remedial and should be carried out in separate institutions or separate sections of institutions. This has been laid down internationally both in the Standard Minimum Rules of the United Nations [1959] and in separate United Nations reports on the treatment of young adult offenders.

So it was that three- or six-month detention centres, the conceptual 'short, sharp shock' of 1948, looked set to become the standard short-term custodial sentence for those judged either insufficiently disturbed to merit approved school or insufficiently wicked to merit Borstal—Borstal now to be reincarnate as the *standard* longer-term custodial solution from 1961 but with shorter elements of custody and longer elements of after-care.

Mention of approved schools prompts a return to discussion of those two other influential reports, that on *Disturbances at the Carlton House* [senior] *Approved School* (OP, 1960b) and that on the long-awaited (Ingleby) *Committee on Children and Young Persons* (OP, 1960c). (Complexities abound here since Ingleby chose to disagree with some of the recommendations made in the two earlier reports.) Broadly speaking, the advocates of decriminiliz-ation for juvenile justice for the under-14s (the key figures behind pressure for appointment of the Ingleby Committee in 1956) had hoped for a programme which would see more recourse to a (money-dispensing) local-authority-run system of social service based on the Children's Departments established in 1948 (one which would prevent children coming before the courts), greater employment of fit person or supervision orders to keep an eye on these children and to bring them back to court for renewed assessment of their needs. Though their terms of reference had been careful to exclude the Ingleby Committee from recommending establishment of a preventive social-work service, a close reading well indicates their support for these ideas (OP, 1960c: 5–20, 154). Indeed, later there was an unseemly row in the House of Lords during passage of the subsequent Children and Young Persons Bill. Their recommendation on raising the age of criminal responsibility from 8 to 12 (OP, 1960c: 154 (8)) might actually have recommended 14 had not the Home Office and Lord Ingleby reminded them of the opposition felt by the local police forces who would have to liaise with whatever social service was involved.[41] (For the Ingleby Committee both local authority Children's Officers and local Police Chiefs were something of a spectre at their feast; neither of these interests was represented amongst those distinguished magistrates, pyschiatrists and local councillors who actually comprised the committee of inquiry—yet both carried immense weight in the outcome of discussions.)

All these aspects were in a sense the 'radical' side of Ingleby—not radical enough for such contemporary commentators on the left as D.V. Donnison or Peggy Jay, no doubt—but too radical for the Government. The Government's view was that additional employment of supervision orders would be unsuitable, nor was any profligate social service tending to undermine those principles of personal responsibility enshrined in the application of the National Assistance Act's 'wage stop' procedure to be desired. Similarly, it seemed politically unthinkable that (in such circumstances of rising juvenile crime) one should be discussing any move to raise the age of criminal responsibility above age 10.[42] Discounting the more radical ideas that had to be abandoned, much that remained seemed merely more punitive:

— recommendations that the minimum age for attendance at one of the 40-odd junior attendance centres now established at police stations in larger urban areas should now be lowered from 12 to 10 (OP, 1960c: 159 (62));
— recognition of the post-Korean inflation which would involve raising a level of fines set in 1879 by five-fold (OP, 1960c: 159 (57));
— encouragement to magistrates that they should now reverse the self-imposed restraint on imposition of separate sentences for different 'counts' proved against the same offender.

This last point was something which had followed on Lord Chief Justice Parker's judgment in the case of *Regina v. Evans* (1958)[43]—this judgment had been to the effect that a probation order could not be thus imposed as a form of after-care additional to detention in a centre (OP, 1960c: 159 (58)).

Finally, in the case of approved schools (and though no recommendation to nationalization or uniform local-authority control was concurrently made), the Committee were eager to press ahead with closed facilities for refractory cases (OP, 1960c: 164 (114 & 115))—something already recommended to the Home Office by some local authorities as early as 1952 (OP, 1955: 39, 135–6). This was something definitely supported by the recommendation of the Carlton House in (OP, 1960b: 47, 52–3) and already long since extensively practised in place of other punishments in the girls' schools (OP, 1952: 11–12).

Recommendation 503 (OP, 1960c: 143) ran to the effect that in the case of those aged 16 'residential training orders' might be made by magistrates—thus helping to blur the distinction between committal to approved school or Borstal. In the event this last recommendation was the only one not realized by the subsequent Act of Parliament in 1961—though minimum age for committal to Borstal via Quarter Sessions and Assizes was to be lowered from 16 to 15.

Talk of committals to Borstal via the narrow gateway provided by Quarter Sessions and Assizes naturally raised anew some of those issues already discussed in relation to the period 1949–53. First, just how far was it possible to match up disposals by the courts against any official aims either of more deterrent custodial punishments or, indeed, of other more liberal objectives. Clearly the official governing principles to reform of the penal system remained those of 1938 — to continue the abolition of judicial corporal punishment (this is merely a confirmation of the trend observed before abolition in the period from 1913 down to 1930) and secondly to persist with the aim of keeping those under 21 out of prisons containing adults. The reality remained that while formal abolition of whipping involved an extremely difficult political balancing act, this also aggravated demands from the right for some more punitive custodial penalty.

Meanwhile, rapid growth in numbers of convicted offenders also meant that such custodial facilities as existed were always inadequate. Any preceding period of contraction always involved abandonment of existing premises on grounds of economy. Such had been the case not only with prisons — in the period from 1889 to 1932 — but also with approved schools from 1922 to 1927 and again from 1952 to 1955. Before the War one major proposal for removing young people from prison had been to abolish remand of the unruly to prison by permitting magistrates direct committal to Borstal. As with detention centres, when so many more had come into existence in the mid-1960s, the whole idea of direct committal was fraught with difficulties. Places had to be rationed — in the case of detention centre orders this was achieved by executive advice that no place was vacant so no such order could be made. Intervening remand to prison in the case of borstal or senior approved schools was a deterrent to justices making such orders. The absence of the separate 'remand centres' that had been promised in 1948 always meant that (with the population of juvenile offenders steadily rising in absolute terms) the number of such offenders actually going to prison before allocation to borstal or senior approved school also steadily increased. By the end of our period absolute numbers of those under 16 so imprisoned on remand still remained higher than at any date since 1910.

So far I have largely ignored proposals emanating both from the post-war Howard League (Fry, *et al.*, 1947: 18–20) and from the Fabian Society (Donnison and Stewart, 1958) that, following some European countries, all court proceedings with juveniles under 14 should now be placed upon a welfare basis — orders being made without proceeding to conviction. As I have already suggested, a lot of this pressure was actually of cross-party character emanating from such groups of advanced thinkers as those found on the London Juvenile Courts Consultative Committee (a high-powered group over which the Home Office kept a watching brief (OP, 1951: 60). Whether this should actually be regarded as a liberalizing movement naturally remains open to question. An academic such as Glanville Williams ultimately supported such exponents of this plan as Margery Fry, Madeleine Robinson, Eileen Younghusband or John Bowlby because he also saw within it some hope that the 'knowledge-of-wrong' test (*doli incapax*—an idea which *theoretically* prevented the most ill-educated and morally-warped of offenders from receiving punishment or 'treatment') might now be abandoned (Williams, 1954: 495–6). (As some contemporaries had in fact commented in 1955, they seriously doubted whether most juvenile court magistrates still applied that test anyway; Morrah, 1955: 349–50.)

By the time the Ingleby Committee had reported in 1960 they also had imbibed this new social-work ethos of the Children's Officers and had placed some faith in the possibility that as cautioning had expanded so the police might also now be willing to consult with local authorities on social-work grounds, whether they should or should not prosecute offences committed by those aged 10 to 12 or 10 to 14, as the case might be settled. Unlike unlimited police discretion to caution—something which bypassed social workers altogether—this whole area was one fraught with difficulty, not least because it presupposed exactly that type of open collusion between police and local-authority workers or even councillors which had first led to appointment of a Royal Commission on the Police on 20 December 1959. Though existent patterns of change were confirmed, this was done tentatively (outside any statutory framework) by the terms of a circular on operation of Parts I and III of the Children and Young Persons Act 1963, numbered H.O.C. 20/64.

Even influential figures in the Labour Party were divided on such matters in 1963. Like many JPs outside London, Mary Stewart, joint author, with D.V. Donnison, of the more radical Fabian pamphlet of 1958—*The Child and the Social Services*—clearly felt rather more anxiety about abandoning the criminal jurisdiction of the juvenile court in December 1962—when she, Donnison and Peggy Jay had issued a new pamphlet in the Fabian Research Series on *The Ingleby Report: Three Critical Essays*.

In fact, one finds very little of either Donnison's or Baroness Wootton's apparent contemporary dismissal of criminal jurisdiction for children in this bold opening statement of Stewart's essay on the future of 'The Juvenile Court', much of which sounds like Ruth Morrah, JP, chiding John Watson in *The Spectator* of 1955 (Stewart, 1962: 18):

> . . . the Juvenile Court, like adult courts, is the guardian of civil liberties without which democracy cannot survive. In practice this means that a child must be regarded as innocent in law unless proved guilty; that when arrested or removed from home for his own safety, he must be taken before a court at the earliest opportunity; that in court he has the right to state his case and to question those who testify against him, that he has the right of appeal to a higher court and the right to legal aid; and that his parents are entitled to know upon what facts the Bench has based its choice of treatment.

Prefatory to these remarks she thought it (Stewart, 1962: 17):

> . . . of interest to note that in countries such as Sweden, wherein the detection and treatment of juvenile delinquency, the emphasis is on 'welfare' rather than on 'justice' and the 'rights of man' in a legal and constitutional sense, the problem [of crime] is no less acute than it is in Britain.

Central to Stewart's views in 1962 was not the diversion or informality proposed in 1958 but separation—splitting the 'Juvenile Court (for 13 to 17-year-olds) from a 'Welfare Court' (for under-13s) with non-criminal care or protection proceedings only permitted in the latter, save only that '*Rules of evidence would be observed*'. Behind the new rhetoric here, however, still lay the reality that in well over 90 per cent of juvenile court proceedings rules of evidence were already scarcely used: legally-unrepresented, most children and young persons were not challenging assertions to their guilt. As for Stewart's central proposal—the split that would result in a system of separate 'welfare' and 'Juvenile' courts (for the under-18s), one is necessarily to see the greatest part of her preoccupation as, in fact, looking backwards to an era before 1933, a long-established, almost old-fashioned concern with 'contamination'—indeed, what we see here are the concerns of the (Aarvold) *Inter-Departmental Committee on Magistrates Courts in London* (OP, 1962: 27–9). None of the passage that follows looks forward to a brave new world where 'delinquent', 'maladjusted', 'neglected' were all seen as essentially the same; I quote: it is *not* (Stewart, 1962: 19–20):

> . . . desirable that teenagers charged with serious offences should share waiting rooms with young delinquents from primary schools or with children who have been brought before the court solely because it is said that they have been neglected or ill-treated at home. Some courts can provide separate waiting rooms for the different categories of young people but many can do no more than provide separate accommodation for 'custody cases' who may represent only a very small proportion of those waiting to go in to court. Some parents and children will be fortunate and will wait for only a short time before their turn comes. Others may have to wait several hours. A few will wait all day. Among these will be parents and children acutely anxious about the outcome of their cases. Nor is this their only cause of anxiety. Fathers may be worrying about the loss of time from work, mothers about children left unprotected at home. The problem of waiting cannot be dismissed lightly as one simply of administrative inefficiency; . . . the problem reflects the difficulty of dealing in the same court on the same day with problems originating from so many different sources. Some of the young people in the waiting room will have been brought in from girls' or boys' remand homes, or a boys' remand centre; others will have come from a police station. Many will have come from their own homes in response to a summons or following a remand on bail or an adjournment, if they are being dealt with under civil proceedings. Since pleas are not taken in advance and cases are not settled out of court, it is often not possible to predict whether a hearing will last five minutes or an hour or more . . .

Views such as these were not, of course, the only way in which those attached to the Labour cause seem divided before publication of the Longford study-group document: *Crime: A Challenge to Us All* (Labour Party, 1964), or the later Home Office White Paper on *The Child, The Family and the Young Offender* (OP, 1965). Many on the left actively disliked the idea of therapeutic social work with offenders—a dislike that went back to the turn of the century at least. As Donnison and Stewart well summarized this point in 1958: 'Socialists have [long] been prone to view social work as at best a mere sticking plaster on the sores of society . . .' (Donnison and Stewart, 1958: 2). It was, in fact, only as so many on the left (men like Anthony Crosland or Longford) had in the mid-1950s come to perceive juvenile crime as evidence for the failure of the 'Welfare state', that scope for remedial social work now seemed to expand wider to involve longer-term interventions and expenditure (Crosland, 1956; Pakenham and Opie, 1958: 17; Wootton, 1961).

Notes

1. This chapter (from a paper presented at the LSE/ICBH Summer School on 6 July 1988) takes its origin from the 1984 ESRC 'Crime and Criminal Justice Initiative'. A history of theory and practice in the field of English criminal justice 1945–75 was sponsored by an ESRC committee then sitting under the chairmanship of the late Sir Athur Peterson. Exceptional approval of conditional access to revelant Home Office papers was later agreed with the grantholders (A.E. Bottoms and S.J. Stevenson) at a meeting held on 22 January 1985. This chapter provides some synopsis of one chapter of a book which should go to press in 1990.
2. Statutes: 8 Edw.7, c.67 (1908).
3. ibid, s.102(1).
4. 8 Edw.7, c.67 (1908).
5. 8 Edw.7, c.59 (1908), s.1(1)(b).
6. ibid, s.3.
7. ibid, ss. 10–16.
8. 7 Edw.7, c.17 (1907), s.1.
9. 1 Edw.7, c.20, s.4(1).
10. See 29 and 30 Vict., c.117 (1866), ss. 14, 18–19; and 29 and 30 Vict., c.118 (1866), ss. 26, 27, 28, respectively.
11. 23 Geo.5, c.12 (1933), Part IV, ss. 79–81.
12. Official Report, House of Lords [hereafter H.L.Deb.], 26 May 1932, col.450.
13. Home Office papers, 884,452/1A (this in Public Record Office class HO 45/21,948).
14. ACTO/4/14–20.
15. CRI/67 12/8/34.
16. Cf. Summary Jurisdiction Act 1879, 42 and 43 Vict., c.49, s.10(1)(d); and s.11(1).

17. Parl. papers, 1947–8, ii, 113–14.
18. H.L.Deb., 3 June 1948, cols. 295–303: 'partially' successful because the original amendment (withdrawn) was to delete Clause 18 ('Detention in a Detention Centre') in favour of attendance centres.
19. ACTO/4/18; and CRI/67 12/8/15 ('Alternatives to imprisonment').
20. H.L.Deb., 23 November 1938, cols. 513, 512.
21. ibid, 513.
22. ibid, 514.
23. ibid, 528–9.
24. ibid, 522.
25. ibid, 536.
26. ibid, 517–18.
27. Brief details of the voluntary efforts made by each of these appear in the *Dictionary of National Biography, 1941–1950*, pp. 658–61; ibid, *1931–1940*, 587–8; Bailey (1987), 10–11.
28. Future Home Secretary Henry Brooke was among those voting for restoration of judicial corporal punishment during a free vote on Second Reading of Wing Cdr Bullus's 'Criminal Justice (Amendment) Bill' on 13 February 1953: *H.C.Deb.*, col. 839. Despite the ministerial line of resistance coming from the Home Office, even the Prime Minister was ambivalent on the issue: see M. Gilbert (1988), *Never Despair: Winston S. Churchill, 1945–1965*, London, Heinemann, 776–7.
29. See J.H. Bagot (1941), *Juvenile Delinquency: a Comparative Study of the Position in Liverpool and England and Wales*, London, Jonathan Cape, p. 86, especially, since his recommendations here clearly form the basis of the subsequent police-juvenile liaison scheme operating in Liverpool from 1952.
30. POL. 89/1/13, 14.
31. CHN. 85/1/4, 6, 9, 10.
32. 42 & 43 Vict., c.49, ss.10(1)(c) and 11(1).
33. See 'True moral welfare', *The Church Times*, 4 December 1953, p. 874; also 'Home Secretary on father's role', *The Times*, 25 January 1954, p. 3, col. 1.
34. 'Deprived children', *The Times*, 24 September 1954, p. 9, col. 3; 'Care in short-stay foster homes', ibid, 1 October 1954, p. 4, col. 7; 'Bench as "Social Guardian" ', ibid, 15 October 1954, p. 5, co;. 2; 'Deprived children', ibid, 15 October 1954, p. 9, cols. 6–7; 'Family welfare', ibid, 16 March 1955, p. 9, cols. 5–6. All but the last (a collective letter with Fry and Rosamund Fisher as lead signatories) were sent in by Hilda Lewis, Gordon Trasler, D.H. Stott and John Bowlby.
35. *The Times*, 23 November 1955, p. 11, col. 7.
36. See, for example, John Watson and Alan Moberly, 'Combating child delinquency: restoring the status of the family', *The Times*, 30 November 1948, p. 5; and letters in reply: Margery Fry, Madeleine Robinson, Barbara Wootton and Eileen Younghusband, ibid, 3 December 1948, p. 5; also Rosamund Fisher, 'Child welfare', ibid, 8 December 1948, p. 5.
37. 6 & 7 Eliz.2, c.48.
38. See H.C.Deb., 7 March 1958, col. 1579; '. . . an anti-Teddy boy Bill. I am bound to say that I had Teddy boys in mind.' (Geoffrey Stevens MP, Portsmouth Langstone).
39. 9 & 10 Eliz.2, c.39 (1961); see Parts I (ss.1–10) and II (ss.11–19).

40. 11 & 12 Eliz.2, c.37 (1963), Part I.
41. H.L.Deb., 20 November 1962, cols. 858, 859, 841.
42. CHN/61 75/2/25, 32, 54; CHN.115/3/51.
43. [1958] 3 All England Reports, 673 (Court of Criminal Appeal).

References

Allen, M. and Nicholson, M. (1975), *Memoirs of an Uneducated Lady: Lady Allen of Hurtwood*, London, Thames & Hudson.

Bailey, V. (1987), *Delinquency and Citizenship: reclaiming the young offender, 1914–1948*, Oxford, Clarendon Press.

Bowlby, J. (1951) *Maternal Care and Mental Health*, Geneva World Health Organization.

Child Guidance Council (1938), *Bibliography of Child Psychology 1928–1938*, London, Child Guidance Council.

Churchill, R.F.E.S. (1964), *The fight for the Tory leadership: a contemporary chronicle*, London, Heinemann.

Crosland, C.A.R. (1956), *The Future of Socialism*, London, Jonathan Cape.

Donnison, D.V. and Stewart, M. (1958), *The Child and the Social Services*, London, Fabian Research Series, No. 196.

Fry, M., Grabinska, W., Grunhut, M., Mannheim, M., Rackham, C.D. (1947), *Lawless Youth: a challenge to the new Europe. A policy for the Juvenile Courts prepared by the International Committee of the Howard League for Penal Reform, 1942–1945*, London, Geo. Allen & Unwin.

Fyvel, T.R. (1961), *The Insecure Offender: rebellious youth in the Welfare State*, London, Chatto and Windus.

Hattersley, R. (1972), 'Immigration', in D. McKie and C. Cook (eds), *The Decade of Disillusion: British Politics in the Sixties*, London, Macmillan. London, 182–96.

Hyde, H. Montgomery (1986), *A Tangled Web: Sex Scandals in British Politics and Society*, London, Constable.

Labour Party, *Crime—a challenge to us all. Report of the Labour Party's Study Group* (1964), London, Labour Party.

Macadam, I. and Cleeve, M. (eds), (1959), *The Annual Register of World Events; a review of the year 1958*, London, Longmans.

McKenzie, R.T. (1971), 'A lifetime in the Jungle—Lord Butler in conversation with Robert McKenzie' *The Listener*, vol. 86, no. 2208, 22 July 1971.

Marwick, A. (1965), *The Deluge: British Society and the First World War*, London, Bodley Head.

Millham, S., Bullock, R., Hosie, I. (1978), *Locking Up Children: secure provision within the child-care system*, Farnborough, Hants, Saxon House.

Morrah, R. (1955), 'Erring Child or Criminal?', *The Spectator*, March 25 1955, 350–1.

National Council of Social Service and the Hygiene Committee of the Women's Group on Public Welfare (1943), *Our Towns: a close-up*, Oxford University Press.

OP (1927), *Report of the Departmental Committee on the Treatment of Young Offenders*, HMSO, Cmd. 2831.

OP (1938), *Departmental Committee on Corporal Punishment*, HMSO, Cmd. 5684.

OP (1939), *Reports by H.M. Inspector of Constabulary for the year ended 29th September 1938*, HC, 83.

OP (1942), *Social Insurance and Allied Services*, HMSO, Cmd. 6404.

OP (1943a), *The Prime Minster's Committee of Enquiry into Detention Barracks*, HMSO, Cmd. 6484.

OP (1943b), *Hereford Juvenile Court Inquiry. Report of the Tribunal appointed under the Tribunals of Inquiry (Evidence) Act, 1921*, HMSO, Cmd. 6485.

OP (1945), *The Boarding out of Dennis and Terence O'Neill at Bank Farm, Minsterley and the Steps taken to Supervise their Welfare*, HMSO, Cmd. 6636.

OP (1946), *Report of the Care of Children Committee*, HMSO, Cmd. 6922.

OP (1948), *Out of School*, HMSO, non-parl.; report from the Central Advisory Council for Education (England).

OP (1949), *Citizens Growing Up—At Home in School and After*, HMSO, non-parl.; pamphlet by the Ministry of Education.

OP (1951), *Sixth Report of the Work of the* [Home Office] *Children's Department May 1951*, HMSO, non-parl.

OP (1952), *Report of a Committee to Review Punishments in Prisons, Borstal Institutions, Approved Schools and Remand Homes: Parts III and IV*, HMSO, Cmd. 8429.

OP (1955), *Seventh Report on the Work of the* [Home Office] *Children's Department, November 1955*, HMSO, non-parl.

OP (1957a), *Homosexual Offences and Prostitution*, HMSO, Cmnd. 247.

OP (1957b), *Defence: Outline of Future Policy*, HMSO, Cmnd. 124.

OP (1959), *The Treatment of Young Offenders*, HMSO, non-parl.; a report by the Advisory Council on the Treatment of Offenders.

OP (1960a), *The Youth Service in England and Wales*, HMSO, Cmnd. 929.

OP (1960b), *Disturbances at the Carlton House Approved School on August 29th and 30th 1959*, HMSO, Cmnd. 937.

OP (1960c), *Report of the Committee on Children and Young Persons*, HMSO, Cmnd. 1191.

OP (1961), *Corporal Punishment*, HMSO, Cmnd. 1213; a report by the Advisory Council on the Treatment of Offenders.

OP (1962), *Report of the Inter-Departmental Committee on Magistrates' Courts in London*, HMSO, Cmnd. 1606.

OP (1965), *The Child, the Family and the Young Offender*, HMSO, Cmnd. 2742.

Packman, J. (1981) *The Child's Generation: child care policy in Britain*, 2nd ed., Oxford, Basil Blackwell and Martin Robertson.

Pakenham, F. with Opie, R. (1958), *Causes of Crime*, London, Weidenfeld & Nicolson.

Penton, J.C., (1946–7) (Lt Col, R.A.M.C.), 'Lessons from the Army for penal reformers: selection of personnel applied to delinquency', *The Howard Journal*, vol. III, no.2, 81–5.

Rathbone, E.F. (1949), *Family allowances; a new ed of 'The disinherited family'; with an epilogue by Lord Beveridge, and a new chapter on the family allowances movement, 1924–47 by Eva M. Hubback*, London, Allen & Unwin, 1949.

Rock, P. and Cohen, S., 'The Teddy Boy', in Bogdanor, V., and Skidelsky, R. (eds), *The Age of Affluence, 1951–64* (1970), London, Macmillan.

Stewart, M. (1962), 'The juvenile court', in Donnison, D.V., Jay, P. and Stewart, M. (eds), *The Ingleby Report: three critical essays*, London, Fabian Research Series, 231.

Titmuss, R.M. (1950), *Problems of Social Policy*, HMSO, 1950.

Watson, J.A.F. (1943), 'The children's magistrate and the child guidance clinic', *Mental Health*, vol. IV, No.1. London, 4–7.

Watson, J.A.F. (1950), *The Child and the Magistrate*, 6th edn, London, Jonathan Cape.

Watson, J.A.F. (1951), 'The Juvenile Court, Today and Tomorrow', *Eleventh Clarke Hall Lecture*.

Watson, J.A.F. (1955), 'The Erring Child as a Criminal?', *The Listener*, March 17, 476–7.

Wieldblood, P. (1955), *Against the Law*, London, Weidenfeld & Nicolson.

Williams, G. (1954), 'The Criminal Responsibility of Children', *Criminal Law Review*, 493–500.

Winnicott, C., Shepherd, R., Davis, M. (eds) (1984), *D.W. Winnicott: Deprivation and Delinquency*, London, Tavistock Publications.

Wootton, B. (1961), 'The Juvenile Courts', *Criminal Law Review*, 669–77.

6 The impact of the retirement debate on post-war retirement trends

Sarah Harper

The immediate post-war period saw an increasing withdrawal of elderly workers from the economic labour force. While a trend towards retirement at earlier ages can be identified throughout the century, the period 1945–64 is of particular interest, not only because the rate of withdrawal was intensified, and spread throughout the classes and professions, but also because this growth in retirement coincided with unprecedented peacetime employment opportunities. The following will examine this spread in the post-war decades of retirement from the paid labour market, focusing in particular on the debate arising from this trend, and its impact upon the retirement process. The key issues to be resolved are why an ever increasing number of older workers abruptly withdraw from the labour market at a time when opportunities for employment were at their peacetime highest, when government policies, at least overtly, and media and medical propaganda was attempting to retain the elderly in employment, and when contemporary surveys suggest that the workers themselves did not desire such an abrupt retirement.

The following discussion draws on contemporary political reports, and social, economic and medical survey data, referring to published and unpublished material produced between 1945 and 1970. Most attention in such material was given to male workers, whose abrupt transition from full-time economic employment, to full-time retirement, was clearly of a different nature to the experience of their female co-workers; this latter group typically withdrawing from part-time employment at a more staggered rate. By virtue of this contemporary focus, and the very different experiences of the genders, this assessment will refer to male retirement only.

Retirement trends

There had been a clear trend towards earlier and more complete withdrawal from the labour force for several decades. The rate of retirement during the immediate post-war years, however, was particularly striking, in particular given the labour market opportunities of the time.

The 1931 to 1961 censuses show a continuous withdrawal from paid labour by men over 65. The percentage of men aged 65–69 who were retired doubled between 1931 and 1961, standing at 60 per cent in that latter year. Similarily there was an increase in retirement for the over-70s from 63 per cent to 90 per cent during this time. The 50 per cent growth in retirement for the 65–69 group between 1931 and 1951 is particularly significant as the first census was taken during a period of high unemployment when the employment opportunities of the elderly were at a low level, whilst in 1951 the exact opposite conditions prevailed.

This trend towards male retirement at a fixed and earlier age than had been previously customary, gave rise to a considerable amount of published discussion and research. Among this material were a variety of surveys assessing attitudes to work and retirement. The main sources on this question are the surveys by the Ministry of Labour in 1945 and 1950 (Thomas and Osbourne, 1945, 1950) and by the Ministry of Pensions and National Insurance in 1956 (HMSO, 1956) supplemented by smaller surveys continued throughout this period (Anderson and Cowan, 1956; Richardson, 1956b; Le Gros Clark, 1954). There are obviously problems in drawing conclusions from such a variety of material, carried out for different purposes, and assessing various groups of workers and retired; however broad indications can be drawn. These surveys all suggest that around 10 per cent of all men reaching retiring age were chronically ill and retired at that time for health reasons. Of greater significance, however, are the indications that the primary attitude to retirement among men over 55 was negative. Indeed of those who had already retired, over half had either been compulsory retired, or had done so due to the strain of the job. In addition these surveys also suggested that many older workers would be happy to exchange full-time employment for part-time work, an option which few employers appeared willing to accommodate.

There are thus clear indications that the growth in retirement was as much associated with involuntary criteria, as with an increase in the *desire* to cease work at a fixed age. This is of particular interest when one considers that throughout this period both employers and workers were subject to a variety of material circulating through a variety of mediums, which was encouraging the retention of the older worker. The eugenistic writings of the inter-war years were being restated and this 'alarming trend towards the deterioration of the age structure' was accompanied by a debate on the implications of an ever increasing retired population, and on the ageing of the entire workforce itself.

The retirement debate

This 'retirement debate' is of interest not only because it reveals aspects of the experiences and the societal perceptions of the elderly in this period, but also because it involved conscious efforts by influential groups and individuals to redefine the roles and status of this age group. The situation was approached from two stances—the fate of the national economy, and the health and personal welfare of the retired themselves.

The first argument, that of national economy, was the main approach adopted by politicians, demographers and economists. It had two broad themes: first the dependency argument, namely that the ageing of the labour force would create an unbalanced ratio of workers to dependents, with severe social and economic consequences; second that industry would positively benefit from the retention of its older workers.

The dependency argument

The dependency argument began to be aired in a variety of official documents. While the ratio of workers to dependents might not be any higher than in the past, it was argued that dependent elderly were far more expensive than dependent children. Parish and Peacock (1954), for example, calculated that expenditure on the elderly by social services was five times that spent on children. Shenfield (1957) similarily argued that, while the number of old people had risen by two and a half times between 1910 and 1954, the proportion of national income transferred to them during this time had quadrupled. The methods of these calculations leave much to be desired. No account, for example, was taken of the contribution of the elderly in terms of personal savings and services, nor the public savings on reduced child expenditure; the emphasis focused clearly on the *burden of cost* in supporting elderly people. Regardless of this, however, such figures were reproduced without question in a variety of documents throughout this period.

Pointing to the predictions of a continued low birth rate, demographers advocated the increased retention of the elderly in the workforce. Both the Economic Survey (HMSO, 1947) and the Royal Commission on Population (HMSO, 1948) called for an increase in the elderly working population, arguing for more flexible working arrangements to ensure this. Retaining large numbers of elderly workers was seen to tackle the problem both by positively contributing to the national economy and also easing the labour shortage, and by relieving the financial burden on the Exchequer from the cost of pensions and public services for the elderly. The discussion was taken up in the Philips Report (HMSO, 1954) in 1954. While accepting that, under certain circumstances, the current pension policies could be maintained, the Philips Committee stressed the magnitude of the commitments being entered into on behalf of future generations of taxpayers. The Government Actuary estimated that the expenditure of the National Insurance Fund would rise from £535 million in 1954/55 to £917 million in 1979, with a deficit of £364 million to be accounted for. About two-thirds of this expenditure would be on retirement pensions—with current expenditure in this area already higher than that part of the insurance contribution assigned for this purpose (HMSO, 1954: para. 161). Indeed the Philips Report was so concerned about the increasing proportion of elderly people in the population that it thought some rise in minimum pension age inevitable. It thus recommended that the age should ultimately be raised to 68 for men and 63 for women, and perhaps more controversially suggested a tighter link between contributions and benefits.

Benefits for industry

Concurrent with these arguments was a growing body of research, mainly produced by social scientists, suggesting that industry would *positively* benefit from the retention of large numbers of its older workers. Welford, working for the Cambridge Unit, for example, argued that not only would there be an immediate increase in production but also that the disruption of high labour turnover would be delayed for several years, (Welford, 1953). The Cambridge group had set out to identify the nature of the work for which the older worker was most suited, and best possible methods of retraining. They concluded that while there were major changes in capacity with age, these could all be overcome through simple retraining and an alteration in the work environment (Welford, 1958, 1962a, 1962b). Such conclusions were heavily supported by other research emerging at this time, for example the work by the occupational psychologist Belbin on retraining, and the prolific Le Gros Clark, who was one of the first to recognize the importance of a versatile workforce. (Belbin, 1956, 1958; Belbin, Downs and Moore 1964; Le Gros Clark, 1954).

Retirement impact

Social scientists, many of them funded by the Nuffield Foundation, were also propounding a third element to the discussion: that the individual severely suffered both mentally and in physical health by an abrupt and premature withdrawal from full time employment. Supported by the medical profession, the 'retirement-impact' hypothesis (McMahon and Ford, 1955), having been out of favour during the depression years, was resurrected.

'The weight of medical support is that sudden demise of mental and bodily functions, previously regularly exercised, such as may happen through retirement, is likely to cause atrophy and degeneration' declared Shenfield (1957: 59).

'The literature is overwhelming', stated Drs Anderson and Cowan, 'in its indications that retirement is detrimental to the health of older men' (Anderson and Cowan, 1956: 1346).

Indeed the literature was not only *not* overwhelming, in Britain it was negligible, while in the United States there were strong supporters on both sides of the debate (Granick, 1950, 1952; Taietz *et al.*, 1956; McMahon and Ford, 1955). With the exception of certain areas of mental health, there appeared little clear medical evidence in support of such a hypothesis. Yet the theory that retirement led to ill health, deterioration and death appeared to have been widely held at this time (Emerson, 1959), encouraged and disseminated by both government releases, as well as the popular press. As a 1954 Ministry of Health report described:

'After 6 weeks of this existence [retirement], life began to pall. He became unsettled, restless and irritable . . . He felt he was too old to attempt anything new. Eventually getting up in the morning became an effort, and in a short time all his interest in everything flagged. The peace of death came to him soon' (Ministry of Health, 2954: 7).

The impact of the retirement debate

It is clearly difficult to ascertain the degree and extent to which such material was reaching wider post-war society. An examination of popular channels of communication, such as the mass media, and the use of contemporary survey material assessing the dissemination of aspects of the debate, does, however, provide a broad indication.

Much of the debate was reflected in government circulars. A series of documents, two reports from the National Advisory Committee in 1953 and 1955, and the brochure 'The Older Worker and his Job' produced by the Department of Scientific and Industrial Research in 1960, all calling for the retention of the older worker, and for access to employment for all ages, were distributed to industry and other employers, and news items concerning the wastage of elderly talent, appeared in the national press until at least 1965. However, while the question of industrial receptiveness to political and research publications is clearly a matter for further investigation, contemporary surveys of the time indicated that industry was either unaware of this component of the debate, or was choosing to ignore it. Indeed a major theme emerging from these surveys was the lack of attention being paid by employers to the age structure of the work force, and a consequent lack of encouragement of the elderly to perceive themselves as a viable economic body. Contemporary surveys (Industrial Welfare Society, 1951; Fleming,

1955, 1963; indicated that industry was either unaware of the debate, despite the government publications, or was choosing to ignore it. Fleming's surveys of the iron and steel industry in 1952 (Fleming, 1955) and the Sheffield cutlery industry some 10 years later (Fleming, 1963), for example, revealed that not only were employers unaware of the age structure of their establishments, but that positive employment steps were all orientated towards youth employment. Indeed no assessment appears to have ever been made as to whether it was economically viable to employ older workers. (Industrial Welfare Society, 1951). As Heron and Chown concluded in 1961 'Industry simply does not acknowledge a problem of ageing' (1961: 16).

Yet while Fleming and others were reporting such ignorance among employers, Rose's work with unemployed older workers revealed that they were all too aware that the government was asking people to stay on at work after retirement age (Rose 1953). The samples are small, yet the indications are that the employers were equally aware of the government message, but were choosing to ignore it.

It was not only knowledge of government wishes that had reached the elderly worker, he appeared also well aware of the other side of the debate: that retirement led to death and deterioration. Emerson (1959: 206) revealed that both those who continue working and those who retire: 'appear to be to some extent affected by rather garbled information concerning retirement impact' and a variety of studies reported fear among workers that the cessation of employment would lead to a rapid deterioration in health and mobility (Nuffield, 1963; Groombridge, 1960; Townsend, 1955).

It was a message that was being picked up by the media, and examples are to be found in variety of publications. Throughout the 1950s and early 1960s references are to be found in *The Times*; the *Nursing Mirror* (December, 1957) and *Nursing Times* (August, 1957) both ran articles in 1957 on the importance of employment for preserving health in old age; the Tory *Crossbow* (1961) suggested that retirement hastened senility, a theme strongly supported by the Socialist Medical Association (1964: 3), who stated: 'forced retirement is a definite threat to health'. Indeed as late as 1971 the *Shropshire Journal*, and the *Salford City Reporter* ran news items on the importance of preserving mental and physical health through employment.

Social services were quick to take up the theme, the 1953 British National Conference on Social Work warned of the problems of abrupt retirement, and a series of social services and voluntary organizations worked throughout the decade to keep elderly men in employment, including the Employment Fellowship and National Old People's Welfare Committee—(NOPWC). Though small in scale the instigation of workshops at this time, for example, indicates the concern at keeping the old gainfully occupied.

The consolidation of the retirement tradition

It is thus clear that throughout the 1950s men continued to withdraw from economic employment, at a time when current opinion was that the elderly should be retained within the labour force, for the good of the country and for the good of the individual. Why was this tradition so consolidated and established at this time, a period of unprecedented peace time labour shortage?

There appear to be four main areas of discussion. Firstly we must attempt to discover the actual degree of commitment to the retention of the elderly worker held by the two political parties at the time, and similarily assess the position and influence of the trade union movement. Secondly, we should examine the impact of the new pension policies on the decision to retire. Thirdly we need to assess the impact of labour market restructuring and the increasing bureaucratization of industry on the position of the elderly worker; and, finally, the implications of technological change.

The political parties and trade union movement

On the surface both the Labour and Conservative parties supported the employment of the elderly worker, though the former had always been historically committed to earlier rather than later retirement. However behind the scenes the picture appears more obscure. For example the Ministry of Labour (through dissemination of information to employers) and the Ministry of Insurance (through slightly increasing the earnings allowance) under the 1945–51 Labour Government, was seen to encourage the deferment of retirement beyond 65, and employment of elderly workers. Yet while Attlee in a 1946 public broadcast, and again a few months before his defeat, was appealing to employers and worker's associations to adjust trade practices to facilitate the employment of older workers, minutes from the Ministry of Labour reveal that special action to retain older workers was generally thought inappropriate (Ministry of Labour, 11254/1946).

The picture is similar throughout the 1950s under a Conservative Government who in principal were less fettered than the Labour Party, since they held no traditional commitment to early retirement. The 1951 Conservative Party Manifesto stated that: 'the care and comfort of the elderly is a sacred trust . . . some of them prefer to remain in work and there must be encouragement for them to do so.'

Following their election the Conservative government introduced a more flexible retirement policy for civil servants. In 1952 the Ministry of Labour and National Service issued a memorandum, 'Employment of Older Men and Women', which argued that all willing to work must have access, regardless of age, calling for a radical change of outlook on the part of employers, workers, and general public. 'Age sixty-five for men and sixty for women ought no longer to be regarded as normal retiring age.'

Appealing to employers to make special provision to enable older people to continue, or indeed to return to employment, the Ministry offered the help of its industrial rehabilitation units in cases where lack of confidence or low morale were obstacles to the re-employment of older people. It then established the National Advisory Committee on the Employment of Older Men and Women (the Watkins Committee). In the first of its two reports in 1953 the Committee strongly opposed the maintenance of an arbitrary retirement age, arguing that the test for employment should be *capacity* not age. The Government, however, ignored this recommendation, as it did the recommendation from the Philips Report, a year later, that among other things, retirement age should be increased by two years. (It should here be noted that the rationale behind these recommendations from the two committees was of course based on very different criteria). Early in 1959 the Watkinson Committee was replaced by an interdepartmental committee assigned to co-ordinate research on the employment of older men and women. This was itself abolished two years later, in 1961, because the Minister of Labour felt that collaboration between government departments could be secured without a special committee. As the NOPWC noted in 1963: 'Since then there has been no apparent official action to promote the employment of elderly people.' Indeed the internal reports of the Ministry of Labour during this period, place more emphasis on consideration of pension rights than on the retention and retraining of the older worker (Ministry of Labour 1760/4/5/6/7).

The Conservative Government thus ignored many suggestions made by the Philips Committee and other smaller reports, and despite continual calls from pressure groups, MPs and campaigning bodies to abolish or at least raise the earnings allowance to allow part-time work by the retired, very little change was made to the pension policy, indeed much of its action in this area appears but cosmetic. It would seem that for both parties the spectre of unemployment, particularly of the young, was still so strong in member's minds that priority would always be given in the last resort to younger rather than older workers.

The trade union movement was an important force, at both the national and local level, in negotiating rights for elderly workers: for example during the enquiry into supplementary pensions for manual workers in nationalized industries (1950–52). However as a body the movement was contrary in its approach to the elderly worker. While the TUC, dealing as it did with a variety of membership policies, attitudes and practices at a time of diversity in available pension schemes, had no firm views on the 'problems of retirement', in practice two main objectives remained central to the movement: early retirement and adequate state pensions. On the one hand it was felt that, the worker, and the manual worker in particular, destroyed by years of labour, had a right to a period of respite at the end of his life; on the other early retirement had long been advocated as a means of cutting unemployment and of encouraging the promotion of younger workers. Even during this period of labour shortage, unemployment was present in certain occupations and regions (notably shipbuilding and iron and steel). Similarly the TUC was concerned that the retention of older workers would block promotion and thus the wage increments of the young.

The TUC representatives on the Philips Committee thus issued a minority report opposing the Committee's recommendation to raise the minimum pension age (TUC, 1957). In addition, they supported the principle that receipt of the National Insurance pension was conditional on retirement, fearing that employers might treat pensions as a subsidy for wages if paid automatically at 65 (TUC, 1957). Indeed by the early 1960s the informal stance of the mid-1950s (Roberts, 1954) was officially declared, and the 'right to work' was extended to the right to work irrespective of age, *only* in cases where the labour of older workers was needed in addition to the full employment of younger men with families (Green, 1963).

Pension policies

The 1946 National Insurance Act provided a flat rate contributory pension for the insured over 60 for women and 65 for men, paid to those who had withdrawn from full time employment. In addition under the earnings rule, up to £5 per week could be earned before deductions were taken from the pension. Those over 70, 65 for women, received a flat rate non-contributory pension. In 1948 the National Assistance Act provided means tested National Assistance as a safety net.

The pension rights under the 1946 Act, allowed for the first time a choice for the elderly between subsistence existence, or continued labour, and it seems that many took up the first option. However it is clear the industry also took up the option of removing large numbers of its workforce once they reached pensionable age.

Neither the Beveridge Report nor the National Insurance Act intended state pensions to remove able elderly workers from the labour market. Warning against the spread of early retirement, Beveridge recommended a system of increased pension rates as an incentive to defer retirement. Indeed the earnings allowance was intended to *discourage* retirement at the minimum age (Hansard, vol. 432, no. 150, c. 1380–1472). Furthermore higher pensions were payable to those who remained in work beyond this age, rising by annual increments for all retiring up to the age of 70. The Philips Committee presumed that so many would take advantage of this scheme that the pension Bill would be raised by £60million due to earned pension increments alone. Yet survey material from the period suggests a direct relationship between economic hardship and the desire to continue working beyond retirement age. (Shenfield, 1957; Pearson, 1957a). Of particular importance in this respect are the Ministry of Labour's two investigations into the employment of one thousand workers over 55 (Thomas and Osbourne, 1945, 1950). Carried out either side of the National Insurance Act of 1948, they provide insight into the immediate effects of the introduction of improved pensions for all workers. Drawing on a comparison between those eligible and not eligible for a pension, Thomas and Osbourne strongly suggested that the effects of pension provision was an important factor in encouraging retirement: those eligible for pensions who were still in employment had fallen from 44 per cent to 30 per cent, while those over 60 not eligible for pensions and still working had actually increased.

The bureaucratization of industry

It is also clear that employers, coping with increasingly bureaucratized and heavily administered industries, also used retirement age as a convenient tool for regulating the work force. Though data is scarce it does appear that if anything, and despite government recommendations otherwise, employers steadily shifted towards more fixed retirement policies as the period progressed. In 1944 the Ministry of Labour's survey revealed that over three-quarters of firms had flexible pension schemes, as did Shenfield's survey of the Midlands manufacturing industry in 1954 (Shenfield, 1957). Yet by the early 1960s half of the 55 large industries surveyed by the Acton Society Trust (1960), and two-thirds of the industry on Merseyside (Heron and Chown, 1961), had a rigid policy. Major industries, such as chemical industry, iron and steel works, and the nationalized coal mines and railways, had all produced rigid retirement policies by the mid-1960s.

Although policies varied according to occupational structure and size of company—(Hannah, 1986) provides a detailed analysis of this—large organizations were considered more likely to instigate rigid retirement policies than small (Action Society Trust 1960), and increasing technology (Le Gros Clark, 1968) and complicated administrative structures (Green, 1963) were also likely to encourage rigid policies. Overall it does appear that the general trend was towards making it more difficult for people to stay on in full-time employment after 65, with a clear transition towards rigidity in policy (Heron and Chown, 1961).

What is also clear is that while in most cases the elderly worker was not even consciously considered, if they were it was typically with negative connotations (Industrial Welfare Society, 1951). Many of these assumptions were based on the difficulties many older workers had with the increasing speed and pace of new technology. In these conditions it is not surprising that few industries adopted a policy for retaining older workers. As Shenfield

(1957: 84) wrote 'to remove discrimination against the older worker is far more urgent for men aged 50–65 years, than for men over pension age'.

Technological change

From the late 1940s the Ministry of Labour was promoting mechanization as a means of boosting production. While heralded by some as a means of retaining the older worker through an easing of working conditions (Shenfield 1957), it was becoming increasingly clear that such transformations in employment were detrimental to the elderly worker. In particular, the increased pace and intensity associated with mechanization and production line techniques demanded the very skills which the aged worker found difficult (Nuffield Foundation, 1963). Indeed such were the problems experienced by the older worker with speed and pace, that a higher percentage were actually employed on heavy manual jobs, than on lighter speed work (Clay, 1960). Le Gros Clark's analysis of retirement rates from different occupations illustrated this. Employment requiring teams of workers operating to a pre-established pace had the highest rates of retirement, while high skilled crafts benefited from the accumulation of experience with age, and had the lowest retirement figures. In between full skilled and partially skilled jobs, these having some freedom to allow the individuals control over their work load, and adjust rather than retire, (Le Gros Clark, 1968).

Many of the lighter 'alternative' jobs, adopted by the aged worker, as he moved towards full-time retirement (Pearson 1957a/b), were similarly being replaced by machinery (Le Gros Clark, 1968) and alterations in the transport system, and a decline in 'personal services' also had an impact.

Conclusion

It is thus clear that a tradition of full-time retirement for all workers at pensionable age became established during this period, despite a labour market which was acting against this trend, and some evidence that the elderly worker would have preferred to have withdrawn gradually from employment through a process of part-time work. The Governments not only appeared unwilling to support the frequently made request to abolish or alter the Earnings Allowance, to allow such part-time employment but also made no steps to positively encourage employers to retain, and indeed retrain, their elderly workforce. Employers coping with the gradual transformation of industries through mechanization and improved production methods, thus took advantage of full-time, abrupt retirement as a means of rationalization, an administrative tool which facilitated efficient regulation and control over the workforce. The elderly worker, finding the workplace an increasingly negative environment in which to work, withdrew, not only owing to the provision of minimum state pension for all, but also because the wider community began to accept that it was 'normal' for cessation of labour to occur at a fixed chronological age. The elderly worker knew that retirement would be the common experience of his peer group and came to accept it.

The retirement debate thus appears to have had little lasting impact upon the post-war retirement process. The early 1960s saw the growth and spread of retirement schemes, and the general acceptance of preparation for, rather than anxiety over, the period of life beyond full-time employment. As a spokesman for Unilever said at the Industrial Welfare Conference in 1960: 'In the olden days retirement was considered to be synonymous with the first step through the cemetery; nowadays . . . retirement should be the entry into a period of continued usefulness' (Hubbard, 1962: 5).

References

Acton Society Trust (1960), *Retirement: a study of current attitudes and practices*, Acton Society Trust.

Anderson, W. and Cowan, N. (1956), 'Work and retirement: influences on the health of older men', *The Lancet*, December, 1344–48.

Belbin, E. (1956), 'The effects of propaganda on recall recognition and behaviour', *British Psychology*, 259–70.

Belbin, E. (1958), 'Methods of training older workers', *Ergonomics* **1**, 207–211.

Belbin, E., Downs, S. and Moore, B. (1964), '"Unlearning" and its relationship to age' *Ergonomics*, 7, 419–27.

Clay, H. (1960), *The Older Worker and His Pension*, DSIR/HMSO.

Emerson, A. (1959), 'The First Years of Retirement', *Occupational Psychology*, **34**, 197–208.

Fleming, C. (1955), *Ageing in an Industry: an age-compositional investigation of workforces in the British iron and steel industry;* 1952–3 Mimeo, 1–76.

Fleming, C. (1963), 'The age factor in the Sheffield cutlery industry', *Vita Humana*, **6**, 4, 177–212.

Granick, S. (1950), 'Studies of psychopathology in later maturity: a review', *J. Gerontology*, 5, 361–9.

Granick, S. (1952), 'Adjustment of older people in two Florida communities', *J. Gerontology*, 7, 419–25.

Green, G. (1963), *The Trade Unions*. Preparation for Retirement First National Conference, September 1963.

Groombridge, B. (1960), *Education and Retirement*. The National Institute of Adult Education.

Hannah, L. (1986), *Inventing Retirement: The development of occupational pensions in Great Britain*, Cambridge University Press.

Heron, A. and Chown, S. (1960), 'Semi-skilled and over forty', *International Research Seminar on Social and Psychological Aspects of Ageing*. Berkley, California, August.

Heron, A. and Chown, S. (1961), 'Ageing and the semi-skilled' Medical Research Council Memo, **40**, 1–49.

HMSO (1947), Economic Survey. Cmd. 7046.

HMSO (1948), Royal Commission on Population. Cmd. 7695.

HMSO (1952), Employment of Older Men and Women. The Economic and Social Effects of the Increasing Proportion of Older People in the Population. Ministry of Labour and National Service.

HMSO (1953), Employment of Older Men and Women. Advisory Committee of the Ministry of Labour and National Service. First Report. Cmd. 8963.

HMSO (1954), Report of the Committee on the Economic and Financial Problems of the Provision for Old Age. Cmd. 9333.

HMSO (1955), Employment of Older Men and Women. Advisory Committee of the Ministry of Labour and National Service, Second Report, Cmd. 8963.

HMSO (1956), Reasons Given for Retiring or for Continuing to Work. Report of an Enquiry by the Ministry of Pensions and National Insurance.

HMSO (1956b), Report of the Committee on the Taxation Treatment of Provisions for Retirement. Cmd. 9063.

HMSO (1958), Provision for Old Age. Cmd. 538.

Hubbard, L. (1962), 'Preparation for Retirement Committee', *Society of Housing Managers Quarterly Journal*, **5**, 10–11.

Industrial Welfare Society (1951), *The Employment of Elderly Workers*, Industrial Welfare Society.

Le Gros Clark, F. (1954), *The Later Working Life in the Building Industry*, Nuffield Foundation.

Le Gros Clark, F. (1959), *Age and the Working Lives of Men*, Nuffield Foundation.

Le Gros Clark, F. (1966), *Work, Age and Leisure*, Nuffield Foundation.

Le Gros Clark, F. (1968), *Pensioners in Search of a Job*, Nuffield Foundation.

McMahon, C. and Ford, T. (1955), 'Surviving the first five years of retirement', *J. Gerontology*, **10**, 212–15.

Ministry of Health, (1954), Unpublished Memo.

Ministry of Labour, unpublished memos 1945–55.

National Old People's Welfare Committee (1961), *Employment and Workshops for the Elderly*, National Old People's Welfare Committee.

National Old People's Welfare Committee (1962), Untitled Memo.

National Old People's Welfare Committee (1963), *Employment and Workshops for the Elderly*. National Old People's Welfare Committee.

Nuffield Foundation (1963), *Workers Nearing Retirement*, Nuffield Foundation.

Parish, F. and Peacock, A. (1954), 'Economics of dependence', *Economica*, **21**, 84.

Pearson, M. (1957a), 'The transition from work to retirement: I', *Occupational Psychology*, **31**, 80–88.

Pearson, M. (1957b), 'The transition from work to retirement: II', *Occupational Psychology*, **31**, 139–49.

Richardson, I. (1953), 'Age and work', *British J. Industrial Medicine*, **10**, 269–84.

Richardson, I. (1956a), 'A socio-medical study of 200 unemployed men', *Medical Officer*, **96**, 165–170.

Richardson, I. (1956b), 'Retirement: a socio-medical study of 266 men', *Scottish Medical J.*, **1**, 281–391.

Roberts, A. (1954), 'British trade union attitudes to the employment of older men and women', *Third Congress of the International Association of Gerontology*.

Rose, A. (1953), *The Older Unemployed Man in Hull*, University College of Hull, Department of Social Studies.

Shenfield, B. (1957), *Social Policies for Old Age*, Routledge and Kegan Paul.

Socialist Medical Association, 1964, *Poverty and Old People*, SMA discussion document.

Taietz, P., Steirs, G. and Barron, M. (1956), *Adjustment to Retirement in Rural New York State*. Bulletin 919, New York State College of Medicine.

Thomas, G. and Osbourne, B. (1945/50), *Older people and their Employment*, Central Office of Information.

Townsend, P. (1955), 'The Construction of Retirement', *Transactions of the Association of Industrial Medical Officers*, **5**.

TUC (1957), *Annual Report*.

Welford, A. (1953), 'Extending the employment of older people' *BMJ*, November, 1193–7.

Welford, A. (1958), *Ageing and Human Skill*, Oxford University Press.

Welford, A. (1962a), 'On changes of performance with age', *The Lancet*, February, 335–9.

Welford, A. (1962b), 'On changes of performance with age: a correction and methological note', *Ergonomics*, **5**, 581–2.

7 Britain, the 1947 Asian Relations Conference, and regional co-operation in South-East Asia

Tilman Remme

In October 1949, the British Cabinet under Prime Minister Clement Attlee endorsed a paper which made 'regional co-operation' official British policy in South and South-East Asia:

> The aim of the United Kingdom should be to build up some sort of regional association in South-East Asia in partnership with the association of the Atlantic Powers . . . The immediate object of a wider association of the West, including the Pacific members of the Commonwealth and the South-East Asian countries, would be to prevent the spread of communism and to resist Russian expansion: its long-term object would be to create a system of friendly partnership between East and West and to improve economic and social conditions in South-East Asia and the Far East.[1]

In January 1950, the British Foreign Secretary Ernest Bevin took measures to implement London's regional policy. He encouraged Commonwealth Foreign Ministers meeting in Colombo to establish a consultative committee in order to examine methods of co-ordinating development activities in South and South-East Asia.[2] This subsequently led to the Colombo Plan, an 'aggregate of bilateral arrangements involving foreign aid for the economic development of South and Southeast Asia' (Singh, 1966: p. 170), which eventually included 23 Asian as well as Western countries from inside and outside the Commonwealth.

The aims of the 1949 Cabinet paper on regional co-operation were twofold: first, to fight the advance of communism by creating prosperous conditions in South-East Asia, an area still suffering from the destruction caused by the Second World War and now under threat from communist guerilla activities. It was felt that Western technical and financial aid would best be distributed on a regional basis, an idea inspired partly by the distribution of Marshall aid through the OEEC in Europe. The paper's second and long-term aim was to create an international organization which would ensure a lasting British role in a post-colonial South and South-East Asia. But how had Britain's commitment to regional co-operation come about?

The Cabinet paper was in fact the outcome of years of interdepartmental debating in London and Singapore. Broadly speaking, there were two lines of thought. The Colonial Office, which as late as 1944 had supported the idea of creating regional commissions in the world's colonial areas had, after the War, opposed any new plans for regional co-operation in South-East Asia. It feared that a regional commission might lead to international and United States interference in the region's British, French and Dutch colonies. The Foreign Office, on the other hand, supported the idea of a regional organization following the Japanese surrender in August 1945. The war had demonstrated South-East Asia's strategic importance for India and Australia. Its future defence would require improved co-ordination between the individual British territories as well as co-operation between the regional powers, Britain, France, the Netherlands and Thailand. Postwar relief and reconstruction too required concerted international action on a regional basis. In the long term, the Foreign Office also hoped that a regional organization might consolidate British hegemony in postwar South-East Asia.[3]

It was to take more than four years of scrutiny, debate and development before regional co-operation became official British policy in South-East Asia (including South Asia). Apart from facing opposition by the Colonial Office, the Foreign Office's plans were affected by three political factors. First, Britain faced the difficult task of postwar administration and relief in South-East Asia and the threat of famine in the region during 1946. Secondly, Asian nationalism advanced and led to the process of decolonization in South and South-East Asia after the transfer of power in India in August 1947. Finally, the shift of the Cold War to South-East Asia was prompted by the Malayan Emergency and by decisive communist victories in China in 1948.

Britain's regional plans were in a sense facilitated by both the threat of famine after the War and the advance of communism in 1948/49, as they constituted mutual enemies for the South and South-East Asian governments. Britain saw herself in the best position to co-ordinate the fight against these enemies. On the other hand, Asian nationalism and the appearance of an increasingly independent India interfered with British plans. The tendency of 'Asia for Asians' and of anti-colonial solidarity fostered by the new Indian Prime Minister, Jawaharlal Nehru, conflicted with London's newly evolving concept in 1947 of British-led regional co-operation between the colonial powers and the new Asian states.

This chapter explores some of the effects of Asian nationalism on Britain's regional plans. Particular attention is given to the proceedings of the Asian Relations conference in 1947, and to London's initial assessment of the meeting. Although not fully appreciated at the time, the conference had an indirect, yet crucial impact on the regional politics of South and South-East Asia. The second part of the chapter sheds light on the Foreign Office's regional policy prior to the meeting. It then assesses Britain's reaction to the growth of exclusively Asian regionalism in the wake of the Asian

Relations Conference, and the meeting's significance for British regional policy in 1949.

The Asian Relations Conference: Signs of Asia's new self-confidence

The Indian Council of World Affairs, an unofficial and little-known organization dealing with the study of international relations, announced on 13 September 1946 that an Inter-Asian Relations Conference would be held in Delhi the following February or March.[4] The conference organizers emphasized that the proceedings would be of an unofficial and cultural nature only, that no resolutions would be passed, and that the agenda would explicitly exclude questions of defence and security.[5] Despite this, the mere fact that 32 countries, including both Japan and the Soviet Union's Asian republics, were to be invited to a specifically and exclusively Asian conference, was of profound political significance. Never before had representatives from the whole of Asia come together to freely discuss problems of common interest such as racial conflicts, the transition from colonial to national economies, and Asian economic co-operation. The event was given political credibility by its support from Pandit Jawaharlal Nehru, at the time the senior member of the Indian Interim Government and one of Asia's most prominent politicians, especially as the conference was his idea. Nehru had first mentioned plans for an all-Asian meeting in December 1945. In March 1946, following a tour of South-East Asia, he used the Indian Council of World Affairs to promote a gathering on Indian soil. Eventually, Nehru stood down as chairman of the Conference's organizing committee and was replaced by Mrs Sarojini Naidu, the Council's president. Nehru personally issued the invitations to the Conference, however, and he lent his full support and prestige to the meeting, soon referred to as Nehru's conference.[6]

If the idea of an all-Asian gathering was unprecedented, it was its timing which gave the Conference particular significance, as India was now on the brink of independence. In May 1946, the report of the British Cabinet Mission to the subcontinent, while failing to provide a solution to the problem of Indian unity or partition, had given 'conclusive evidence of the British desire to withdraw from India at the earliest possible moment' (Mansergh, 1958: 218). In early September, the Indian Interim Government assumed office, and the Indian Constituent Assembly declared in December that India would become an independent sovereign republic. After the British government's commitment on 20 February 1947 to quit India within the next 16 months, both India and Pakistan attained independence in August 1947—a watershed in Asian history which led to the independence of Burma and Ceylon in early 1948 and marked the beginning of the end of the European colonial empires in Asia. At the same time, countries in South-East Asia such as Indonesia and Vietnam, after declaring their independence in

1945, were struggling against the return of the Dutch and the French after the end of the Japanese occupation. In Malaya, the British were facing unprecedented opposition to their constitutional reform plans while the Philippines officially gained independence from the United States on 4 July 1946. To many Asians, the holding of an Asian Relations Conference at such a time was a further sign of Asia's new self-confidence, and solidarity, in standing up to colonial rule.

The Conference was to be of profound significance for British policy in South and South-East Asia. First, it was a sign of growing independence in Indian foreign policy. More importantly, and this London did not immediately realize, the conference was to inspire a trend for exclusively Asian co-operation in South-East Asia which directly contravened British plans. At the beginning of 1947 the Foreign Office was secretly contemplating the creation of a regional organization in South-East Asia. Its centre would be in Singapore, and it was to be dominated by Britain. Under the impression of advancing self-government in Asia, the Foreign Office hoped that such an organization would one day bind newly independent states like Burma, Ceylon, Indonesia and Indochina closely to Britain and the West. The Foreign Office was also optimistic about including India in Britain's planned regional system.

However, until the Asian Relations Conference in March 1947 the Foreign Office underestimated Asian opposition to such a British-inspired organization. As the conference was to reveal, the smaller countries in South and South-East Asia were highly sensitive to anything reeking of Western imperialism. They also mistrusted Indian and Chinese desires for leadership in Asia. Instead, many politicians from South and South-East Asia supported exclusively Asian co-operation between the smaller countries directed against the colonial powers. While in the event no new alignments were created, the Conference did inspire a flurry of international proposals for exclusively Asian regional co-operation in South and South-East Asia during the following years. In the short run, this unexpected trend towards Asian regionalism forced the Foreign Office to postpone its own ambitious regional policy, as it was grasping the strength of Asian susceptibilities to British hegemonial designs. In the long term London tried to find a compromise between Asian and British concepts of regional co-operation.

Immediately after the Conference's announcement, however, British officials were still largely unaware of the meeting's potential significance for regional co-operation in South-East Asia, although the India Office suspected it would be 'hostile to western "imperialism" ', and regarded it as a sign of Indian ambitions to lead the South-East Asian independence movements.[7] Sir David Monteath, the Permanent Under-Secretary at the India Office, described Nehru's invitations as an 'example of the expansive tendencies of the Interim Government in foreign affairs.[8] The Foreign Office, on the other hand, was more disturbed by the news that Soviet delegates would attend the conference. In December, Christopher Warner, the head of the Northern Department recently transformed from Russophile to staunch anti-Soviet (Rothwell, 1982: 256ff), could 'hardly think that delegations from the Soviet Asiatic Republics will not be highly organized to make the maximum political use of the Conference'. He feared that the meeting was 'likely to be rather similar to conferences called under Russian auspices, which are attended by non-political delegations who then find themselves forced into discussions of resolutions of a highly political nature and compelled to vote on them.'[9]

Britain's suspicion of the meeting remained partly because of a lack of political information. Only weeks before the conference, London knew only of a 'tentatively approved agenda' providing a 'forum for the airing of everyone's political views' and of a plan for groups of delegates to produce reports to be considered in plenary discussions.[10] In November 1946, the Colonial Office enquired whether the Governors of Malaya and Singapore should pass on invitations to non-Indian associations and individuals.[11] A decision was made on the highest level by Lord Pethick-Lawrence, the Secretary of State for India and Burma, who, following the Labour Government's policy of preparing India for self-government and eventual independence, favoured 'as many Indians as possible having to deal with practical matters and taking part in conferences of this kind'.[12] Accordingly, India Office officials, while noting that the proceedings might take an objectionable course, supported the transmission of invitations [13] and adopted an attitude of reluctant co-operation. Pethick-Lawrence's decision was also binding for the Foreign Office which in March 1947 grudgingly granted visas to the Soviet delegates.[14]

Immediately before the Conference, London instructed the British High commissioner in India, Sir Terence Shone (whose staff were to attend the opening plenary session) to cable information of conference discussions on issues such as nationalist movements in foreign and British colonial territories, regional co-operation with special reference to economic and welfare matters, as well as the popularity of the British Council and opportunities for its development.[15] The Foreign and India Offices approached Dr Nicholas Mansergh, an academic from London's Royal Institute of International Affairs (Chatham House), who was one of two British observers during the Conference entitled to attend the group discussions, which were closed to the press. Mansergh was asked to write a comprehensive and confidential report about the conference and to stay in touch with Shone's staff as well as the Reuters correspondent covering the event to ensure fair reporting.[16]

Four days before the opening of the Conference, a telegram from the Cabinet Office, drafted by the Foreign Office, warned Shone that the Soviet delegates would attack British 'colonial methods and imperialist reactionaries'. Unless the discussion of political issues was excluded from the Conference, the Soviets would have every opportunity to damage British interests. Shone was advised to mobilize the support of friendly delegates and to influence press and new agencies to mitigate the effect of unfriendly resolutions; Reuters had already promised the Foreign Office to edit reports on the Conference in its London office.

Shone was also asked to influence local journalists. Should the conference develop on undesirable lines, the High Commissioner should consider mentioning British concerns to Nehru, who might co-operate in limiting the damage, since he was probably 'no more anxious than we are to promote Soviet leadership in Asia'. The worst outcome of the conference, the telegram stated, would be the establishment of a permanent or semi-permanent Inter-Asian body including the Soviet Asian Republics and excluding Britain. If a permanent secretariat were created, the authorities should be convinced to include a suitable British representative in its membership.[17]

Conference proceedings. Asian unity put to the test

While Whitehall tried to protect British interests in advance of the conference, Nehru's invitations received an overwhelming response: 28 out of the 36 countries eventually invited sent delegations.[18] though invitations were originally issued to the heads of Asian countries, most of the delegates represented unofficial bodies and organizations dealing with cultural affairs or international relations, supported by a small number of observers of greater political weight.[19] Since not every country had a national government or sent high-ranking officials, delegations varied in quality as well as quantity. By number, the dominant delegation at the conference was the Indian, whose 51 representatives, including Nehru, made up almost a quarter of the Conference.[20] The Chinese, in contrast, were represented by only eight officials from the Kuomintang government, who nevertheless exercised disproportionate influence. From South-East Asia, Thailand and the Philippines attended as fully independent countries, while Indonesia and Burma sent members of their nationalist leadership. Malaya, in the absence of such a body, was represented by a more radical group of labour leaders (Thompson and Adloff, 1947: 98). Indochina sent three pro-French delegates from Cambodia, Cochin-China and Laos, who were confused frequently with the pro-communist delegation representing the Democratic Republic of Vietnam. From South Asia, apart from the Indians, delegates from Afghanistan, Nepal and Tibet attended, while Ceylon sent some of its nationalist leaders. From the Middle East, Turkey, Iran, Egypt and a delegation from the Hebrew University in Palestine attended the conference. Transjordan, Iraq, Lebanon, Yemen and Saudi Arabia had no delegations but, according to the organizers, were represented by an observer from the Arab League.[21] The Soviet Union sent delegations from six Asian republics, while from East Asia, China, Mongolia and the American controlled part of Korea were represented. Only Japan was completely unrepresented as the Allied control authority forbade her to send delegates to international conferences.

Despite initial antagonism between some of the delegations — Arab and Jewish delegates almost came to blows and China disputed Tibet's right to attend — opposition to colonial rule served as an ideological bond between most participants. Werner Levi wrote in 1952:

> The organizers were aware of the limitations of Asian solidarity and expected no miracles . . . Nevertheless, many delegates came to New Delhi with as much enthusiasm for a united Asia as there had ever been. There was not in the foreseeable future another period in which Asians, flushed by achieved and anticipated victories in the struggle for freedom, would be so enthusiastic about cooperation and so willing to push divisions into the background. Whatever the conference could achieve would be the maximum at that stage of Asian political developments. (Levi, 1952: 36)

Despite anti-colonial sentiment, the language of the Conference was English, and a garden party held by the new Viceroy of India, Lord Mountbatten, was attended by most delegates and produced 'the most favourable reactions'.[22] The British High Commissioner commented that the Indians wanted to show that India could entertain in style, even if the host were an English Viceroy.[23] The organizing committee also invited observers belonging to cultural institutions such as Chatham House and the Institute of Pacific Relations from Britain, the United States, Australia, the Soviet Union and the United Nations.[24] While the colonial powers were to be criticized, the Indian hosts did not want the meeting to be a platform for militants.

The Conference opened on 23 March 1947 with a plenary session in the Old Fort auditorium in New Delhi. In the inaugural address, Nehru made the most significant speech of the day. He stressed the historical significance of the Conference: 'We stand at the end of an era and at the threshold of a new period of history. . . . Asia, after a long period of quiescence, has suddenly become important again in world affairs.' Nehru then dispelled fears that India might use the occasion to establish a leading role in Asia. He emphasized that although the conference happened to be convened in India, the idea had arisen simultaneously in many Asian countries and they faced a common task on an equal basis. Despite this assurance, Nehru did hint that India had a special role to play. Apart from the fact that she was emerging into freedom and independence, India was the 'natural centre and focal point of the many forces at work in Asia'. Nehru insisted, 'We have no designs against anybody,' and supported the United Nations, but added that, in order to have ' "One World", we must . . . Think of the countries of Asia co-operating together for that larger ideal'. Nehru hoped that some 'permanent Asian Institute for the study of common problems and to bring about closer relations', as well as a School of Asian Studies would emerge from the Conference. (Asian Relations Organization, 1948: 26ff)

After the opening plenary session, the conference split up into Round Table Groups dealing with the following topics: (1) national freedom movements; (2) migration and racial problems; (3) economic development and social services; (4) cultural problems; and (5) women's problems. (Asian Relations Organization, 1948: 4) It was in these groups that the actual work of the Conference took place. Although the agenda did not explicitly include the issue of Asian unity or co-operation, it was of such importance to many delegates that it arose constantly during the discussions. Indeed, the group discussions soon tested the idea of continental unity, revealing some intractable obstacles to all-Asian co-operation. The central problem was the smaller countries' mistrust of the bigger ones. No sooner was Western exploitation denounced, the Chatham House observer reported, than fears developed of Indian and Chinese economic dominance once the Western powers had gone.[25] Furthermore, neither India nor China wanted to see the other emerge from the Conference as the leader of Asia. Added to this were racial prejudices and, to a minor degree, differences over economic policies and the role of foreign capital in the economic development of Asia.

According to Dr Mansergh's report to the Foreign Office, five factions emerged during the Conference: India, China, the South-East Asian perimeter (including Indonesia, Malaya, Vietnam, Ceylon, Burma and Thailand), the Middle East states and the Soviet Union. Of these five, the Middle East countries played the least important role, feeling 'quasi-detached' from the Conference and, according to American observers from the Institute of Pacific Relations, appearing not to regard themselves as Asians. One reason for the Arab states' reserved attitude lay in the Indian Muslim League's opposition to the Conference.[26] Furthermore, the Soviet delegation played a much less influential role than the Foreign Office had expected, making a generally poor impression which only improved after the showing of a propaganda film of the 1946 May Day parade in Moscow. Observers soon identified the Soviets' main aim during the Conference as preventing the creation of an Asian bloc, a goal which coincided with Western interests. Otherwise, apart from trumpeting Moscow's achievements, the delegates of the Soviet Asian republics contributed little, avoiding, to London's surprise, any direct criticism of Britain's role in Asia.[27]

By contrast, the Indian delegation was one of the most active. According to Mr W.W. Russell, the second Chatham House observer, the Indians pursued two strategic aims largely dictated by Nehru. First, they assured the great powers and the smaller Asian countries that India had no intention of promoting an Asian bloc; secondly, they ensured the formation of a permanent Indian-based inter-Asian organization, satisfying the ambitions of the Indian Congress leaders for a large say in Asian affairs.[28] Achievement of the first aim was the easier task. Nehru and other leading Indian figures such as Krishna Menon continually emphasized that they did not intend to create an Asian bloc. This was accepted by the Foreign Office and Soviet delegates were also satisfied. Pursuing their second goal, however, the Indians soon ran into trouble. Their aim of acquiring, implicitly or explicitly, some kind of leadership in Asia encountered resistance from the well-coordinated and relatively high-powered Chinese delegation. The Chinese played their hand more skilfully, showing full understanding of their unpopularity in South-East Asia and leaving a most favourable impression. Much to Nehru's annoyance, the Chinese succeeded not only in persuading the delegates that they, not India, should host the next conference, but also forestalled the establishment of a permanent Asian organization under Indian leadership.[29] The organization that was created instead consisted of only national units with loose contact between them, and without a central co-ordinating office.

The Indian delegation suffered from a split between the political element following Nehru and the promoters of the conference in the Indian Council of World Affairs. The two alignments squabbled over minor procedural questions, at times preventing the expression of a coherent Indian view. Nehru was also under sustained attack from the Muslim League, which had announced a boycott of the conference on 20 March and denounced it as a thinly diguised attempt on the part of the 'Hindu Congress' to boost itself politically.[30] Throughout the proceedings *Dawn*, the League's main press organ, nourished the smaller countries' suspicions of Nehru:

> Skilfully he has worked himself into some sort of all Asian leadership. This is just what this ambitious Hindu leader had intended—to thrust himself upon the Asian nations as their leader and through his attainment of that prestige and eminence to further the expansionist designs of Indian Hinduism.[31]

While India and China were opposing and, to a degree, neutralizing one another, the South-East Asian countries were anxious to assert themselves, conscious of the fact that they were not strong enough to stand on their own feet economically or politically. The South-East Asians were united by their opposition to colonial rule in Asia, and their morale rose further on the triumphant arrival towards the end of the conference of the Indonesian Prime Minister, Dr Sutan Sjahrir, whose government, on 25 March, received *de facto* recognition by the Netherlands in parts of Indonesia.[32] Their deep mistrust of both India and China, according to Mansergh's report to the Foreign Office, was apparent at all times, and it was only the smaller countries' even greater dislike of Western imperialism which persuaded them to accept Chinese or Indian leadership as the lesser evil.[33]

South-East Asian fear of India and China was especially strong in the discussion group dealing with national freedom movements. A Burmese delegate recalled that India had been a tool in the hands of British imperialism for subjugating her neighbours, and he feared that one day European capitalism and exploitation in Burma might be replaced by 'brown exploitation'. (Asian Relations Organization, 1948: 73) Another Burmese delegate stated that it was 'terrible to be ruled by a Western power, but . . . even more so to be ruled by an Asian power'. (Levi, 1952: 36) As a delegate from Ceylon pointed out, small countries like Ceylon, Burma, Malaya and Indonesia might face Chinese and Indian aggression not necessarily of a political, but of an economic or demographic nature. In Ceylon and Malaya, he explained, there was considerable hatred of Chinese and Indian groups, who were doing well under the colonial government and who did not want to see change. (Asian Relations Organization, 1948: 79) The unpopularity of the Chinese and Indian immigrants in South-East Asia, Mansergh observed, was quite unmistakable: in the group on racial problems and inter-Asian migration an Indonesian delegate explained that the Chinese were associated with Dutch rule, and a delegate from Ceylon added that he wasn't 'at all surprised that the Chinese were murdered in Indonesia'.[34] According to an Australian observer, the discussions in this group 'disclosed a degree of racial exclusion and discriminatory administrative practices by Asians against Asians not generally appreciated elsewhere'. (Packer, 1947: 5)

The South-East Asian delegations also shared the more positive ambition of co-operation in the development of their economies, which they perceived as lagging behind even their limited political progress. In the group on economic development and social services, the South-East Asian countries agreed that none of them could aim at self-sufficiency and that their objective must be the creation of a planned economy over the South-East Asian region. This had been impossible because of the restrictive practices of the colonial powers; only full political freedom would make such planning feasible. Later on in the economic and social group, South-East Asian delegates even went on to suggest the creation of a South-East Asian or continental bloc. India, though sharing with the South-East Asian delegates a mistrust of foreign capital, was alarmed by such talk of exclusive economic alignments: Krishna Menon, Secretary of the India League, warned that an Asian economic bloc would lead to confrontation with the West and would mean 'putting a rope around our necks'.[35]

Unimpressed by these Indian reservations, the South-East Asian group continued to argue for anti-colonial collaboration on a continental or a regional basis. After the Malayan chairman of the group on national freedom movements demanded the liquidation of the British Empire, another Malayan delegate suggested a neutral bloc on the Asian continent, or failing that, one in South-East Asia. An Indonesian delegate went even further, suggesting, as a measure of inter-Asian co-operation in the 'non-political sphere,' the acceleration of withdrawal of all foreign troops from Asia, and of the achievement of full independence. Encouraged by such remarks, the leader of the nationalist Vietnamese delegation appealed for assistance in the war against the French. India should accord recognition to the government of Vietnam, persuade the United Nations to take up the Vietnamese question, and stop French reinforcements. The Vietnamese demand for active anti-colonial co-operation was the most far reaching of the whole conference, and Nehru swiftly delivered a reply, warning delegates against positive assistance to national movements. Such intervention by India would bring a world war; any expectation of it was unrealistic.[36]

Despite the differences in the group discussions, the Conference displayed political unanimity towards the end of the proceedings. During the concluding plenary sessions, it was announced that the Steering Committee, consisting of delegation leaders, Nehru and Mrs Naidu, had decided to set up an 'Asian Relations Organization', which would be composed of national units, one in each country, and which was to:

(a) promote the study and understanding of Asian problems and relations in their Asian and world aspects;
(b) foster friendly relations and co-operation among the peoples of Asia and those between them and the rest of the world; and
(c) further the progress and well-being of the peoples of Asia.

As a first step towards the creation of this planned organization, a provisional General Council was appointed, to which Nehru was unanimously elected President, with an Indian and a Chinese secretary.[37] However, the organization was less than Nehru originally hoped, as it lacked a central secretariat which could co-ordinate the organization's work and which Nehru originally intended to be situated in India.

The Asian Relations Conference ended on 2 April 1947. The final plenary session was attended by an enthusiastic audience of 25,000 and speakers described the conference as a landmark in Asian history. Mahatma Gandhi, who had arrived for the end of the conference, emphasized that, above all, Asia had a spiritual message to carry to the West. The conference closed with an impassioned speech by Mrs Naidu, hailing the coming of a new age in Asia, and ending with the words:

> Fellow Asians, as I called you the other day, my comrades, my kinsmen, arise; remember the night of darkness is over. Together, men and women, let us march forward to the dawn. (Asian Relations Organization, 1948: 254)

Despite such emphatic rhetoric and solidarity against colonial rule, the Conference revealed that all-Asian unity was too grandiose to be contemplated seriously. The Middle Eastern countries were barely willing even to communicate with the subcontinent, East and South-East Asia; Indian and Chinese ambitions proved inherently incompatible; while the Soviet Union feared the emergence of an Asian grouping it could not control.

For Nehru and the Indian delegation, the Conference's outcome was disappointing. On the one hand, the meeting enhanced Indian prestige as an independent political force in Asia and Nehru's reputation as a statesman. On the other, Indian plans to assume the moral, if not political, leadership in Asia clearly failed during the Conference. The region's smaller countries had displayed considerable reservations, if not hostility, towards Indian influence or hegemony. Furthermore, the Chinese managed to block an Asian organization with a permanent secretariat passed in India. The Chinese also convinced the Conference's steering committee that the next Asian Relations Conference should be held not in India but in China in two years' time.

The delegates from the South-East Asian perimeter, in contrast, had reason to be pleased with the conference's outcome. Not only did they succeed in putting India (and China) in their place but they also discovered a unity of purpose, displaying for the first time a mutual desire for economic and political co-operation in South-East Asia. This stimulus for regional co-operation in South-East Asia was perhaps the most significant outcome of the Asian Relations Conference.

Aftermath: Diverging British assessments

Contrary to Foreign Office advice, British observers and officials kept a low profile during the Asian Relations Conference. As Shone cabled London soon after the opening session, the High Commission might be accused of interfering in the proceedings if it lobbied the press and delegates. This would lead to anti-British press attacks and difficulties with the Indian authorities. The Soviet Union was less influential than expected, and Nehru had indicated that the Conference was unlikely to pass resolutions, except for the establishment of a permanent organization perhaps on the lines of the Pacific Relations Conference.[38] Immediately before the end of the Conference, the Foreign Office asked Shone and Mansergh to insist upon British membership in any new organization including the Soviet Union.[39] Shone, however, warned 'while the Pan Asiatic sentiments engendered by the conference are still warm we should go slow in pressing upon the newly formed organisation our claims to representation'.[40] In his final report to London, Shone argued that insistence on British membership might 'attribute greater importance to the organisation than the terms of reference and their implementation warrant'.[41] A conversation between Nehru and Mansergh two weeks after the Conference indicated that the new Asian Relations Organization was unlikely to play any significant part in international diplomacy, reinforcing Shone's view.[42]

The Foreign Office eventually dropped the issue of British membership. In July, Mansergh told an interdepartmental meeting in London that the Asian Relations Organization might have lasted, had it been controlled by India. However, the Chinese opposed Indian leadership and would either kill the organization at the next conference or arrange it to work against Indian wishes.[43] After India's failure to establish a permanent Asian organization under its leadership, Nehru was not inclined to follow the Steering Committee's alternative of a limited organization and a second conference under Chinese auspices.[44] The Asian Relations Organization never developed; its main achievement was publication of the 1947 Asian Relations Conference's proceedings. The second Asian Relations Conference never occured after it was postponed by the communist revolution in China in 1949.

London's fears of anti-British agitation before the Asian Relations Conference had been unfounded. According to Mansergh's report to the Foreign Office, the Soviet delegates were not unfriendly to London and refrained from any direct attacks on Britain. Nor was there any pointed hostility towards the British from other Asian countries, apart from the Egyptian and Malayan delegations, although Britain did not receive any compliments either. In general, Mansergh argued:

> The attitude towards Britain may best be described as somewhat patronising. Britain represented the imperialism that was retreating. Delegates could therefore afford to be tolerant and kind. This rather provocative tolerance was most noticeable amongst the Indian delegates.[45]

Shone shared Mansergh's impression of limited anti-British feeling during the Conference, and he noted that India, on the verge of independence, was less ready than before to espouse freedom movements elsewhere. Nevertheless, Shone suspected from unofficial contacts and from reading between the lines of press interviews that many delegates, notably the Malayans, regretted that the conference was not more hostile to Britain.[46] At the Foreign Office R.M.A. Hankey commented, 'It is distressing that the British should be held in so little esteem even though the management of the Conference and the fact that it was largely held in the English language is a tribute to what we have done in Asia.' The Conference had encouraged a 'tendency of Asia for the Asiatics which is sure to work greatly to our disadvantage and to be exploited by the Soviet to their advantage in the long run.[47]

Mansergh's report warned the Foreign Office not to underestimate the wider significance of the Conference. In its continental context, Mansergh argued, the meeting could only be described with the hackneyed phrase 'the awakening of a Continent'. Although it revealed deep divisions in Asian opinion and destroyed any prospect of a continental grouping, the most important fact was that the Conference took place. Though appeals for active aid to nationalist freedom movements fell on deaf ears, the sentiment created by the conference would prevent imperialist forces from gaining lost ground and would make it very difficult for the Dutch in Indonesia and the French in Indochina to re-establish their authority. Mansergh also noted a feeling of political solidarity among delegates from South-East Asia. Finally, Mansergh reported the general feeling of the conference that the time was ripe for Asian countries to play their part in world affairs, especially through the United

Nations, where Asian countries would 'like to paddle their own canoe' and where they would enlist help from other powers to remove the remaining vestiges of imperialist control in Asia.[48]

Mansergh's report created a division of opinion at the Colonial Office where one official, J.S. Bennett, believed the conference was of

> The greatest importance in considering the future of the Asiatic countries—particularly South-East Asia—and the future British (European) position there. The conference was in a way memorable for what it did not do. It did not launch out into old-fashioned diatribes against imperialism, or not to any great extent. An entirely new tone is to be seen. It is not basically unfriendly to the West—except on the issue of political or economic domination. But there is a quiet assumption throughout that, politically at any rate, the Western powers are on the way out. The Asiatics felt strong enough, and responsible enough, not to preach forceful intervention in the remaining Western colonies in Asia. They are confident that moral pressure will see the end of the business in a few more years.[49]

The Asian Relations Conference, according to Bennett, resembled the conference at Alexandria in 1944 which led to the formation of the Arab League and turned a divided and mainly colonial region into a considerable bloc in world affairs. He conluded:

> All this is long-term, of course. But not so very. From our point of view, I would suppose that the chief moral is in regard to the time-table within which we must work in the South-East Asia colonial territories.[50]

The majority of Colonial Office officials, in the best tradition of divide and rule, emphasized signs of Asian disagreement. H.T. Bourdillon, a Malayan expert at the Colonial Office, warned of misleading comparisons to the formation of the Arab League:

> The nations which congregated at Delhi . . . make up at least half the population of the globe and have no unity of any kind, except the practically meaningless description of being 'Eastern' as opposed to 'Western' peoples. It does not absolutely follow from this that the Delhi Conference could not have been the birth-place of a new Asian solidarity, but unfortunately the record of the Conference itself gives little evidence of such a development.

On the contrary, Bourdillon asserted, the meeting had produced much evidence of disunity both between and within the participating countries. He concluded:

> In South East Asia as elsewhere, our prime concern must be the welfare, needs and progress of the colonies with which we are dealing, and not the real or supposed pressure of outside events. We must watch outside events and take account of them, but we must not allow them to dictate to us.[51]

Bourdillon was supported by another official, Mayle, who minuted, 'We certainly ought not to allow ourselves to be driven, by this development, into granting constitutional advances where the peoples are not ready for them.' He predicted that 'this Conference would rather have a depressing effect on nationalistic movements in South East Asia'. Nehru's intimation that Indian assistance would have to be confined to moral backing must have disappointed many, particularly the Malayan delegation. Mayle even suggested using the Conference's outcome for propaganda purposes, with publicity in Malaya stressing Nehru's attitude towards nationalist movements in South East Asia.[52] Only Bennett dissented, writing on 22 August 1947, seven days after India and Pakistan gained independence:

> Personally I still stick by my minute of 21st May, and by the lesson to be drawn from that approach, namely that there can only be *one* 'Western' policy towards Asia, and the policy must be the one which we ourselves have set in the largest Asiatic state, India . . . If these papers were brought up again in another year it would be interesting to see how far this reading of the situation has turned out to be sound. [3]

Events soon proved Bennett right. Apart from India and Pakistan, Burma and Ceylon won independence from Britain in 1948. The Dutch, under growing internal and international pressure left Indonesia by the end of 1949, while France gave up Indochina after her humiliating defeat at Dien Bien Phu in 1954. In 1957, Malaya gained independence from Britain, much earlier than colonial officials would have thought possible in 1947.

While it is difficult to assess the Asian Relations Conference's direct influence on the process of decolonisation in South and South-East Asia, it is evident that the meeting encouraged Asian initiatives for regional co-operation in South-East Asia. Only weeks after the conference Aung San, the leader of the Burmese nationalists, called for a South-East Asian economic union of Burma, Indonesia, Thailand, Indochina and Malaya. In Thailand, plans were made in July and September 1947 for a Pan South-East Asian Union and a South-East Asia League. In 1949, unsuccessful efforts were made for a conference in Bangkok on economic and political matters in South-East Asia, to be attended by Thailand, India, Burma and the Philippines (Vandenbosch and Butwell, 1957: 246ff). The Philippines, who had arrived too late to play a full role at the Asian Relations Conference, jumped on the regional bandwagon, convening a conference of South and South-East Asian countries in Baguio in the summer of 1950, although the initiative proved unfruitful due to its strictly anti-communist stance. More importantly, India, after the second Dutch 'police action' against Indonesian nationalists in December 1948, convened a conference on Indonesia in January 1949. During the meeting, Ceylon tabled formal proposals for closer political and economic co-operation between India, Pakistan, Burma, Indonesia, New Zealand and Australia (Vandenbosch and Butwell, 1957: 246ff).

For London, the problem was that all of the Asian proposals for regional co-operation excluded Britain. Despite their lack of success, the trend towards exclusively Asian co-operation, fuelled by anti-colonial sentiments, was not encouraging for Britain's own regional policy.

British regional designs, 1944–1947

Between 1944 and 1947, the concepts behind British plans for regional co-operation in South-East Asia underwent major changes. Initially, both the Colonial Office and the Foreign Office were thinking in terms of regional co-operation primarily between the colonial powers. By 1947, however, the Foreign Office contemplated involving the new Asian states, including India, in a regional organization. What had not changed were the long-term aims behind the Foreign Office's regional plans: the consolidation and expansion of British influence in South-East Asia. Developments following the Asian Relations Conference soon called into question whether these aims were still realistic.

In December 1944, the Churchill government endorsed a major paper drafted by the Colonial Office and titled 'International Aspects of Colonial Policy'. It envisaged a worldwide system of international regional commissions in colonial areas, including South-East Asia, providing international collaboration on issues such as health or social welfare in the colonies. The commissions would include the colonial powers as members, though outside powers like the United States would also be represented, giving them a minimum say in the internal affairs of European colonies. The 1944 paper was part of the Anglo-American wartime debate on the future of colonial empires. The paper's British authors intended to counter demands by the United States for international supervision or trusteeship of colonial territories in the postwar era, by proposing the somewhat vague compromise formula of regional co-operation in colonial areas. The Colonial Office's scheme also aimed at transforming into proper colonies the mandated territories which Britain and France had taken over from Germany and Turkey after the First World War.[54]

However, the Colonial Office's plans were short-lived. At Yalta in February 1945 Churchill unwittingly accepted discussing the mandates and the issue of trusteeship during the forthcoming San Francisco Conference on the United Nations. Instead of replacing the mandates, the Colonial Secretary Oliver Stanley subsequently lamented, Britain's proposals now meant 'throwing the whole Colonial Empire open to discussion by this motley assembly [the UN—author's note], a procedure which I should regard as hazardous in extreme'.[55] The Colonial Office consequently dropped its plans, fearing they might lead to international interference in Britain's colonial territories without replacing the mandates or putting an end to the debate on trusteeship in return. After the failure of its worldwide colonial scheme the Colonial Office remained highly suspicious of similar new proposals.

After the Japanese surrender in August 1945, however, the Foreign Office picked up the regional initiative. It pursued the idea of creating an international regional organization to cement British influence in South-East Asia.[56] A Foreign Office proposal at the end of 1945 to establish a regional commission dominated by a British Minister Resident was blocked by the Colonial Office on grounds of possible international meddling in colonial affairs through such an organization. Nevertheless, the Foreign Office succeeded in appointing Lord Killearn as Special Commissioner in Singapore in February 1946. At the time, South-East Asia was threatened by famine resulting from wartime destruction. Killearn was therefore instructed to take measures to alleviate the critical shortage of rice and other foodstuffs in South-East Asia, defined as Thailand, Indochina, Indonesia, Malaya, Borneo, Ceylon and Burma.[57] Killearn's Special Commission soon developed into South-East Asia's first regional organization, providing international co-operation on the technical level. The Special Commissioner, with the help of his expert staff, soon organized regular international meetings in Singapore (so-called monthly Liaison Officers' Meetings) to co-ordinate the supply and distribution of food in the region. He also convened a series of specialized regional conferences between August 1946 and January 1948 dealing with topics like nutrition fisheries, social welfare and statistics.[58] The Foreign Office and Killearn hoped that the technical co-operation organized under the Special Commission's roof could one day be extended to economic, political and possibly even defence co-operation.

During the Commonwealth Prime Ministers' Meeting in April 1946, the British Foreign Secretary Ernest Bevin first voiced Foreign Office plans for regional co-operation on an international platform. Bevin suggested Killearn's organization as the focus around which Britain, Australia, New Zealand and India could develop South-East Asia. Bevin explained to the Australians that he wanted to raise the region's standard of living, pointing to South-East Asia's resources and her vast and untapped market.[59] Apparently, Bevin wanted to bait Australia into a defence commitment to South-East Asia proposed by the British Chiefs of Staff during the conference. The Australian delegation welcomed the creation of a regional commission, but refused to commit itself to South-East Asian defence. At the same time the Colonial Office, taken by complete surprise by Bevin's proposal, reiterated its concern that a regional commission in South-East Asia would lead to international interference in the region's European colonies, particularly because of the contemporary troubles in Indochina and Indonesia.[60] As a result, Britain qualified Bevin's proposal. At the end of the Prime Ministers' Meeting, the Colonial Secretary, George Hall, stated that, although a regional commission was desirable in South-East Asia, the time was not ripe for it. Even so, this formula, a compromise between the Colonial Office and the Foreign Office, constituted Britain's first postwar commitment to the principle of regional co-operation in South-East Asia.

Until the Prime Ministers' Meeting, the Foreign Office had been thinking of regional co-operation as co-operation with the colonial powers in South-East Asia. However, the increasing prospect of Indian independence forced the Foreign Office to revise its regional concepts. In April 1946, one official argued that Indian independence was likely to accelerate the independence or dominion status of Burma and Ceylon, and the establishment of more or less independent states in Indonesia, Indochina, the Philippines and Korea. India, moreover, would be the leading partner in this new group of independent Asian states.[61] The Foreign Office agreed, concluding that any regional commission in South-East Asia would be meaningless unless it included representatives of an independent India.[62]

Although subsequent news of Nehru's plans for and exclusively Asian conference suggested that India might not even want to be part of a British sponsored regional organization in South-East Asia,[63] the Foreign Office remained optimistic about the inclusion of India and other fledgling Asian states in its regional plans. At the beginning of 1947, a Foreign Office memorandum argued:

> All the Colonial territories of South East Asia look forward to a future of greater self-government or total independence. At the same time they are looking to other countries for help, guidance and example.

Though Soviet interference was seen as looming in the background, the peoples of the region were still disposed to look to Britain and the USA:

> We ought to grasp the opportunity which this tendency gives us, firstly by promoting rehabilitation . . . and secondly by offering them the advice and help they need in developing their lives on modern lines.

The Special Commission was a valuable means of centralizing these efforts as it was already organizing regional co-operation on a technical level. The paper concluded:

> As confidence grows it should be possible to progress towards regional collaboration in political matters also. Out aim should be to develop Singapore as a centre for the radiation of British influence . . .[64]

A second paper added that although the political troubles in Indochina and Indonesia made collaboration difficult for the moment, it was desired to:

> . . . build up a regional system, with Singapore as its centre, which should not only strengthen the political ties between the territories concerned and facilitate a defensive strategy, but also prove of considerable economic and financial benefit to the United Kingdom.[65]

In a third paper Esler Dening, the head of the Far Eastern department emphasized the Indian connection:

> With out imminent withdrawal from India and Burma, South-East Asia becomes of even greater significance as a strategic link between the United Kingdom, Africa and Australia. Though it is believed that our influence will not entirely disappear from India and Burma, its focus will be centred in South-East Asia, and geographically the centre is Singapore. It may well be that closer contacts of the U.K. with India and Burma will be maintained through some organisation such as that of the Special Commissioner in Singapore, in view of the great distance from the U.K.[66]

Taken together, the three memoranda suggested that Britain should eventually expand the scope of the commission in Singapore in order to influence and guide the about-to-be independent countries of South-East Asia along pro-British lines, and to maintain a close British link with India and Burma after their independence. At the same time, the other two colonial powers, France and the Netherlands, would be of only secondary importance in such a regional scheme. As Dening argued in the third paper:

> We must not appear to be ganging up with the Western Powers against Eastern peoples striving for independence. Rather should our aim be to contrive a general partnership between independent or about-to-be independent Eastern peoples and the Western Powers who by their past experience are best able to give them help and, in our case, to some extent protection.[67]

The limits of British regional policy in South-East Asia

However, other countries' regional proposals in the wake of the Asian Relations Conference soon threatened Britain's lead in South-East Asian regionalism which it had established through the Special Commission. Weeks before the conference, a first challenge came from the Australian Minister for External Affairs, H.V. Evatt, who called for a 'regional instrumentality' to be established concerned with the interest of all peoples in South-East Asia and the Western Pacific,[68] and for a conference of 13 countries, including the colonial powers, the independent countries in South-East Asia as well as India and the United States to discuss defence, trade and cultural relations in the Indian Ocean and the South-West Pacific area. The British were not pleased with Evatt's independent initiative. Sir David Monteath at the India Office described it as a 'counterblast' to the Asian Relations Conference.[69] The Foreign Office, apart from objecting to Australia taking the lead on regional co-operation, thought Evatt's regional initiative premature. Any attempt to present:

> . . . a cut-and-dried policy of United Kingdom or Australian manufacture would
> be likely to frustrate our main object of securing the wholehearted and friendly
> cooperation of India and Burma, whether they remain in the Commonwealth or
> not.[70]

While Britain persuaded Australia for the time being to abandon her regional ideas,[71] she was unable to prevent other countries from launching regional proposals more hostile to the European colonial powers. As a result, Britain temporarily lost the initiative in the field of regional co-operation in South-East Asia. The feeling of anti-colonial solidarity in Asia butressed by the Asian Relations Conference was sustained in the following year by opposition, particularly in Burma and India, to the Netherlands' and France's hardline colonial policies in Indochina and Indonesia. In such an atmosphere, the Foreign Office found itself unable to implement its regional plans for South-East Asia (which still included the French and the Dutch) and to expand the Special Commission's functions to economic and political co-operation in Asia.

Other factors contributed to the temporary demise of Britain's regional policies. On 18 March 1947 the UN created the Economic Commission for Asia and the Far East (ECAFE), originally including Britain, France, the Netherlands, the United States, Australia, the Soviet Union, India, China, Thailand and the Philippines.[72] Despite its wider geographical scope and its lack of funds and expertise, ECAFE, because of its UN background, had greater credibility as an inter-governmental organization for the economic development of South-East Asia. ECAFE soon emerged as the UN's competitor to Britain's regional organization in Singapore and tried to assume the Special Commission's regional functions. Furthermore, the moderate improvement of the rice situation in South-East Asia [73] threatened the Singapore organization's main *raison d'être*. Eventually, Britain's increasing financial difficulties forced London to merge the Special Commission with the Governor-General's Office in Malaya, a Colonial Office post, by the spring of 1948.[74] Although the new combined post of Commissioner General, taken over by the former Governor-General Malcolm MacDonald, incorporated the Special Commission's international department, it failed to maintain the level of regional co-operation organized by Killearn.[75]

It was the outbreak of communist disturbances in Malaya and Burma in 1948 that gave a new impetus to Britain's regional policy in South-East Asia. At the Commonwealth Prime Ministers' Meeting in October 1948, attended for the first time by independent India, Pakistan and Ceylon, Bevin emphasized the common threat of communism in the Far East and suggested regular Commonwealth consultation to put South-East Asia's political and economic life on a firm footing.[76] In December 1948, after decisive communist victories in the Chinese civil war threatened to increase communist disturbances throughout South-East Asia, the Cabinet agreed to consult the interested Commonwealth countries, as well as Burma, Thailand, France, the Netherlands and the United States, on means to deal with the situation.[77]

In October 1949, the Attlee Government endorsed the Cabinet paper which made the creation of 'some sort of regional association' to contain communism, ensure a friendly partnership between East and West and improve the economic and social conditions in South and South-East Asia an official goal in British policy. Britain's new regional scheme took into account lessons first taught by the Asian Relations Conference. It no longer explicitly included French and Dutch participation, unacceptable to Asian countries, but centred on co-operation initially within the Commonwealth. The Cabinet paper saw India as 'the key to the whole problem of South-East Asian regional cooperation'. Because India mistrusted Western imperialism, she was trying to steer clear of the West's struggle with Moscow and believed in her destiny as the leader of the Asian peoples. However, though India was capable of leading South-East Asia, 'the Asian countries appear to fear and mistrust domination by one of their number as much as they disliked European domination'. The paper therefore concluded that Britain was in the best position to play 'a major (if unobtrusive) part in organising South-East Asia for regional political, economic and military co-operation'; but much was to be said 'for using a Commonwealth rather than a purely United Kingdom approach to achieve our aims'. Collaboration initially through the Commonwealth would dispel Indian suspicions of British intentions and at the same time satisfy the smaller Asian countries that regional collaboration was not another term for Greater India.[78]

Thus during the Commonwealth Meeting on Foreign Affairs in Colombo in January 1950, Britain encouraged Ceylon and Australia to take the lead in promoting regional co-operation in South-East Asia. The resulting Colombo Plan never developed into the kind of effective regional organization Britain had envisaged in early 1947, and it failed to be extended to political or defence co-operation as the authors of the 1949 Cabinet paper had hoped it would. Indian and South-East Asian fears of Western dominance were too great to allow this. Nor was the plan's impact on Asia's economic development as significant as originally hoped, the scale of Western aid was too small compared with Asia's extensive needs. But however limited the degree of regional co-operation within the Colombo Plan, the fact that it was negotiated and included Western and Asian powers was a success for Britain's policy in South-East Asia. Immediately after the Asian Relations Conference such a compromise between British and Asian concepts of regional co-operation had looked highly unlikely. The British had shown themselves flexible in taking into account Asia's anti-colonial feelings, while playing on the smaller countries' fears of Indian dominance. London was also grasping that any prospects for British hegemony in postwar South and South-East Asia were finally over.

Notes

1. The paper, CAB(49)207, is still classified. However, FO minutes show that it consisted of two planning papers drafted by the Permanent Undersecretary's Committee: PUSC (32), 28 July 1949, 'The United Kingdom in South-East Asia and the Far East'; and PUSC (53), 20 August 1949, 'Regional co-operation in South-East Asia and the Far East'. Both can be found in FO 371, 76030, F 17397. The Cabinet paper was endorsed on 27 October 1949, see CAB 128/16, CM(49) 62nd, 27 October 1949, Item 8. See also Tarling, 1986, p. 24, and Ovendale, 1982, p. 455.

   All primary sources referred to or quoted in this article are kept at the Public Record Office in London, unless stated otherwise.
2. CAB 133/78, FMM(50)6, 12 January 1950; FMM(50)8, 13 January 1950; and FMM(50)10th, 13 January 1950.
3. See for example FO 371, 46328, F 3944, memo by Dening, 26 June 1945; and FO 371, 46424, F 12106, Dening (SEAC) to Bevin, 30 November 1945. For further evidence see my forthcoming thesis, 'Britain and Regional cooperation in South-East Asia, 1945–50'.
4. FO 371, 54729, W11239 newspaper cutting from the *Hindustan Times*, 13 September 1946. The conference was actually convened in New Delhi, and its official title was 'Asian Relations Conference'.
5. See Fifield, 1958, p. 450; *The Economist*, 29 March 1947; Asian Relations Organization, 1948, p. 3; also FO 371, 63539, F 921, memo by W.R. Owain Jones, India Office (IO), 3 January 1947.
6. Singh (1966), p. 4; also Asian Relations Organization, 1948, p. 2; and FO 371, 63539, F920, memo by W.R. Owain Jones, IO, 3 January 1947.

   Nehru first mentioned his idea on 25 December 1945 in an interview with a correspondent for the *Manchester Guardian* and the *Hindu*.
7. CO 537/1478, Donaldson, IO, to Allen, Foreign Office (FO), 22 August 1946.
8. FO 371, 54729, W 11239, Monteath, IO, to Sargent, FO, 30 September 1946.
9. FO 371, 54729, W 12230, minute by Warner, FO, 9 December 1946.
10. FO 371, 63539, F 2815, FO minute, 4 March 1947.
11. FO 371, 54729, W 11968, J.S. Bennett, Colonial Office, CO, to J.P. Gibson, IO, 25 November 1946.
12. FO 371, 54729, W 12230, minute by Warner, FO, 9 December 1946, quoting the Secretary of State for India.

    He was quoted by the India Office as saying: 'In general, I think that the more Indians engage in practical problems and in discussions such as these, the better.' See India Office Library and Records, London (IOLR), L/P†S/12/4637, file page 555, note for record, 4 December 1946.
13. FO 371, 54729, W12186, Donaldson, IO, to J.S. Bennett, CO, 11 December 1946.
14. FO 371, 63539, F 3129. FO to Moscow, tel. 1021, 8 March 1947.
15. FO 371, 63540, F 3874, despatch No. 11 from J.D. Peek, Secretary of the Cabinet, to UK High Commissioner in India, 17 March 1947.
16. FO 371, 63539, F 2615, minute by Turner, 14 March 1947.

    The idea that a 'responsible British correspondent' should be sent by Reuters originated with Lord Killearn, Britain's Special Commissioner in South-East Asia.

17. FO 371, 63540, F 3836, Cabinet Office to UK High Commissioner in India, tel. UKRI 150, 19 March 1947.
18. Asian Relations Organization, p. 263; also FO 371, 63539, F 921, memo by W.R. Owain Jones, 3 January 1947.
19. FO 371, 63541, F 7102, confidential report dated 16 April 1947 by Dr P.N.S. Mansergh on the Inter-Asian Relations Conference.
20. As it turned out, this proved to be to India's disadvantage: too many conflicting political and economic views were reflected, preventing a considered statement of outlook being placed before the conference by the Indians. See Mansergh, 1948, p. 104f.
21. CO 537/2092, despatch no. 36 from UK High Commissioner in India, Sir Terence Stone, 25 April 1947, file item 74.
22. Viceroy's Personal Report No. 1, 2 April 1947 in Mansergh, (1982), p. 94, IOLR L/P&J/10/79, file pages 522–5.
    See also Fifield, 1958, p. 449.
23. CO 537/2092, despatch no. 36 from UK High Commissioner in India, 25 April 1947, file item 74.
    Nehru made a great effort to ensure that delegates were feeling at ease, for example by taking them on personal tours outside the conference—personal interview with (now: Professor) Nicholas Mansergh, 8 June 1987. The author is most grateful for Professor Mansergh's excellent account of the conference, forty years after the event.
24. Of the Western countries, only New Zealand declined invitations to send observers, displaying unwillingness to be drawn into Asian affairs. See FO 371, 63539, F 2615, despatch no. 13 from the UK High Commissioner in India to the Cabinet Office, 30 January 1946.
25. FO 371, 63541, F 7102, report by Dr Mansergh.
26. Thompson and Adloff, 1947: p. 98; also FO 371, 63541, F 7102, report by Dr Mansergh.
    Mahomed Ali Jinnah, the president of the All-India Muslim League, when passing through Egypt prior to the conference, had made a considerable effort to convince leading Muslims that the conference was organized as an anti-Muslim move, putting the Middle East states in a somewhat awkward position at the meeting. See FO 371, 63540, F 3539, British Legation, Beirut, to External Affairs Department, New Delhi, 3 March 1947.
27. FO 371, 63541, F 7102, report by Dr Mansergh.
    Though British documents do not mention the creation of an Asian bloc explicitly as a potential danger, there is little doubt that London would have overtly opposed an exclusive Asian alignment.
28. FO 371, 63541, F 7102, Confidential Report by W.W. Russell, dated 16 April 1947, on the Indian delegation and its contribution.
29. FO 371, 63541, F 7102, report by Dr Mansergh; also Fifield, (1958), p. 450 and Levi, (1952), p. 38. Sino-Indian antagonism, though a dominating feature, does not seem to have spoilt the cordial atmosphere during the conference. For a description of the Chinese delegation see: IOLR, L/P†S/12/4637, file pages 35–38, memo by the China Institute of Pacific Relations, 8 April 1947.
30. FO 371, 63540, F 3954, BBC despatch, 20 March 1947.
31. FO 371, 63541, F 7102, report by Russell, 16 April 1947.

32. The enthusiastic mood of the South East Asian delegates was pointed out to the author in an interview with Professor Nicholas Mansergh, 8 June 1987.
33. FO 371, 63541, F 7102, report by Dr Mansergh.
34. FO 371, 63541, F 7102, report by Dr Mansergh.
35. FO 371, 63541, F 7102, report by Dr Mansergh.
    An unnamed guest nevertheless replied that the dangers of an economic bloc had been exaggerated and that the bloc may be merely for co-operative purposes on common problems. Discussing a borrowers' council for South-East Asia might be useful, he pointed out. Asian Relations Organization, p. 114.
36. FO 371, 63541, F 7102, report by Dr Mansergh, and Asian Relations Organization, p. 75ff.
37. CO 537/2092, despatch no. 36 from UK High Commissioner in India, 25 April 1947, file item 74.
38. FO 371, 63540, F4328, UK High Commissioner in India to Cabinet Office, tel. IRKU 195, 26 March 1947.
39. FO 371, 63541, F 4378, Cabinet Office to UK High Commissioner in India, tel. UKRI 183, 1 April 1947.
40. FO 371, 63541, F4813, UK High Commissioner in India to Cabinet Office, tel IRKU 220, 3 April 1947.
    In one of its new minutes on the conference's outcome, the IO noted: 'Sir T. Shone advises—with great cogency, I think—that we should not press too obtrusively to put a finger into this Asiatic (Asian, according to P. Nehru) pie. If we part, or remain, friends with India, Burma etc, we shall be invited anyway: it will be a mistake to invite ourselves.' IOLR L/P+S/12/4637, minute by Donaldson, 12 June 1947.
41. CO 537/2092, despatch no. 38 from UK High Commissioner in India, 25 April 1947, file item 76.
42. FO 371, 63541, F 5926. Note by Dr. Mansergh on a conversation with Pandit Jawaharlal Nehru on 14 April 1947; see also IOLR L/P+S/12/4637. UK High Commissioner to Ministry of Defence, tel. IRKU 254, 17 April 1946, file page 139, reporting on the conversation, and IOLR L/P+S/12/4637, Shone to Monteath, 23 April 1947, file page 126.
43. FO 371, 63541, F 7102, record of a meeting held in the India Office, 3 July 1947. The India Office, in its main file on the conference (IOLR, L/P+S/12/4637), largely refrained from commenting on the event's outcome and political implications.
44. Interview with Professor Mansergh, 8 June 1987.
45. FO 371, 63541, F 7102, report by Dr Mansergh.
46. CO 537/2092, despatch no. 38 from UK High Commissioner in India, 25 April 1947, file item 76.
47. FO 371, 63541, F 7102, minute by Hankey, 9 May 1947.
48. FO 371, 63541, F 7102, report by Dr Mansergh.
49. CO 537/2092, minute by Bennett, 21 May 1947.
50. CO 537/2092, minute by Bennett, 21 May 1947.
51. Co 537/2092, minute by Bourdillon, 26 May 1947.
52. CO 537/2092, minute by Mayle, 28 May 1947.
53. CO 537/2092, minute by Bennett, 22 August 1947.
54. CAB 66/59, W.P. (44)738, 16 December 1944. On the Anglo-American debate

on the future of colonial territories see Louis, 1977.

55. CAB 66/63, W.P. (45)200, Annexed memo by Stanley, 19 March 1945.
56. The idea was originally inspired by the existence in the immediate post-war period of the British led South East Asia Command. See for example FO 371, 54020, F 5385, Jacob, War Office (WO) to Dixon, FO, 13 September 1945; and *ibid.*, memorandum by Sterndale Bennett, 19 September 1945.
57. FO 371, 54018, F 3117, FO to SEAC, tel. 377, 1 March 1946, containing Killearn's political directive, and CAB 134/678, S.E.A.F. (46)34, 13 March 1946, containing the food directive.
58. CAB 21/1956, Killearn to Bevin, 27 March 1948, 'Work of the Special Commission in South-East Asia'.
59. CAB 133/86, P.M.M. (46), 1st meeting, 23 April 1946.
60. CO 537, 1437, memorandum dated 29 April 1946.
61. FO 371, 53995, F 7340, memo by Stent titled 'The Forthcoming Situation in Asia', dated 24 April 1946 but circulated in May.
62. FO 371, 53995, F 7340, minute by Allen, 8 May 1946.
63. CO 537/1478, Donaldson, IO, to Allen, FO, 22 August 1946.
64. FO 371, 63549, F 2616, memo titled 'British Policy in South-East Asia', 24 January 1947.
65. FO 371, 63549, F 2616, 'Stock-taking' memorandum compiled by Esler Dening, 22 February 1947.
66. FO 371, 63547, F 1969, memo by Dening titled 'South-East Asia', 7 February 1947.
67. FO 371, 63547, F 1969, memo by Dening titled 'South-East Asia', 7 February 1947.
    On Britain's efforts in 1947 to publicly distance herself from Dutch and French colonial policy in South-East Asia while at the same time seeking covert co-operation with the local authorities in the fight against communist guerilla forces, see my forthcoming thesis 'Britain and Regional Cooperation in South-East Asia, 1945–50'.
68. FO 371, 63552, F 3458, extract from a statement by Dr. Evatt, 26 February 1947.
69. FO 371, 63552, F 4334, Monteath, IO, to Sargent, FO, 26 March 1947.
70. FO 371, 63552, F 3269, FO to Singapore, tel. 858, 8 April 1947.
71. FO 371, 63543, F 5642, UK High Commissioner in Australia to Dominions Office (DO), following for FO from Killearn, tel. 280, 24 April 1947.
72. On ECAFE see Singh, 1966.
73. See CAB 21/1956, Killearn to Bevin, 27 March 1946, 'Work of the Special Commission in South-East Asia'.
74. FO 371, 63543, F 7625, meeting at the Treasury, 24 April 1947.
75. These conclusions are based on my forthcoming thesis, 'Britain and Regional Cooperation in South-East Asia, 1945–50'.
76. CAB 133/88. P.M.M. (48) 3rd Meeting, 12 October 1948.
77. CAB 129/31, C.P. (48)299, 9 December 1949.
78. FO 371, 76030, F 17397, PUSC (32), 28 July 1948 and PUSC (53), 20 August 1949. See also note 1.

References

Asian Relations Organization (1948), *Asian Relations—being a Report of the Proceedings and Documentation of the First Asian Relations Conference, New Delhi, March–April 1947*, New Delhi, Asian Relations Organization.

Fifield, R. (1958), *The Diplomacy of Southeast Asia, 1945–1958*, New York, Harper.

Levi, W. (1952), *Free India in Asia*, Minneapolis, University of Minnesota Press.

Louis, W. (1977), *Imperialism at Bay, 1941–1945: The United States and the Dissolution of the British Empire*, Oxford, Clarendon.

Mansergh, N. (1948), *The Commonwealth and the Nations*, London, Royal Institute of International Affairs.

Mansergh, N. (1958), *Survey of British Commonwealth Affairs: Problems of Wartime Co-operation and Post-War Change, 1939–1952*, London, Oxford University Press.

Mansergh, N. (1982), *The Transfer of Power, 1942–47*, vol. X, London, HMSO.

Ovendale, R. (1982), 'Britain, the United States, and the Cold War in Southeast Asia, 1949–1950', *International Affairs*, vol. 58, no. 3, Summer 1982.

Packer, G. (1947), 'The Asian Relations Conference: The Group Discussions', *The Australian Outlook*, vol. 1 no. 2, June 1947.

Rothwell, V. (1982), *Britain and the Cold War*, London, Cape.

Singh, L.P. (1966), *The Politics of Economic Cooperation in Asia*, Columbia, Missouri University of Missouri Press.

Tarling, N. (1966), 'The United Kingdom and the Origins of the Colombo Plan', *Commonwealth and Comparative Politics*, vol. 24, no. 1.

Thompson, V. and Adloff, R. (1947), 'Asian Unity: Force or Facade', *Far Eastern Survey*, vol. 16, no. 9, 7 May 1947, p. 98.

Vandenbosch, A. and Butwell, R.A. (1957), *Southeast Asia among the World Powers*, Lexington, Kentucky; University of Kentucky Press.

8 Counterinsurgency and colonial defence

A.J. Stockwell

Defence policy and colonial security: the appraisal of 1954–5[1]

Some may doubt whether counterinsurgency, or rather its study, is a proper subject for the historian. It might be said that research on recent history is difficult enough without taking on a topic on which the official record is bound to be restricted if not inaccessible. Indeed, although there is a wealth of literature, which is largely informed by the personal experiences of counterinsurgents, about the causes of insurrection in colonial territories and methods of combating it, little has been written with the benefit of government archives.[2] The major exception is Anthony Short's *The Communist Insurrection in Malaya, 1948–1960*.[3] Short was at first provided with full access to the secret files of the Malayan/Malaysian government which later unaccountably withdrew its support and tried to block publication of the finished work. Short is now in the process of completely re-writing his study of the Emergency, adding to it material that has been opened at the Public Record Office at Kew since his original book appeared. However, though superabundant in many fields, the holdings at Kew are slim on counterinsurgency be it in Malaya or Cyprus or Kenya or elsewhere. One finds the ephemeral detail of monthly political intelligence reports but promising leads on policy still disappear into thickets of files that have been 'retained' or remain 'closed' beyond the 'thirty-year rule'.[4]

If, then, the historian is on shaky ground when tackling counterinsurgency, it would appear doubly perverse of him to take, as I shall here, 1954 as the starting-point for a discussion of it. After all, Britain had withdrawn from Palestine in May 1948, she had been engaged in the Malayan Emergency from June 1948 and had been fighting the Mau Mau in Kenya since the declaration of emergency there in October 1952. Moreover, British government appeared to be in the grip of paralysis at this time. Ministers were already drained of major policy initiatives although they were positively brimming with political intrigue. Indeed, to read recent political biography is

135

to marvel that any government business got done at all in the last year of Churchill's second administration.[5] So far as defence and foreign policy were concerned, neither continuity nor change but rather drift seems characteristic of 1954–5. Churchill, already inert but still dominant, mistrusted his Foreign Secretary's diplomacy and frequently questioned his suitability as heir. Eden, nervy and in poor health, resented the Prime Minister's summitry and fretted at his reluctance to leave 10 Downing Street. The succession issue increasingly consumed the interests and energies of other senior ministers too, such as Lord Salisbury, R.A. Butler and Harold Macmillan. All were distracted from their departmental duties.

There is, however, a case for starting this discussion in 1954 and it is as follows. First, one can argue that the year marks the end of one phase and the start of another in British global strategy, although it must be admitted that there was no stark break with the past, that many measures were part of a continuing pattern of post-war policy and that some of the novelties were shortlived or alternatively took a long time coming to fruition. Secondly, this reappraisal of Britain's world position contributed to a stocktaking exercise as regards the internal security of her colonies. Thirdly, for a moment in 1954–5 a shutter flickers open onto government files to reveal the dim outline of 'the official mind' at work on problems of insurgency and counterinsurgency, and to shed a little more light on what we already know from the published record. Let us first consider what ministers and service chiefs still referred to as 'Britain's global strategy' before turning to its repercussions upon colonial defence.

At first sight the most striking feature of Britain's foreign policy in 1954 was that chain of agreements strung across Europe, the Middle East and South-East Asia. As it turned out, none of these arrangements were all that effective. In Europe the European Defence Community was stillborn.[6] In the Middle East hopes for a regional pact involving the Americans (a MEATO or MEDO) came to nought, while the Anglo-Egyption treaty (October 1954) did not save Eden from disaster two years later.[7] As for South-East Asia, the treaty organization (SEATO), which was set up after conferences at Geneva (April–July 1954) and Manila (September 1954), had the effect of increasing rather than reducing Britain's military obligations in the area.[8] This is not the place to examine Eden's foreign policy [9] but it is appropriate in setting the context within which colonial security was appraised to point out that the agreements of 1954 were subtle, if not very successful, attempts to temper the wind to the shorn lamb. Seen in this light, they appear to continue rather than depart from the course of post-war foreign policy whose central objective was to transfer to allies (notably the Americans) many of the burdens and much of the cost of policing the world without—and this was central to government thinking—surrendering Britain's global influence.[10]

There is a second development during these months of muddling which was less obvious at the time but probably more significant both for long-term strategy and the contemporary review of colonial security. Following a fresh appreciation provided by the Chiefs of Staff, the Cabinet Defence Committee took tentative but nonetheless notable steps along a track which is usually located in the post-Suez era. The radical 'switch of resources' presented in the Sandys' Defence White Paper of 1957 has its origins in high level ruminations three years earlier. Given the financial constraints upon the defence budget and the declining threat of world war 'as its character grows more devastating', the Cabinet Defence Committee came down in favour of building up Britain's nuclear deterrent in order to prevent the outbreak of a major war rather than expenditure on conventional weapons and forces. This was an important marker for the future.[11]

These adjustments in foreign and defence policies—regional pacts and nuclear deterrence—clearly had implications for colonial defence. Surely there was a *prima facie* case for decolonization: the strategic value of a territorial empire had diminished in an era when small bases, redeployment and dispersal were the hallmarks of warfare. Likewise, the cost of administering and defending colonies, particularly those devouring British lives and materials in brutish wars that went under the name of 'states of emergency', together with the slender profits of colonial development over which the shadows had lengthened since the notorious East African groundnuts scheme, seemed to reinforce the argument favouring end of empire. It was, indeed, recognized that emergencies in 'Malaya, Kenya and British Guiana are a large drain upon United Kingdom money and men', and the Minister of Defence noted that two years' National Service was an increasingly expensive method of maintaining distant garrisons.[12] Yet nobody in high office was advocating either the wholesale abandonment of colonial commitments or even withdrawal from specific troublespots.

There may well have been much sentimental attachment to such territories on the part of politicians and generals who had, after all, been brought up as Victorians. Apart from that, however, they believed that empire carried a value in terms of national prestige and international influence that warranted its retention. Moreover, the economic case against colonies was by no means clear-cut in the mid 1950s, as is indicated in the series of cost-benefit analyses which were produced in response to Prime Minister Macmillan's call for an imperial balance sheet a few years later.[13] Furthermore, in spite of, or rather because of, the emerging equilibrium in nuclear power between East and West [14] and the consequent swing to deterrence strategy, colonies actually acquired an enhanced strategic significance. Their very vulnerability as Britain's soft underbelly necessitated, it was held, improvements in their protection. Harold Macmillan, who had become Minister of Defence in October 1954, argued at the time and repeated in his memoirs that the corollary to the improbability of a third world war was the greater likelihood of aggravated Cold War in the Colonies. 'If we are defeated here', he wrote in a Cabinet Paper at the end of 1954, 'much of our effort in Western Europe will be wasted.' Macmillan felt that communists might either inspire trouble in the colonies or exploit existing unrest which stemmed from nationalism and tribalism. In either case, Britain had to prepare for an intensification of colonial subversion.[15]

The question of the internal security of the colonies highlighted an imperial dilemma. The colonies were regarded as too important to lose yet their defence was proving too costly for Britain to bear, at least on her own. How was their security to be assured? Who was to pay for it? If colonial defence depended upon colonial collaboration might it not precipitate a series of political bargains culminating in colonial independence? These were not new problems, of course. The defence burden had stretched to breaking-point the connection between Britain and the thirteen North American Colonies after 1763. A century later, Robert Godley of the War Office seeking ways of withdrawing troops from self-governing colonies as part of the army reform and redeployment which came to a head after the Crimean war, accepted that Britain had an 'obligation . . . of assisting her Colonies to defend themselves against foreign enemies' but stated that she was 'by no means bound to relieve [the colonies] of the whole responsibility of self-defence'.[16] Throughout the nineteenth century Britain had turned the men and materials of India to the tasks of defending the Raj and extending empire elsewhere, and during the First World War one and a half million Indian soldiers served in theatres outside South Asia. In the hard times following 1918 Britain had leaned naturally but heavily upon Indian resources to police the peace and occupy her newly acquired Mandates in the Middle East.[17] Such metropolitan demands had been at first resented by Indians and then used by them as levers to extract concessions from Britain. In 1945-7 the British military faced manpower shortages throughout the world; for example, fear of mutiny and nationalist resistance inhibited South East Asia Command in its deployment of Indian troops in the reoccupation of the Dutch East Indies after the Japanese surrender.[18] Again, in the second half of 1950, when Britain's commitments included the Malayan Emergency and the Korean war in addition to NATO, West Germany and the strategic reserve that was being built up in anticipation of world war, Attlee had considered the use of colonial troops on overseas duties as well as in the routine tasks of internal defence.[19] Attlee's suggestion was not pursued at the time but by the middle of 1954 battalions from The King's African Rifles and other African regiments (as well as a battalion from the Fijian Regiment) were posted in Malaya where previously it had been held that black troops would be unacceptable.

What was required to achieve and maintain security in the colonies was, it was argued in 1954-5, the more effective use of British and colonial resources. Effectiveness depended in turn upon defence organization, the intelligence services and the co-operation of colonial peoples. The review of defence programmes and expenditure which went to Cabinet in November 1954 included the following statement:

Everything possible should be done to build up local Colonial forces in order to reduce the demands on our own Army. We shall not get quick relief in this way, but the point is of such importance that we consider this question should now be studied by Ministers and pursued as a deliberate policy. In this study we suggest that special attention should be given to the possibility of strengthening Colonial police and security services. These are the front line of defence against subversion and we are informed that recent experience has revealed defects in their organisation. Efficient police forces and Intelligence Services are the best way of smelling out and suppressing subversive movements at an early stage, and may save heavy expenditure on military reinforcements. They are an insurance we cannot afford to neglect.[20]

On 5 November the Cabinet endorsed the view expressed in this paper that local colonial forces and, in particular, colonial police and security sevices, should be enlarged and improved.[21]

At the same time Cabinet appeared to be reaching out to grasp the nettles of defence organization and the intelligence services in general. Anxiety had been frequently expressed by successive governments about shortcomings in both areas, and improvements had already been attempted at both metropolitan and colonial levels. In Whitehall, however, responsibility for defence was still fragmented and the Minister of Defence languished in virtual powerlessness. Between 1940 and 1945, and also for a short time during his second government, Churchill had been his own Minister of Defence. In effect he had been a Minister without a Ministry and, while the arrangement had provided leadership and strategic direction and had rescued the Prime Minister from the encumbrances of departmental duties, it did not solve for all time the problems of co-ordinating the activities of the semi-autonomous services. In 1950 Attlee appointed Shinwell as Minister of Defence in the hope that improvements could be made but the Labour government fell before major structural changes were carried out. Field-Marshal Alexander, who succeeded Churchill at Defence in March 1952, was not an administrative success. When Macmillan became Minister in October 1954, he found himself occupying an anomalous position between the Prime Minister and the separate service ministers and their professional advisers.

This experience convinced Macmillan of the need for the closer union of the services and Ministry of Defence, a reform that he would encourage when he himself became Prime Minister. In the meantime, defence disorganization compounded flaws in intelligence gathering and consequently placed at risk Britain's colonies and other overseas commitments. If the communists were to launch a centrally directed campaign of protest and resistance within Britain's colonies, as was firmly believed, the British would automatically be at a disadvantage for want of their own centrally co-ordinated machinery. Macmillan complained at the end of November 1954:

No one is wholly responsible—it's partly Defence, partly Colonial Office, partly Foreign Office. There's no central anti-Communist organisation with any drive in it. 'Cold War' alarms me more than 'Hot war'. For we are not really winning it, and the Russians have a central position . . . and a well-directed effort, with strong representation (through the Communist party) in every country.[22]

Similarly outside Whitehall and on the periphery, the organization of defence and the intelligence services had been so flawed in the colonies that the British had been taken by surprise by the Malayan communists in 1948 and by the Mau Mau in 1952. Since then major improvements in three key areas— namely, the collection of intelligence, the co-ordination of administrative, police and military activities, and the conquest of hearts and minds—had been pioneered in Malaya and adapted to the circumstances of insurgencies elsewhere. Given the expected increase in communist subversion in the mid 1950s, now was the moment to take stock: to examine past failures, face up to current problems and plan for future successes.

It was with an eye to confronting the problems of organization, intelligence and colonial contributions that Macmillan urged the appointment of a Ministerial Committee on security in the colonies. The Cabinet agreed and on 25 January 1955 the Committee, which was chaired by Lord Swinton, formally invited General Templer (who had already been sounded by Macmillan) to undertake an examination of events leading up to the 'troubles' in Malaya, British Guiana, Cyprus and elsewhere, and of the immediate action that had been taken in each case. Six months earlier Templer had returned to the War Office from Malaya, where he had spent just over two years as High Commissioner and Director of Operations, and he was now waiting to take up the post of Chief of the Imperial General Staff which would fall vacant in the Spring of 1955. Templer's experience in military intelligence during the Second World War and more especially his success in turning the tide in the Malayan Emergency made him the obvious choice to head this enquiry. Templer submitted his report, *Security in the Colonies*, on 23 April, the day of the announcement of his appointment as CIGS.[23]

Although the press got wind of the enquiry and produced some startling headlines (such as 'WINSTON PICKS TEMPLER—Big Shake-up of Empire Defence Begins', on the front page of the *Sunday Express* on 6 March 1954) they could not make much of the innocuous statement which the government fed them about Templer 'conducting an enquiry into the organization and nature of colonial military forces, at the request of the War Office and the Colonial Office' or of his visits to Cyprus and Uganda.[24] Perhaps it was at this time that Peter Wright was lobbying Templer for his support in a proposal to involve MI5 in Cyprus, but the reference in *Spycatcher* is unreliable: the date is not given and Templer is misspelt![25]

What is available at the Public Record Office? Not surprisingly, neither Templer's report nor his working papers are open but a few references may be instructive as to Whitehall attitudes. The first is the response of the Far Eastern Department in the Colonial Office to Templer's call for information on the origins of the Malayan Emergency. Secondly, we have the papers of the Official Committee set up to examine the military implications of the report. There are, thirdly, the final report of the Ministerial Committee and the Cabinet conclusions on it.

The minute by R.L. Baxter (Colonial Office), which Templer himself did not see but which is quoted at length in Appendix 8A (p. 149), illustrates the negative thinking of 'the official mind' when on the defensive or consumed with day-to-day business or when called upon to draw general conclusions from past experiences. Thankful, one senses, that Baxter's minute somehow absolved it from the obligation of conducting further research into the matter, the department sent a brief letter regretting that it was unable to provide Templer with the explanation he sought because 'the contemporary material on the files is somewhat meagre', there was 'no authoritative assessment of the trend of events by the High Commissioner' and some of the opinions expressed were 'mutually contradictory'. It was further explained that those serving in the department at the time of the outbreak had long since left or been transferred.[26] Nonetheless, although the matter was allowed to rest so far as the Far Eastern Department was concerned and although Baxter's minute lay dormant until recently unearthed at the Public Record Office, it is interesting to note that this response to the Templer inquiry raised the very questions to which students of the Emergency have been seeking answers ever since.[27]

By the time Templer finished his report, Eden had succeeded Churchill (6 April) and Macmillan had been transferred to the Foreign Office (7 April), his place at the Ministry of Defence being taken by Selwyn Lloyd. The steam seemed to go out of defence reorganization at home and in the colonies and, according to Darby, apart from its recommendations on intelligence, Templer's investigation appears to have had little impact.[28] For example — and here is the second reference to the Templer report to be found at the Public Record Office [29] — on the 27 June 1955 an Official Committee on the Military Implications of General Templer's Report was set up, under the chairmanship of Sir Harold Parker (Permanent Undersecretary at the Ministry of Defence), primarily to examine the system of command and administration necessary to achieve zonal systems of defence in East and West Africa. So it seemed that the universalist approach to ascertaining reasons for insurgency and methods of countering it was deflected either by bureaucratic prevarication or by concern with the particular.

There was an additional reason for this loss of momentum — finance. Although the Ministerial Committee submitted an interim report on the Templer inquiry as early as July 1955, its final report was held up by the question of the UK contribution to the cost of improved housing for colonial police forces. By May 1958, however, Britain's economic position had improved to the extent that Cabinet contemplated the inclusion of this item in the 1959–60 budget. Its task complete, the committee was then disbanded.[30]

Despite the yawning gaps in the official record, the ministerial and official discussions of colonial security in 1954–5 do provide us with an introduction to a range of questions on insurgency and counterinsurgency which agitated government during the 1940s and 1950s.

Diagnoses of insurgency and prescriptions for counterinsurgency

The questions which exercised governments at the time and which have interested students since can perhaps be summarized as follows:

(1) Was insurgency part of a global revolutionary movement or did it arise from problems peculiar to the territory affected?

(2) If it was an aspect of world revolution, in what respects and to what extent should or could Britain match global subversion with a global response?

(3) If, on the other hand, insurgency was a local phenomenon, how far should or could London devolve the responsibility and the cost of counterinsurgency upon the colonial government of the territory concerned?

(4) Were colonial emergencies the outcome of faulty intelligence or were they rather the result of governmental failure to act upon intelligence?

(5) In countering insurgency what was the relative importance of the military campaign and the political and economic programmes?

(6) What was the correct relationship, and the best means of liaison, between military, civil and police authorities in the colonies and between the Colonial Office, Ministry of Defence and services in Whitehall?

(7) Were all dependencies worth fighting for and, if not, at what point was orderly disengagement to replace counterinsurgency as the military objective?

(8) In the event of successful counterinsurgency, at what point was responsibility for internal security to be transferred to a locally elected government?

As regards the origin of insurgencies, this has been explained in terms of both monogenesis and polygenesis. According to the former, all could be traced to the old Adam of Bolshevism. The Zhdanov and Truman doctrines of 1947 partitioned the world into two camps. International communism, centred upon and orchestrated from Moscow, was seen to be spreading through the world. The outlets into Asia were through Calcutta and Beijing: a call to arms was supposedly issued to Asian communist parties at conferences held in Calcutta during February 1948, while Beijing was believed to be actively nurturing insurrection in South-East Asia through a clandestine courier system.[31]

The communist channel into Africa was said to be Cairo but official assessments of the extent and nature of unrest in this continent were less clear-cut than contemporary analyses of subversion in South-East Asia. Although Bevin warned Attlee on 6 November 1948 that 'sooner or later the Russians will make a major drive against our positions in Africa'[32] and although the hand of international communism had been sensed in the Accra riots of February that year, the Secretary of State for the Colonies (Creech Jones) was unwilling 'to take a too alarmist view of communist and other subversive activities in our territories'.[33] Creech Jones accepted that there was a 'real' danger to colonial stability in Africa but felt that it was on the whole locally generated — 'polygenesis' so to speak — from the problems and grievances of particular societies which could then be exploited by the machinations of the Cominform. 'The increasing awareness of the colonial peoples and our failure to give them all the satisfactions they want', he wrote, 'make them an easy prey to subversive influences.'

By 1950 British officials dealing with Africa, or at least those at the London end, were on the whole inclined to fear international communism as the exploiter rather than the initiator of trouble. This is the view conveyed in a secret Foreign Office survey of communism in Africa which was carried out that year in collaboration with the Colonial, Commonwealth Relations and War Offices and with which the US State Department largely agreed. It stressed the difficulties and dangers of generalizing about communist trends in the continent, drew attention to 'striking differences of race, of social evolution and political development encountered everywhere' and concluded that 'Communism in the strict sense is making no headway' in spite of the intensification of Moscow's 'colonial campaign'. The survey pointed out, nonetheless, that 'the Kremlin can doubtless be relied upon to exploit any incipient unrest in colonial or other territories'.[34] Similarly, although advocates of white minority rule in East, Central and South Africa saw the settlers as a bastion against international communism and its fellow traveller, the black nationalist, the official historian of the Mau Mau restrictively defined the outbreak as 'the violent manifestation of a limited nationalistic revolutionary movement confined almost entirely to the Kikuyu tribe'.[35]

The variety as distinct from the universality of subversion was manifest in the case of Cyprus. Here the guerillas fighting in George Grivas's EOKA movement were obviously anti-communist as well as anti-British and anti-Turk. Their objective was *enosis* or union with Greece. In addition to EOKA's insurgency, however, there was a significant communist dimension to Britain's problem in Cyprus. The government feared that AKEL (the Cypriot Communist Party) would take advantage of unrest on the island and that the Soviets would exploit tension between Britain, Greece and Turkey in order to prise Britain's grip from her military bases in the eastern Mediterranean and also make trouble between Britain and her NATO allies.[36] As we have already noted, Macmillan combined both international and local interpretations of insurgency in his prognosis of the communist threat to the colonies in the mid 1950s. As the Cyprus crisis worsened from 1956 so it ceased to be primarily a colonial issue and became increasingly a matter of international importance as first Britain's Foreign Secretary (Macmillan, 1955–7) and then the Prime Minister himself (Macmillan 1957–63) took over the direction of British policy towards the island which in August 1960 achieved independence within the Commonwealth and with the security of British bases assured.

Contemporary diagnoses clearly differed according to the prospectives of observers. Intelligence officers were in the business of finding trouble while governors were inclined to brush it under the carpet. Spycatchers from Malaya's John Dalley, who claimed to have been instrumental in the recall of High Commissioner Gent, to MI5's Peter Wright, whose operation to knock-out Colonel Grivas in Cyprus was aborted as a result of constitutional negotiations during the governmorship of Sir Hugh Foot, lamented the propensity of senior colonial and Colonial Office officials to make a virtue of compromise and inaction.[37] While at times colonial administrators were eager enough to blame Moscow for all their difficulties, they were also tempted to convey an impression of confident government by dismissing insurrection as a little local difficulty. Less than a fortnight after the declaration of the Malayan Emergency (June 1948), the ever-optimistic Malcolm MacDonald, Commissioner General in South-East Asia, stated that it 'should not last more than six months' and suggested that the arrival of Gurney, who had been appointed to succeed Gent as High Commissioner, should be delayed until the end of the year by which time the troubles would be under control.[38]

In Whitehall different departments had *ex officio* differing viewpoints. At the time Cabinet decided to recognize the regime of Mao Zedong (1950), the Colonial Office claimed that Malayan insurrection was being inflamed by China and complained that recognition would hamper the Malayan authorities in handling recalcitrant Chinese. The Foreign Office, on the other hand, argued that Malaya's problems lay in Malaya itself and not in mainland China.[39] China's intervention in the Korean war in late November 1950, however, gave a fillip to 'proto-domino' theories and, as the French position in Indochina deteriorated from the summer of 1953 onwards, so the Colonial and Foreign Offices accepted that Malayan security was interlocked with the stability of South-East Asia as a whole and that a Vietminh victory in Indochina would have serious repercussions upon British dependencies in the region.[40]

Later analysts of insurgency have focused upon the local circumstances in which specific unrest arose and particular movements operated. As regards the communist-led risings which occurred throughout South-East Asia in March–September 1948, for example, there is still considerable controversy, as R.B. Smith has recently reminded us,as to whether they were 'the outcome of a deliberate international communist strategy or merely the product of coincidental decisions by individual communist parties'.[41]

As with diagnoses of insurgency, so prescriptions for counterinsurgency varied with the viewpoint and position of the makers and executors of policy. Soldiers grew impatient with the methods of administrators who in turn were wearied by the simplistic recipes of men of action. The colonial government would appeal through the Colonial Office for more troops in order to release police from paramilitary duties and make them available for normal policing. The Ministry of Defence would try to shift expenditure from the Defence to the Colonial budget or from London to the locality, or draw the police and colonial forces further into counterinsurgency so as to reduce the demands made upon British troops.[42]

In the debate over methods of counterinsurgency some emphasized logistics while others stressed the importance of psychological warfare; some favoured military methods while others preferred the police to play the major role; some concentrated on destroying the enemy while others insisted on the importance of cultivating friends among the local population. It was soon appreciated that counterinsurgency had economic and political dimensions as well as military. First the Labour government and then the Conservatives accepted the importance of economic development in the maintenance of political stability in Asia and recognized in the Commonwealth's Colombo Plan (January 1950) a trusty weapon in the struggle for influence in Asia. Four temperamentally very different men, Bevin, Eden, MacDonald and Templer, were at one in their commitment to Cold War; yet all believed that communism in Asia could not be checked by military means alone and that the solution lay as much in political as military methods.

In the heat of battle and on the anvil of experience a number of key principles for counterinsurgency were hammered out. The first was co-ordination of effort by all branches and between the different levels of government from the district office through government house to Whitehall. Malaya was a trial ground here: in the early years of the Emergency central direction was dogged by a federal constitution, by feuding between civil, police and military authorities and by lack of overall direction. The establishment of War Executive Councils at state as well as federal level and the appointment of Templer as both civil and military supremo were major reforms in the command structure. The second principle, 'know the enemy', placed a premium on the collection and utilization of intelligence; here, once more, lessons from Malaya were subsequently applied elsewhere. Food denial operations and resettlement schemes ('New Villages'), pioneered by General Briggs in Malaya (1950–1) and adapted to Kenya, were aspects of a third principle, namely 'isolate the enemy'. Other features of this were the notorious regulations imposing curfews, allowing detention without trial and providing for the 're-education' of surrendered and captured personnel all of which were imposed in Malaya, Kenya and Cyprus. The object was to create 'white areas' where, insurgents having been flushed out, Emergency regulations could be relaxed. The fourth principle, 'destroy the enemy', related to the use of military techniques appropriate to the environment: for example, having been worsted by the Japanese in jungle warfare in 1941–2, the British later developed an unrivalled expertise in the deployment of foot patrols supported by helicopters in the tropical rain forests of Malaya and Borneo. Fifthly, the dictum of 'hearts and minds', which again was principally associated with Templer in Malaya, was the final component of a strategy intended to turn the tables on insurgents by conducting a 'people's war' through the active co-operation of local inhabitants sharing with Britain a clear political aim. Some support might be gained in Britain's multi-ethnic dependencies, of course, by deliberately preferring one community to another, as was done, so it was claimed, in the case of Malaya's Malays and the Turks of Cyprus. Such tactics of unabashed 'divide and rule', however, achieved merely short-term respite while building up enormous problems for the future and were on the whole condemned as poor substitutes for 'nation-building'.

Experience in one operation obviously influenced practice in another. There is, indeed, a linear development from policing the Indian Raj during the 1920s and 1930s through the post-war crises of Palestine, Malaya, Kenya, Cyprus, Borneo and Aden to the troubles in Northern Ireland since 1969. The ripple effect is seen in the activities of generations of more or less honourable schoolboys from Spencer Chapman of Malaya to 'Mad Mitch' of Aden.[43] Of the generals, Kitson and Walker are two who served with distiction in a number of colonial theatres.[44] The length (from 1948 to 1960) and ultimate success of the Malayan campaign plus Britain's continuing activity in South-East Asia until the withdrawal of the legions in 1971, made it a nursery of counterinsurgents, a ground for experiment and the yardstick against which other operations were judged. For example, the expertise of Richard Clutterbuck and Robert Thompson, one a former soldier and the other a former administrator, was rooted in their respective experiences in Malaya.[45]

Of course, there are inherent dangers in theorizing and in transferring techniques and models from one situation to another. For example, in the early days of the Malayan Emergency the army's ideas on how to combat jungle terrorists were, despite the lessons of the Second World War, still derived from an official handbook published in 1906 and based on the campaign against Boer guerillas in South Africa.[46] At the same time wholly inappropriate policing methods were imported into Malaya from Palestine with disastrous results.[47] Another false parallel was drawn between the society for which Malaya's New Villages were devised in the 1950s and that of the Mekong delta where the United States planted Strategic Hamlets in the 1960s. Indeed, the fact that over the years counterinsurgency has more often failed than succeeded leaves one wondering whether the techniques are at fault or whether they are applicable to only some situations or, again, whether techniques were on the whole incidental to the outcome.

It has been calculated that British forces have been engaged in some 70 operations (other than the conventional conflicts in Korea, Suez and the Falklands) since 1945.[48] The main areas of counterinsurgency have been in Ireland (1919–21 and since 1969), Palestine (in the 1920s and 1930s and again in 1943–8), Malaya (1948–60), Kenya (1952–6), Cyprus (1955–9), Borneo (1963–6) and Aden (1964–7). Of the operations listed two startlingly different outcomes were those in Palestine and Malaya. As regards the former Britain failed to ensure the emergence of a stable and friendly successor state that would advance Britain's influence in the Middle East but instead she withdrew leaving bloodshed in her wake, weakening her influence in the region and souring Anglo-American relations. In Malaya, by contrast, Britain transferred power to a co-operative state within the Commonwealth and enhanced her position in South-East Asia. What are the reasons for these contrasting results?

Now it is possible to argue that in limited military terms the Palestinian operation, or at least the evacuation, proved a success. When the decision was taken to withdraw, troops were pulled out with minimum casualties, whereas the Malayan Emergency proved to be a long and enormously costly campaign in terms of men and money. That being the case, why was it decided that orderly disengagement was preferable to continued counterinsurgency in Palestine but not in Malaya? The answer lies in the contemporary assessment of costs and benefits. On 6 July 1945, two months after Victory in Europe and ten days before the Potsdam Conference, Churchill considered the post-war settlement of Palestine and wrote as follows to his Colonial Secretary and Chiefs of Staff.

> The whole question of Palestine must be settled at the peace-table, though it may be touched upon at the Conference at Potsdam. I do not think we should take the responsibility upon ourselves of managing this very difficult place while the Americans sit back and criticise. Have you ever addressed yourselves to the idea that we should ask them to take it over? I believe we should be stronger the more they are drawn into the Mediterranean. At any rate, the fact that we show no desire to keep the mandate will be a great help. *I am not aware of the slightest advantage which has ever accrued to Great Britain from this painful and thankless task* [authors emphases]. Somebody else should have their turn now. However, the Chiefs of Staff should examine the matter from the strategic point of view.[49]

The insistence of the Chiefs of Staff that Palestine was strategically crucial prolonged Britain's mandate by another three years. Britain's conflicting obligations to Arab and Jew together with American obstructionism meant that the prospect of a solution to the problem of Palestine receded further and further into the distance. When, in February 1947, the Attlee Cabinet decided to refer the issue to the United Nations, they were, in effect, admitting that the strategic value of Palestine was now outweighed by the damage it inflicted upon Britain.[50]

Malaya's worth, by contrast, vastly surpassed that of Palestine and warranted the costs of counterinsurgency even during the financial crises of 1948–55. If Malaya fell, then, it was held, Britain would lose a key dollar-earner and an important supplier of commodities. In addition, any repeat of the 1941–2 debacle would damage Britain's relations with the Common-wealth, the USA and with the independent states of Asia, and would aggravate the instability of a crucial theatre of the Cold War.

The reasons for Britain's decision to fight for Malaya are clear but her eventual success in the Emergency was not simply fathered by the thought. Good intentions and abundant determination were not enough. Although it was in Malaya that so many of the principles and practices of post-war counterinsurgency were developed, Britain enjoyed advantages which were not of her own making nor subject to her control. Unlike Palestine, Malaya did not drive a wedge between the British and Americans; on the contrary the government of the USA admired and imitated British efforts against communism in South-East Asia. Furthermore, the economy of Malaya was not irreparably damaged by guerrilla warfare and in fact benefited consider-ably from the prices boom during the Korean war. Moreover, the Chinese-dominated Malayan Communist Party (MCP) suffered two fundamental weaknesses; on the one hand, unlike the Vietminh, it was largely cut off from outside assistance and, on the other, it was unable to rally to its support the largest and essentially rural community of the Malays. The British, therefore, had a natural ally in the United Malays National Organization which from 1952 became the dominant partner in the political Alliance of Malay, Chinese and, later, Indian communal parties.

Once the Alliance had established its popular credentials in the landslide election victory of 1955 and once the Malayan leadership had demonstrated their 'soundness' on communism by refusing to concede to the MCP's request for political recognition, the British concluded that the balance of advantage lay in transferring to Malayan ministers control over internal security. The British agreed to do this in advance of the grant of full independence—to answer the last question posed at the start of this section—not because they themselves had established full mastery over the country but because they had found in the Alliance something they had lacked in Palestine and which the Americans would fail to find outside the vicinity of Saigon, namely a locally well-rooted and widely supported collaborator in the pursuit of counterinsurgency.

Contrasting results of counterinsurgency operations therefore suggest that, while techniques had their uses and men were wise to pay attention to guidelines born of experience elsewhere, success also depended upon circum-stances beyond the control of both soldiers and politicians.

APPENDIX 8A

A Colonial Office view on the reasons for the outbreak of insurrection in Malaya in 1948

Extract from a minute by R.L. Baxter (Colonial Office, Far Eastern Department), 8 February 1955, Public Record Office, CO 1030/16.

The events leading up to the Emergency in Malaya took place nearly seven years ago. The memory of them has dimmed, but their history has yet to be written. As Mr Perry Robinson has shown, the material with which to write such a history 'is, from a historian's point of view, scanty and awkward'.[51] It is certainly not to be found in London. The only contemporary material that I have been able to discover here is on the one hand the verbose and uninformative reports of the Malayan Security Service and on the other a flood of telegrams from the High Commissioner and later the Commissioner General dealing with particular points as they arose . . . [Baxter goes on to suggest two possible approaches, of which one was a straight chronological account of events.] Alternatively we might attempt some sort of post-mortem examination drawing attention to any failures on the part of the Government or its security services which may have contributed to the troubles. This would be very much more difficult. I cannot find that any such post-mortem has yet been attempted: the nearest approach to one is perhaps [High Commissioner] Sir Henry Gurney's despatch of the 30th May 1949[52] . . . but this deals more with the grand lessons of the Emergency. Some of the questions that would have to be answered have already been the subject of bitter controversy. Did the Malayan Security Service give adequate warning of the Emergency? Mr MacDonald [Commissioner General, SE Asia 1948–55] thought that it did: Sir E. Gent [High Commissioner, Federation of Malaya 1948] that it did not. If not, did its deficiencies derive from its isolation from the two police forces [of Malaya and Singapore], its inexperience, its lack of tried agents, or the personality of Colonel Dalley [Director, Malayan Security Service]? did the M.S.S. err in devoting too much time to the study of unimportant Malay factions, while ignoring the Chinese? If so, why? How many of its officers were Chinese? Was Loi Tak (the Secretary General of the M.C.P. [Malayan Communist Party]) a British agent after the war as he had been before it; and if so can it be that the authorities relied too much on his ability to keep the Party quiet? Or was it rather that after two years of wrestling with the Malayan Union [a constitutional innovation that provoked Malay opposition] the Administration as a whole was too exclusively occupied with Malay affairs and had not begun to think at all in terms of the 'cold war'? How did the Government keep in touch with the Chinese in the absence of a Chinese Protectorate?[53] These are the sort of questions that spring to mind on a preliminary glance through the papers. To answer them after nearly seven years would entail much research, and since the papers have to be brought from Hayes I think that we have not the material which would enable us to come to any definite conclusions.

Notes

1. This section has benefited from collaboration with Dr A.N. Porter during the writing of our *British Imperial Policy and Decolonization, 1938–64: Volume 1 1938–51, Volume 2 1951–64*, London, Macmillan, 1987 and 1989.
2. For example, General The Lord Bourne, 'The Direction of Anti-Guerilla Operations', *Brassey's Annual 1964*; R. Clutterbuck, *Guerillas and Terrorists*, London, Faber and Faber, 1977; Kitson, *Low Intensity Operations*, London, Faber and Faber, 1971; Sir Robert Thompson, *Defeating Communist Insurgency*, London, Chatto and Windus, 1966.
3. A. Short, *The Communist Insurrection in Malaya 1948–1960*, London, Frederick Muller, 1975.
4. 'Retained' files are those that have not been transferred to the Public Record Office from their originating Department or its successor (e.g. The Foreign and Commonwealth Office). 'Closed' files are those which, having been transferred to the PRO, remain embargoed for 50, 75 or possibly 100 years.
5. For example, Carlton, *Anthony Eden: A Biography*, London 1981; M. Gilbert, *'Never Despair'. Winston Churchill 1945–1965*, London, Heinemann, 1988; A. Horne, *Macmillan 1894–1956*, London, Macmillan, 1988; A. Howard, *RAB. The Life of R.A. Butler*, London, 1987; R. Rhodes James, *Anthony Eden*, London, Weidenfeld and Nicolson, 1986; D.R. Thorpe, *Selwyn Lloyd*, London, Jonathan Cape, 1989. See also J. Colville, *The Fringes of Power. Downing Street Diaries 1939–55*, London, Hodder and Stoughton, 1985 and Evelyn Shuckburgh, *Descent to Suez: Diaries 1951–56*, London, 1986.
6. The agreement to establish a supranational European Defence Community with common armed forces and containing the members of NATO excluding the UK and USA but including Italy and West Germany, had been signed by the Foreign Ministers concerned on 27 May 1952 but collapsed when the French Assembly refused to ratify it on 30 August 1954. The EDC was abandoned and the looser Western European Union (of the six EDC signatories plus the UK) took its place in May 1955.
7. A Middle East treaty organization was eventually set up in 1955 as the Baghdad Pact of Turkey and Iraq plus Britain, Iran and Pakistan. It did not, however, include the USA and this omission weakened Eden's position at the Suez crisis.
8. Harold Macmillan, *Tides of Fortune 1945–1955*, London, Macmillan, 1969, p. 574.
9. See A. Adamthwaite, 'Overstretched and overstrung: Eden, the Foreign Office and the making of policy, 1951–5', *International Affairs*, **64**, 2 (1988), 241–59; D. Carlton, *Anthony Eden*; R. Rhodes James, *Anthony Eden*; J.W. Young (ed.), *The Foreign Policy of Churchill's peacetime administration, 1951–55*, Leicester University Press, 1988.
10. See 'British overseas obligations', Memo by the Secretary of State for Foreign Affairs (Eden), 18 June 1952, Public Record Office, CAB 129/53, C(52)202.
11. See the review of defence programmes enclosed in the Prime Minister's memo of 3 November 1954, CAB 129/71, C(54)329, and 'Defence: outline of future policy', Cmnd. 124, February 1957, *PP* (1956–57), XXIII, 489.
12. 'Internal security in the Colonies', Memo by the Minister of Defence (Macmillan), 29 December 1954, CAB 129/72, C(54)402. See also H. Macmillan, *Tides of*

Fortune, 1945–1955, London, Macmillan, 1969, p. 574, and A. Horne, *Macmillan 1894–1956*, p. 345.

13. Personal minute from Prime Minister to Lord President of the Council, 28 January 1957, CAB 134/1555, CPC(57)6, and 'Future constitutional development in the colonies—report by the Chairman of the Official Committee on Colonial Policy [Norman Brook], 6 September 1957, CAB 134/1556, CPC(57)30.

14. Growing equilibrium did not mean equality; it was held that the US would be able to maintain its nuclear superiority for the next four or five years, see Report by the Committee on Defence Policy (chaired by Lord Salisbury), 24 July 1954, CAB 129/69: C(54)250.

15. 'Internal security in the Colonies', 29 December 1954, CAB 129/72, C(54)402, and H. Macmillan, *Tides of Fortune 1945–1955*, p. 572.

16. Cited in B. Knox, 'The concept of Empire in the mid-nineteenth century: ideas in the colonial defence inquiries of 1859–1861', *J. Imperial and Commonwealth History*, **XV**, 3 (May 1987), p. 248.

17. See K. Jeffery, *The British Army and the Crisis of Empire 1918–22*, Manchester University Press, 1984.

18. See P. Dennis, *Troubled days of peace: Mountbatten and South East Asia Command, 1945–46*, Manchester University Press, 1987, and H. Tinker, 'The contraction of empire in Asia, 1945–48: the military dimension', *J. Imperial and Commonwealth History*, **XVI**, 2 (January 1988), pp. 218–233.

19. A.N. Porter and A.J. Stockwell, *British Imperial Policy and Decolonization, 1938–1964, Volume 1 1938–51*, London, Macmillan, 1987 pp. 61–2, 360–5.

20. CAB 129/71, C(54)329, 3 November 1954.

21. CAB 128/27 pt. II, CC73(54)1, 5 November 1954.

22. H. Macmillan, *Tides of Fortune*, p. 572 cf. A. Horne, *Macmillan, 1896–1956*, p. 343ff.

23. H. Macmillan, *Tides of Fortune*, pp. 572–3, and J. Cloake, *Templer: Tiger of Malaya*, London, Harrap, 1985, pp. 331–2.

24. Ibid.

25. P. Wright, *Spycatcher*, New York, Viking, 1987, pp. 154–5.

26. CO 1030/16, 17 February 1955.

27. See A. Short, *The Communist Insurrection*, p. 65ff.

28. Phillip Darby, *British Defence Policy East of Suez 1947–1968*, London, Oxford University Press, 1973, p. 73.

29. CAB 130/111, papers for the period 15 July 1955–28 June 1956.

30. Both the interim report [CP(55)89] and the Cabinet minute on it [CM26(55)6, 26 July 1955] have been retained by the Cabinet Office. They are, however, referred to in the committee's final report and the appropriate Cabinet minute of May 1958, see CAB 129/92, C(58)92, 1 May 1958, and CAB 128/32 pt. 1, CC41(58)3, 13 May 1958.

31. For a summary of the debate over the significance of the Calcutta conferences see A. Short, *The Communist Insurrection*, pp. 45–9. The question whether the international communist movement actually devised and executed a coherent strategy across all of South and Southeast Asia in 1950–51 is discussed by R.B. Smith in 'China and Southeast Asia: The Revolutionary Perspective, 1951', *J. Southeast Asian Studies*, **XIX**, 1 (March 1988), pp. 97–110. In this connection one might note the following reference to thinking in 1953: in the summer of

1953, after his return from Malaya as Commissioner of Police, Arthur Young gave a lecture at the Imperial Defence College in which he stated that Chinese Communists in Malaya received instructions from Moscow at six-monthly intervals. When the Foreign Office took the matter up with the Colonial Office, however, it was the CO's view that there was no evidence as to whether or how instructions reached Malaya from Moscow or Beijing, see CO 1022/145.

32. Bevin to Attlee, 6 November 1948, cited by J.D. Hargreaves, *Decolonization in Africa*, London, Longman, 1988, p. 147.

33. Minute by A. Creech Jones, n.d. October 1948, CO 537/4402.

34. 'A Survey of Communism in Africa', paper by the Research Department of the Foreign Office, secret, August 1950, CO 537/5263.

35. F.D. Corfield, *Historical Survey of the Origins and Growth of Mau Mau*, Cmnd. 1030, *Parliamentary Papers* (1959–60), X, p. 7.

36. Greece and Turkey were admitted as parties to the treaty in 1951 (effective from February 1952). From 1955 Britain and Turkey were also members of the Baghdad Pact (CENTO from 1959). Greece left NATO after the Turkish invasion of Cyprus in 1974. By 1979 all the members of CENTO, except the UK, had withdrawn from the organization.

37. Colonel Dalley maintained (e.g. interviews with the author 1–4 November 1971 and 25–28 January 1972) that a paper he wrote towards the end of December 1947 on 'The omissions and commissions of Sir Edward Gent' tipped the scales against Gent when his future as High Commissioner was being considered by the Secretary of State and Commissioner General. For Wright's disparaging comments on the Cyprus settlement negotiated by Sir Hugh Foot and the Colonial Office see *Spycatcher*, pp. 157–8.

38. Commissioner General to Secretary of State, top secret and personal telegram, 29 June 1948, CO 537/3686. See also CO 537/3687 on the appointment of Sir Henry Gurney as High Commissioner.

39. Cf. A.J. Stockwell, 'British Imperial Policy and Decolonization in Malaya, 1942–52', *J. Imperial and Commonwealth History*, **XIII**, 1 (October 1984), p. 78.

40. Cf. 'Political effects that a deterioration of the situation in Indo-China might have in British Colonial and Protected Territories', 13 June 1953, CAB 134/898; and James Cable, *The Geneva Conference of 1954 on Indochina*, London, Macmillan, 1986, pp. 16–19.

41. Smith, 'China and Southeast Asia', p. 97.

42. Stockwell, 'British Imperial Policy and Decolonization in Malaya, 1942–52', pp. 79–82.

43. Lieutenant-Colonel F. Spencer Chapman (1907–71) stayed behind the Japanese lines for most of the Japanese occupation of Malaya and later wrote an account of his adventures in *The Jungle is Neutral*, London, 1948.

   Lieutenant-Colonel Colin Mitchell (b. 1925), having served in Palestine 1945–8, Korea, Cyprus 1958–9 and Borneo 1964, acquired the soubriquet 'Mad Mitch' as commander of the Argyll and Sutherland Highlanders in the occupation of the Crater of Aden in 1967.

44. General Sir Frank Kitson (b. 1926) served in Kenya 1953–5, Malaya 1957 and Cyprus 1962–4. He is the author of *Gangs and Counter Gangs* (1960), *Low Intensity Operations* (1971), *Bunch of Five* (1977) and *Warfare as a Whole* (1987).

   General Sir Walter Walker (b. 1912) served on the North West Frontier before the Second World War, in Burma 1942 and 1944–6, in Malaya 1949–59 and again in Borneo 1962–65 where, as Director of Operations during Confrontation with Indonesia, he brought to bear 'a distillation of the empire's military skills' (Tom Pocock, *East and West of Suez: The Retreat from Empire*, London, The Bodley Head, 1986, p. 124).

45. Richard Clutterbuck (b. 1917) served in Palestine 1947, Malaya 1956–8 and Singapore 1966–8 during the closing stage and aftermath of Confrontation with Indonesia. Having retired as Major-General, he lectured on political conflict at Exeter University (1972–83) and is the author of *The Long, Long War: The Emergency in Malaya, 1948–60* (1967), etc.

   R.C.K. Thompson (b. 1916) entered the Malayan Civil Service in 1938, served as a Chindit during the Burma campaign, returned to Malaya after the Second World War and became closely involved in counterinsurgency, serving for a time as Secretary for Chinese Affairs. When Malaya achieved independence (1957) Thompson stayed on and later became Permanent Secretary for Defence in Kuala Lumpur. After the end of the Emergency (1960) he was appointed as Head of Britain's Advisory Mission to Saigon (1961–5). He was held in high regard by the Americans but became increasingly critical of what he saw as their misapplication in South Vietnam of the Malayan scheme of New Villages. His book, *Defeating Communist Insurgency* (London, 1966) is, according to A. Short (*The Communist Insurrection*, p. 401n) 'the clearest statement of counterinsurgency principles and practice that one can find'.

46. Colonal C.E. Callwell, *Small Wars. Their Principles and Practice*, London, HMSO, 1906, see A. Short, *The Communist Insurrection 1948–60*, p. 138n.

47. Cf. A.J. Stockwell, 'Policing during the Malayan Emergency, 1948–60: Communism, Communalism and Decolonization' in D. Anderson and D. Killingray (eds.), *Policing and Decolonization: Nationalism, Politics, and the Police, 1917–1965*, Manchester, Manchester University Press, forthcoming.

48. Keith Jeffery, 'Intelligence and Counter-Insurgency Operations: Some Reflections on the British Experience', *Intelligence and National Security*, 2, 1 (January 1987), p. 118ff.

49. Prime Minister to Colonial Secretary and Chiefs of Staff, 6 July 1945, in Winston Churchill, *The Second World War*, VI, London, Cassell, 1954, p. 654. The British General Election had been held the day before but the returns were not in and the results were not known until 26 July.

50. See R. Ovendale, 'The Palestine policy of the British Labour Government 1947: The decision to withdraw', *International Affairs*, **56**, 1 (January 1980), pp. 73–93.

51. J.B. Perry Robinson later wrote the book, *Transformation in Malaya*, London, 1956.

52. The file containing this despatch does not appear to be open at the PRO. Sir Charles Arden-Clarke, Governor of the Gold Coast 1949–56, acknowledged the help he derived from Gurney's despatch when handling Nkrumah's Positive Action, see CO 537/5812; I am grateful to Dr Richard Rathbone for this reference to the Gold Coast.

53. From the late 1870s to 1941 the Chinese Protectorate had been a specialist department employing Chinese-speaking Europeans to deal with the affairs of the

Chinese community of Malaya. In their wartime administrative and constitutional planning the British decided to abolish the Protectorate on the liberation of Southeast Asia from the Japanese. In so doing the government lost contact with the Chinese community in Malaya.

9 British naval policy 1945–57

Eric Grove

The period for which documents are now open, 1945–57, was a vital period of transition for the Royal Navy. The service had to come to terms with fundamental changes both in strategy and Britain's position in the world which combined to produce a most unfamiliar environment for Naval policy-makers. It is a tribute to the Naval Staffs of this period that on such a limited timescale the Navy was able to reassess its role so fundamentally and provide itself with a rationale that was to see it safely into the 1960s and beyond. The story also provides an instructive case study of the evolution of British defence policy as a whole in the immediate post-war decade.

The immediate post-war problem facing the Admiralty was demobilization. Not only did the Navy's own massive wartime organization of ships, aircraft and men have to be slimmed down to a peacetime level but its warships, especially the carriers, had to play a part in the massive trooping task required to bring the other services home. Immediate policy decisions were required. A very large number of ships were left over from the War, and more were under construction. Which were to be scrapped or cancelled and which kept? This was to be a familiar problem for the post-war Admiralty that was never short of ships, only the men and money to operate them and keep them up-to-date. The Chancellor, Hugh Dalton, was soon insisting that the Navy be reduced to the minimum in ships and manpower and as was also to be only too usual that minimum was below the minimum level of efficiency as defined by the Naval Staff. The month the War ended the Cabinet's Defence Committee (Operations) discussed the size of the post-war services. The First Lord, Albert Alexander, an unfairly maligned figure in this historian's opinion, put up a brave attempt to define the size of the services in relation to their commitments. The Foreign Secretary Ernest Bevin soon put a stop to that. In a typically homely metaphor he insisted that 'we must cut our coat according to our cloth' thus setting the tone for the entire post-war era of defence policy making.[1]

155

At this Defence Committee meeting the Prime Minister, Clement Attlee, formally conceded American naval supremacy. In February 1946 the same committee decided that the USA would probably be on Britain's side in any future major war and not an enemy but that there was little probability of a major war in the next two to three years. It was estimated that no fleet capable of being a menace would exist for the next few years but anxious eyes were already being cast by the Admiralty at the Soviet Navy, especially once it had digested the lessons of advanced German technology. One of the striking features of Admiralty documents of this period is the seriousness of the perception of the threat that was deemed to be posed by the pre-Gorshkov Soviet fleet.

Manpower was the major problem, as it was to remain. The Cabinet wanted to get Britain back to work as soon as possible, which demanded a high rate of release and more dislocation than the Admiralty would have liked. Attlee could not see why more men than pre-war were required for fewer ships and this led the Admiralty to produce a fascinating study of why a modern fleet was more labour intensive.[2] Ships required more guns crews for anti-aircraft armament; new radar and other electronic equipment had to be manned and maintained by trained personnel; naval aviation, provided by the RAF before the war, now required 24,000 naval personnel; the new combined operations commitment required 5,500 men; and peacetime conscripts had to be trained, a task that the Navy insisted required an additional regular strength of 10,000. Retention was abysmal as the post-war Welfare State offered greater social security than the pre-war world had done and long service recruitment had effectively ceased at the outbreak of war. By 1948 retention had dropped to a mere 22 per cent compared to 61 per cent in 1938; the rate among the lower ranks of stoker and mechanician was a mere 4 per cent![3] It was hoped that improved pay and conditions both ashore and afloat would solve this near crisis situation and it is hardly surprising that better habitability became a high post-war ship design priority.

In 1947 the Ministry of Defence was set up to act as a clearing house between the Treasury and the services. A.V. Alexander was the first Minister charged with the thankless task of seeming unnecessarily stingy and unsupportive to the service departments and over-indulgent and unrealistic to the Chancellor. A Staff Conference with Attlee in the chair decided on three 'pillars' of British strategy, defence of the home base, sea communications and the Middle East. All these had important naval dimensions, the second in particular and they provided the basis for a proper planning process to begin on the shape and size of the post-war fleet. This concentrated on anti-mine and convoy escort forces to protect the flow of shipping. A carrier capability would be maintained to protect convoys from air and subsurface threats in the Atlantic and the threat of heavy air attack in the Mediterranean. Carriers would also assist relatively limited surface forces to cope with Soviet cruisers. This was a sensible priority list although the forces initially asked for by the Navy were far too large, even for a sympathetic Alexander. Its proposed 600 major ship navy that would cost twice the expected £600 million defence budget was almost grotesquely unreasonable in the circumstances.

It had been decided in 1947 that the chances of war in the next five years were slim but would increase in the next five; at any time its chances would be diminished by willingness to show strength (Grove, 1984). The inflated service demands—the Admiralty was not alone—caused Alexander to go further and tell them to plan on the assumption that there would be *no* war in the next five years. The convertibility crisis of August had sharpened Alexander's cost-cutting senses. Not only did this affect future plans; in the shorter term there seemed little alternative but to run down the active fleet to save money and manpower and safeguard the training base. The Home Fleet bore the brunt and by the end of the year was down to a small cruiser, a couple of big destroyers, half a dozen frigates and 20 submarines. A single carrier with 28 aircraft was operational in the Mediterranean where four cruisers, twenty destroyers and two submarines provided the only 'fleet' worthy of the name. A small force of cruisers destroyers and frigates kept the White Ensign visible in the Pacific and tiny squadrons each of a cruiser and a couple of frigates showed the flag in the South Atlantic; another frigate was in the Gulf.[4]

This deployment had a definite ring of the Pax Britannica about it, a large reserve at home but only a weak operational squadron, a relatively strong Mediterranean presence, and small cruiser squadrons spread all over the globe. It was not just imperial nostalgia that kept the distant squadrons deprived, however. They led an active life from the Corfu Channel to the Yangtse and often there was no-one else to sustain Western interests; the buck still stopped at Britain in many parts of the world in the late 1940s. As it was, the run-down of the fleet had an adverse effect on perceptions of British power in the world, especially in Latin America where pressure on British possessions, including the Falklands increased. When the Home Fleet was resuscitated in 1948 reasserting its presence in these waters was a high priority.

The outbreak of the Cold War that year led to some limited naval recovery but the dilemmas remained. What was to be the balance between active and reserve ships? Where were the latter to be deployed? One possible answer was provided by the Harwood Committee that was set the task by the Chiefs of Staff to produce a suggested force posture on an annual expenditure of £700 million a year, the Treasury's best current offer. Its recommendations that emphasized withdrawal to Europe and a concentration on preparations for hot war have a remarkably modern ring about them but they seemed horrific at the time, as was the Chiefs' intention. In their rebuttal of the Committee's recommendations they put the crucial question as follows: 'whether, after the economic exhaustion of the war years we have the power and the resources to maintain the armed forces equipped to modern standards to permit us to play the role of a great power.' A wholesale abandonment of overseas commitment was they answered 'unthinkable'. It would be silly, the Chiefs cogently argued, to forfeit the chance of winning the Cold War or at least working out an acceptable *modus vivendi* with the Russians in order to prepare for a hot war that might never happen.[5] This was a logic that appealed to the Government, which opened the coffers a little more; it was to also to develop steadily as the next decade wore on, much to the Navy's benefit.

In 1949 the Admiralty at last came out with some acceptable plans and their difficult birth was implied in the title; the 'Revised Restricted Fleet'. This was to support the foreign and colonial policy of the Government in peacetime, and to meet the immediate requirements of a war in 1957, in which it would form a nucleus for expansion. It was to consist of two operational fleet carriers, three light fleet carriers, 250 aircraft, 13 cruisers, 38 destroyers, 32 frigates and 20 submarines.[6] An active battleship would be retained with reduced complement for training and prestige and there would be large reserves of frigates and minesweepers. The wartime fleet would provide half the Allied naval effort in the Atlantic and Mediterranean. The emphasis in new construction was clearly on the conversion and later construction of convoy escorts to cope with the latest subsurface and air threats. Large numbers of new minesweepers were, however, top priority as it was assessed that this was the form of naval warfare at which the Russians were most adept.

This was the policy to which the Admiralty was committed when the Korean War broke out in mid-1950. The surprisingly early explosion of the first Soviet nuclear bomb in 1949 had already led the newly formed NATO Alliance to bring forward the planning date for possible war to 1954, something Britain was unwilling to do nationally because of the financial implications. In effect however by the end of 1950 Britain had decided to rearm as fast as she felt she could with the intention of building up the maximum deterrent strength as soon as possible, and of keeping the Americans committed to the defence of Europe. The original 'Fraser Plan', named after the First Sea Lord, which was the naval part of the original £3,600 million three-year rearmament proposals, was replaced by the 'Accelerated Fraser Plan' when Attlee upped rearmament to the £4,700 million level at the end of 1950; at £1,610 million the Navy's new plan made up just over a third of the total.

The emphasis was on quick 'fixes', more conversions, more small craft, more aircraft of existing types and this was to saddle the services, the Navy included, with some equipment that would soon become of little use. The Navy hoped that the bonanza might continue, however, and in 1951 began to put together ambitious proposals for fleet growth, including a large new carrier. These discussions did not go outside the Admiralty, for it was clear that the Government's current plans were breaking down. In the Cabinet's Defence Committee at the beginning of 1951 Chancellor Gaitskell had shown a lofty and Fabian disdain for the consumer goods such as 'Frigidaires' that would have to be foregone by the population to sustain rearmament.[7] That was not the problem, although the Government's narrow victory in the 1950 election was a sign that the country was becoming tired with continued austerity. More pressing problems were labour shortages, especially in drawing office staff, electricians, plumbers, and fitters. Lack of draughtsmen was probably *the* key factor holding up work on ships throughout the immediate post-war period. Materials were also in short supply and labour disputes compounded problems of late delivery of pipes, valves and electrical fittings. Full employment Britain was not a war economy and the Government was in no political position to make more restrictions. The Navy itself was also having problems in manning all the ships it had, despite conscription and a recall of reservists.

Off Korea the Royal Navy played an important role, one that is almost forgotten today. Routine naval operations off Korea's west coast were under British command and for a short time Vice-Admiral Andrewes was in charge of the naval blockade of the entire coast of Korea. British cruisers provided much of the gunfire support for the Inchon landings and, in all. Royal Navy ships fired 170,000 rounds of heavy gunfire at the Korean coast and its Seafire, Sea Fury and Firefly aircraft flew 23,000 sorties. A British (or Australian) light fleet carrier was on station throughout the war. The Royal Navy's carriers had been coming under some attack both from Slessor the Chief of the Air Staff and Shinwell the Minister of Defence in 1950. The former, worried about rumours of the Navy having aspirations to use their carriers in a strike role, had even suggested a unified 'maritime air force' with an emphasis on anti-submarine warfare. This demonstration of the utility of carrier aircraft in attacking ground targets in what would become known a little later as 'warm war' could not have come at a better time.

The future of the carrier force would come to dominate the in-house debate over naval policy when the rearmament plan was first slowed down and then effectively abandoned by the Churchill Government after its 1951 election victory. Butler, the Chancellor, was horrified at the economic situation he had inherited and felt strongly that too much of the output of the 'metal using industries', a term that would dominate defence discussions for the next few years, was being diverted to defence and away from exports. Nuclear weapons allowed strategic logic to be made out of economic necessity and in 1952 the Chiefs of Staff were called into conclave at Greenwich to produce a new paper on 'Defence Policy and global Strategy'. Their remit was to come up with a defence and deterrent policy that would be affordable for some considerable period.

The 1952 Global Strategy Paper [8] argued that as long as deterrent forces were maintained, especially nuclear bombers and adequate ground forces, then the chances of war were so diminished that a smaller rearmament programme was acceptable. If war did indeed break out it would start with a short fierce phase in which the enemy's immediate combat power would be the main target. Sir Rhoderick McGrigor the redoubtable First Sea Lord insisted that naval forces would also have a crucial role to play ensuring Britain's survival in this opening phase. The Soviet submarine threat was assessed as worse than that posed by the German U-boats at the blackest period of the War and left alone it would soon bring Britain to her knees. The main plank of the Naval platform, however, was the period of 'Broken-Backed' war that would follow the first intensive phase. Survival and recovery required sea communications secure from the submarine and the mine. Indeed most of the fighting in this phase might be at sea as Britain and her allies prepared for the next intensive period that would bring victory.

Another theme of Global Strategy that was even better for the Navy was the emphasis on peacetime, 'Cold War' commitments. In a companion paper the Foreign Office argued that it was vital to maintain British prestige around the world for as long as possible, not least to help preserve influence with the United States, that might thus be persuaded eventually to take up British burdens in due course.[9] A visible naval presence was a vital part of this campaign to keep up appearances. The battleship *Vanguard* had a vital role to play in this. She had entered the operational fleet once more, it is said at the insistence of Churchill, but her reduced complement meant that she was usually unable to carry ammunition beyond starshell for her secondary battery; sometimes special shoots were carried out, usually with the forward turrets only. Many other 'active' ships seem to have been on reduced complements that greatly reduced their fighting efficiency. Who, however was to know? The Global Strategy paper might have reduced new frigate construction by 40 per cent but older, familiar vessels were adequate for the increasing emphasis on Cold War functions. This would allow the maintenance of the largest possible fleet at minimum cost. Moreover it would be a fleet that had to look like that of a great power.

This was all to the good as Butler immediately wrote down the Global Strategy figures and insisted that a 'Radical Review' of defence policy begin in 1953. This was carried out on the principle that only those forces that contributed to Britain's world power and status and which were relevant in the first six weeks of hostilities should have any priority. This attacked fundamentally the Navy's 'Broken-Backed' war arguments but even those had their dangers especially with a Prime Minister who saw navies in terms of old unmodernized vessels that would be adequate for this later phase of conflict once they had somehow come out of reserve. If old ships would suffice for war as well as peace there only seemed to be one place to save money, where the Navy was increasingly concentrating its investment funds, the carrier fleet. Churchill's son-in-law Duncan Sandys as Minister of Supply was also quite sure that this was the best place to make savings; for the carrier programme put extra demands on Britain's limited aircraft industry and increasingly seemed to duplicate the land based strategic bomber programme.

This was a fundamental challenge to the Admiralty which did indeed now see strike carriers as its most important forces. A number of factors had contributed to this major reassessment of Admiralty policy. One was the setting up of NATO's Atlantic Command in 1952. The core of Allied Command Atlantic's forces then, as now, was a powerful carrier 'Striking Fleet'. The British, the Admiralty argued, needed to make a contribution to this force both to hold the ring before the Americans arrived, especially in the North, and to give influence over how the nuclear armed American carriers were used when they did come across. Although the strike potential of contemporary British carrier aircraft was low with conventional weapons, nuclear bombs would transform the situation. The promised tactical nuclear bomb would give carrier fighters massive striking power to attack enemy submarines 'at source' early in a conflict. This all fitted in well with the logic of 'Global Strategy' although it raised Air Force fears to such an extent that a deal had to be struck that emphasized the carrier strike role against ships *at sea* rather than in harbour. On this basis in 1952 a new long range strike aircraft, the NA 39 later the Buccaneer, was authorized along with a new fleet carrier to replace the previous programme of modernizing older wartime fleet carriers. This had proved over-expensive and was curtailed at the one ship already taken in hand, *Victorious*. The pressure of the Radical Review caused the Navy to give up its new carrier the following year and replace it with more distant plans for a smaller ship; but the *Victorious* rebuilding, the incomplete *Ark Royal* and *Hermes* and a full programme of new aircraft and new techniques and equipment that would allow their operation from ships already under construction or in service gave the Admiralty everything to fight for.

The Admiralty made much of the prestige argument both in general terms and in relation to the contemporary struggle over NATO naval commands. In a Radical Review meeting on 10 November 1953 Thomas, the First Lord, reminded his fellow service ministers of '. . . The disastrous results which would follow if, in spite of the strategic need, fleet carriers were abolished from the Royal Navy. In the eyes of the rest of the world we would have ceased to be a major power. I must ask you to bear in mind the effect of this on the morale of the Royal Navy and on its confidence in any Board of Admiralty that agreed to such a measure.' In the context of the Foreign Office paper of the previous year these arguments were not without weight. The Minister of Defence tried to suggest compromise proposals in early 1954 that would have completed *Ark Royal* but only with a fighter and anti-submarine warfare air group. This and the cancellation of *Victorious* and *Hermes* would have reduced the Navy to an escort carrier force and the Admiralty fought back hard. Duncan Sandys was ill and the Air Force were made to feel that if this did not stop, a Naval counterattack on Coastal Command was possible. In the event the Navy was allowed to keep its strike carriers on condition it made cuts elsewhere to keep below the Chancellor's proposed figures.

No sooner had this victory been scored than everything was put back into the melting pot by the first terrifying reports of the Bikini thermonuclear bomb tests in March 1954. Practical megaton range bombs were hardly weapons of war fighting and although it took some time for this fundamental fact to sink in some within the Admiralty like Ralph Edwards the Third Sea Lord saw the implications immediately. In a paper entitled 'Future Strategy' he mapped out a future based around a deterrent of a few H-bombs delivered eventually by the Navy and a fleet configured primarily for peacetime and limited war duties.[11] This thinking was too advanced to become consensus opinion within the Admiralty immediately but it would become the basis of the Royal Navy's long term survival.

In the 'H-Bomb Review' of defence policy that took place that summer McGrigor was able to obtain Chiefs of Staff endorsement of the concept of an immediate nuclear attack on the Soviet Navy in its bases as the best way of gaining command of the sea at the outset of a major war. This seemed to vindicate the carrier programme but it was soon under attack again as the Chancellor pointed out that the Services' expenditure plans were still above his planned total of £1,500 million for 1955. Churchill formed a special Committee under Lord Swinton. Duncan Sandys and Nigel Birch were the other members, like the chairman pro-RAF and anti-carrier. Its report struck a chill note for Thomas, McGrigor and their colleagues:

> The three Services are equal in honour and will remain so. But each must vary in size and character as changes take place in the science of war and the course of world events. In the new strategic conditions the relative importance of sea power in our defences is evidently diminishing and there is no sign that this trend will be arrested. There can be no question of having a larger Navy than we need or can afford; and we must make the best use of existing material. It is natural that the Navy should wish to have their share in air power, which is growing in importance. The cost of the Fleet Air Arm, however—already about £70million and expected to rise sharply—appears to impose a burden disproportionate to the results. Moreover the role of the aircraft carrier is already restricted through the every increasing range of shore based aircraft.[12]

The Committee insisted that carriers configured for the escort role were sufficient for 'Broken-Backed' war. The Admiralty went into top gear to counter this attack but it became clear to Philip Newell the very able head of 'M' Branch as the fateful Cabinet meeting drew close on Guy Fawkes night 1954 that a deal might be struck. As he drily minuted:

Fireworks from the Prime Minister may be expected but I suggest the whole object of plugging a half empty carrier in the Defence review Report may be to make certain that the Admiralty accept everything else and feel thankful they are to be spared the last straw.[13]

After a stormy meeting in which McGrigor ably presented all the pro-carrier arguments, Macmillan, the new Defence Minister, suggested a compromise and drafted it before the end of the year. A change of Prime Minister and an election were both imminent. This was no time for resignations from the Admiralty. At the price of its remaining minesweeper programme, the Navy retained strike carriers.

This choice of forces with a 'cold' and 'warm' war relevance rather than forces only useful in 'hot' war was the underlying logic that a triumphant Admiralty described to the world in the 1955 Naval Estimates Statement. Modernized carriers and a mix of modernized and unmodernized cruisers would operate with World War Two destroyers and those modern and modernized frigates that had survived the cutbacks in rearmament. Many plans had been abandoned, a 5,000-ton gun-armed cruiser-destroyer, an east coast gunboat to protect coastal convoys from enemy coastal craft, an ultra austere anti-submarine frigate. A new ocean minesweeper was also cancelled but coastal and inshore minesweepers were coming into service in almost embarrassing numbers and some impressive surface ship plans were still being developed, notably a large missile armed cruiser and a big destroyer for fleet escort.

The responsibility of defending this fleet and developing its logic further passed from McGrigor to Lord Louis Mountbatten in 1955. Churchill had opposed the latter's appointment. The old man recognized Mountbatten would add unscrupulous political skills and enormous social influence to the forensic abilities of the Admiralty's staff, honed by years of interdepart-mental conflict. The Admiralty was already considering a set of preemptive cuts of shore establishments and the Reserve Fleet to help stave off future cuts in more important areas. The new First Sea Lord took over the project in typical style and made it his own, forcing it through with a special 'Way Ahead' Committee. The First Sea Lord also developed the Staff thinking on limited war that he had inherited and saw that it put a new emphasis on amphibious warfare for which he had always had an enthusiasm that was unusual among naval officers. Consideration was given to greater investment in this cinderella of naval warfare and this received a decisive push from the Suez landings. These showed both the weaknesses and the potential of current amphibious forces, old, slow and unseaworthy landing craft side by side with new techniques of amphibious landing using helicopters and improvised commando carriers. HMS *Eagle* also proved that large fleet carriers were the most efficient suppliers of air support. There was also a more general lesson. If one was going to intervene it had to be done quickly when the context was right. Rapidly deployable mobile forces might be one answer.

These ideas were developed alongside older justifications based on broken-backed war to make the Admiralty case in the context of the Defence Review that Eden began in 1956. This had not produced results before the departure of Eden after Suez brought in Macmillan as Prime Minister and the dreaded Duncan Sandys as Defence Minister. Worse was that old enemy of the Navy was endowed with more power than any of his predecessors to sort out defence once and for all. Sandys' major task was to abolish conscription and this dominated his approach. If Royal Marines could be recruited voluntarily then they ought to replace soldiers in garrison duties, the Minister argued. This gave Mountbatten an opportunity to make his amphibious case. Mountbatten was able to score a major triumph by obtaining Chiefs of Staff support for the carrier as a mobile source of air power in limited war. This appealed to Sandys who conquered his old anti-carrier prejudices and kept them in the programme. The Admiralty were less successful in the attempts to get Sandys to take out those famous words from his White Paper about the role of naval forces in general war being 'somewhat uncertain'. Nevertheless the admirals cannot but have been gratified by the assertion that the Royal Navy and Royal Marines were an effective 'means' of bringing power rapidly to bear in peacetime emergencies or limited hostilities'.[14] The price demanded, the cancellation of the missile cruiser (its missiles would instead be mounted in the new destroyers) and the final demise of the battleships seemed small in comparison.

Sandys kept up his attack throughout 1957 but Mountbatten and the Admiralty fought a classic rearguard action. The First Sea Lord built up a powerful constituency among the political elite that made further serious cuts impossible. He engaged in personal diplomacy with Sandys at his house at Broadlands something few other First Sea Lords could have done. He proved flexible on the question of conversion of the home-based carriers into the anti-submarine role as it was more important to be flexible on that point and retain a Navy of 88,000 men in the short- to medium-term than worry about future developments that rested on the long-term acquisition of new equipment. The Admiralty had no intention of keeping its side of the bargain once Sandys had gone, and did not. As Sir Gerald Templer is said to have remarked to Mountbatten, 'Dickie, you're so crooked that if you swallowed a nail you'd shit a corkscrew!' (Ziegler, 1983: 528). The Navy was lucky to have such a man at the helm in one of its most serious bureaucratic crises of the post war era.

The Sandys exercise did the Admiralty a great deal of good. Mountbatten thought he had obtained a more 'reasonable deal' for the Navy than that given the other services (Ziegler, 1985: 554). By the end of 1957 the Royal Navy had indeed acquired a more coherent doctrine than it had ever possessed before, one primarily related to thrusting power ashore 'East of

Suez', although the first steps towards both nuclear submarines and Polaris missiles had also been taken. 'East of Suez' would sustain a carrier force and an increasingly impressive amphibious squadron together with a fleet of modern escorts into the 1960s and beyond. For a few years naval policy would acquire a certain stability, a considerable achievement for the creative tension of the Sandys–Mountbatten combination. The question of the long-term nature of that stability was, however, more open. Indeed, hitching the Navy's wagon so firmly to the twin horses of 'East of Suez' and the carrier created hostages to fortune that would create tricky problems for Mount-batten's successors. By the mid 1960s the embers of the carrier controversy would have been fanned into flame once more, but that is another story. At least there was a Navy to argue about: that, given the challenge, was the Admiralty's fundamental achievement in the period 1945 to 1957.

Notes

The account is based primarily on the author's book *Vanguard to Trident* (London, Bodley Head, 1988) where full citations for sources may be found. Only direct quotations and figures will be referenced separately.

1. DO(45) 11th Meeting 29 September 1945 CAB69/7.
2. 'Size of the Navy', DO(46)97, CAB131/3.
3. 'Manning Difficulties', Admiralty Board memo B595, ADM167/133.
4. Figures from the relevant 'Pink List' in the Naval Library.
5. DO(49)51, CAB131/7.
6. Admiralty Board memo B590, ADM167/133.
7. DO(51) 1st Meeting, CAB131/10.
8. There had been others, not least in 1950 revised in 1951, which seems to have marked a significant swing towards Europe in Britain's strategic priorities. 'Global Strategy Papers' tend still to be closed and not available in the PRO. Their content must be deduced from associated documents.
9. This fascinating and highly significant paper 'British Overseas Obligations' *is* available in the PRO, C(52)202 in CAB129/53.
10. 'The Role of Aircraft Carriers', ADM/24695.
11. 'Future Strategy' is to be found in First Sea Lord's Records ADM205/102.
12. 'Defence Policy', C(54)329, CAB129/71.
13. Note in ADM205/99.
14. 'Defence Outline of Future Policy', Cmnd. 124.

References

Grove, E.J. (1984), 'Post-war ten year rule, myth and reality', *J. Royal United Services Institute*, December 1984.

Grove, E.J. (1988), *Vanguard to Trident*, London, Bodley Head.

Ziegler, P. (1985), *Mountbatten*, London, Collins.

10 Defending the pound: the economics of the Suez crisis, 1956

Lewis Johnman

The thirtieth anniversary in 1986 of the Suez crisis produced and continues to produce an avalanche of studies. The vast majority of these studies has concentrated—perhaps correctly—exclusively on the political, military, diplomatic and imperial aspects of the affair. The major issues examined being typically:

(1) the role of certain key ministers within the British Cabinet, including the Prime Minister Eden, and the accusation that the affair was generated and sustained by a 'Star Chamber' of ministers, officials and top military personnel, which excluded and misled the rest of Cabinet, the Conservative Party and the country.
(2) the extent and the timing of secret collusion between Britain, France and Israel.
(3) the opposition to the operation from the USA and other 'allies'.

Amidst almost all studies little or no consideration has been given to the economic aspects of the crisis and present studies fail to take one much further than the cursory treatment paid to the subject by contemporaries. In a 165-page reflection on Suez in his memoirs, Sir Anthony Eden (1960: 555–6) managed to devote just over half a page to the economic aspects of the crisis. Paradoxically, given his brief treatment of this aspect of the affair Eden concludes that the economic problems were 'a more formidable threat than Marshal Bulganin's'—referring to the Soviet Premier's allegation that the situation could develop into a Third World War and that the Soviet Union would use force—and concedes that the financial situation 'threatened disaster to our whole economic position'. Eden concluded:

> The position was made immediately critical by speculation against sterling, largely in the American market or on American account. Chinese balances were also withdrawn, no doubt for political reasons, and Indian balances reduced. The

166

Chancellor of the Exchequer, Mr Macmillan, later gave the House the figures. During the first half of the year, the gold and dollar reserves of the United Kingdom had been rising. Some pressure against sterling had been expected in the Autumn and allowance had been made for it. The pressure was greatly intensified at the beginning of November. Our reserves fell by $57 million in September, $84 million in October, and $279 million in November. $279 million represented about 15% of our total gold and dollar reserves. This was a gloomy foreboding and decisive within the next few days . . .

Other contemporary actors were as or even more minimal than Eden. Macmillan devotes scant space in his memoirs to his term at the Treasury and has little to say on the economics of Suez. Nor has this shortfall been fully corrected by recent work. Anthony Howard's biography of R.A. Butler contains only one reference to the economic situation which makes the point that Britain was rapidly losing reserves and that there was no possibility of this position being rectified until a ceasefire was announced and Britain declared its readiness to withdraw (Howard, 1987: 273). Robert Rhodes James's (1986: 573; 584) biography repeats Eden's reflections on the loss of gold and dollar reserves and the view that assistance from either the USA or the IMF would be available only in the event of a ceasefire and possibly a withdrawal of Anglo-French forces. Rhodes James does take the issue somewhat further by speculating on the role of Harold Macmillan in the course of events. Macmillan had been one of the most hawkish of ministers in the original series of discussions leading to the decision to invade and according to Rhodes James was also;

The key figure in the surrender—or bowing to the inevitable, as it might be described by others . . . The economic pressure applied by the Americans was severe and the combination of events had made the run on sterling and the evaporation of reserves more frightening to the Treasury. Several of Macmillan's colleagues—and certainly Eden—considered that Macmillan saw the situation in excessively dire terms. Others thought that he was making a deliberate move for the leadership.

Although Rhodes-James' consideration of the economic aspects is also brief he does bring these aspects to centre stage and raises intriguing questions as to the role of Macmillan and the Americans in the affair. Perhaps subconsciously Rhodes-James had in mind the thoughts of Samuel Brittan (1964: 184–5)—Brittan's work is nowhere mentioned in Rhodes-James—but writing in 1964 he raised a number of issues concerning the economic aspects of the crisis. In particular Brittan sought clarification on two issues. Firstly, which Ministry had been responsible for giving totally misleading advice to Eden concerning what he terms 'the supposedly catastrophic effects on the British economy should the Canal be closed', and secondly he speculated on the role of Macmillan. 'Macmillan' he wrote:

had originally been the warmest cheer-leader of the Suez expedition and had originally maintained, on the basis of a personal meeting with Eisenhower, that the Americans would not oppose it. But in a crucial Cabinet meeting in early November, he suddenly changed his mind and threw all his weight behind those who wanted to bring the operation to an end, giving as one of his reasons, 'We can't afford it'. How much then had the run on the reserves really to do with this change of front?

In trying to answer these questions I hope I can hold up for wider scrutiny the general economic aspects of the Suez crisis.

The answer to the first question is that no Ministry specifically gave Eden misleading advice concerning the economic effects of the closure of the canal although almost all departments of Government contributed to the development of an atmosphere of deep pessimism as to what the effects of closure would be. This atmosphere was heightened by the reaction of Cabinet Ministers to the nationalization of the canal. At the Cabinet meeting on 24 August, Lord Home, the Commonwealth Secretary, told Eden: 'I am convinced that we are finished if the Middle East goes and Russia and India and China rule from Africa to the Pacific'. And Alan Lennox-Boyd, the Colonial Secretary, wrote to Eden arguing that: 'If Nasser wins, or even appears to win, we might as well as a government (and indeed as a country) go out of business'.[1] Such judgements certainly contributed to a mood of cataclysm over Suez although Egypt as an issue for Cabinet discussion in 1956 appears in the briefest of minutes in February with a note concerning the prospective meeting between Selwyn Lloyd and the Egyptian Prime Minister, with Lloyd at pains to suggest that the sole aim of Britain in the region was to protect the sources of its oil supplies in the Persian Gulf and to prevent Soviet encroachment.[2] The Aswan Dam project is mentioned briefly in May[3] and the imminent termination of the Anglo-Egyptian agreement is referred to in June.[4] Then in July Cabinet minutes reveal the American decision not to finance the Aswan High Dam and the possible repercussions that this might have for Britain's relations with Egypt with as the minutes noted: 'possibly serious consequences for our trade'.[5] Nasser responded to the ending of finance by nationalizing the canal on 26 July. The following day Eden reported to the Cabinet that: 'any failure on the part of the Western Powers to take the necessary steps to regain control over the Canal would have disastrous consequences for the economic life of the Western Powers . . .'[6] and he invited the Cabinet to consider what course of action Britain could take to safeguard its interests.

Initially the main economic worry centred on oil supplies. Of the 70million tons of oil which went through the Canal from the Persian Gulf, 60million tons were destined for Western Europe, a sum which represented some two-thirds of total Western European needs. It was believed that moving such a volume of oil via the Cape would require twice the tonnage of tankers, that there would be a need to seek alternative supplies in the western hemisphere, and that some form of rationing would be likely.[7] At the Cabinet meeting of 27 July it was agreed that a programme of economic sanctions should be applied on Egypt, more information on the likely economic effects of cänal closure was sought and the Chiefs of Staff empowered to draw up a war plan.[8]

On the same day the Treasury began to formulate plans to block Egyptian sterling balances and although this action of itself was simple enough the Treasury added some important qualifications to the envisaged effects of the action. The Treasury noted that: 'Unless the rest of the sterling area is prepared to join in this economic blockade, HMG must be prepared to receive and reject violent complaints from them.'[9] On the following day with the Suez Canal Co's assets in the UK and France frozen and Egypt expelled from the transferable account area the Foreign Office was telegraphing the British Embassy in Washington that 'We regard it as of the highest importance that the US should align themselves with France and the UK',[10] and asked the Embassy to urge the Americans to support the Anglo-French position. Such early incidents however were enough to weaken confidence in sterling and Sir Leslie Rowan, the Second Secretary at the Treasury was moved to comment in a memo to Macmillan that: 'Yesterday after initial weaknesses the Exchanges improved and *net* we lost no dollars.'[11]

By 6 August the Treasury had become very bleak as to the efficacy of economic sanctions because of the absolute lack of support from almost anywhere in the world. They were especially dismayed by the lack of response from America: '. . . The steps taken by the US on trade fall far short of our action', Europe: 'The most we can count upon is for one or two countries to *consider* action . . .' and the Commonwealth: 'The only Commonwealth Governments which are . . . comtemplating taking action . . . are Australia and the Federation of Rhodesia and Nyasaland.'[12] The Cabinet considered that it was unlikely that economic sanctions could have any effect unless they were maintained over a long time period and the Americans could be persuaded to join in.[13]

As if this prognosis were not gloomy enough a memo from the Joint Permanent Secretary at the Treasury, Sir Edward Bridges, to Macmillan on 8 August deepened the gloom. Bridges warned Macmillan that the Suez Canal affair was already putting the balance of payments and the gold and dollar reserves under considerable strain and warned that even with a successful conclusion to the London conference this was still likely to be the case. He also presented a range of possible scenarios according to the scale of military operations defining these as: 'a limited war, or a not so limited war—a war in which we go it alone, or a war in which we have the Americans with us from the onset'.[14] His conclusion was bleak in that he argued that even without hostilities any duration of the crisis would mean a disturbance of the export trade, a loss of confidence and possibly an Autumn Budget.[15]

Indeed by the time the London conference opened on 16 August, Treasury views as to both the ability of the economy to stand the strain and the likelihood of American assistance continued pessimistic. Fiscally the Treasury was contemplating a six-penny rise in the standard rate of income tax, an increase of between sixpence and one shilling in petrol duty, increases in tobacco duty and perhaps on purchase tax and profits tax. They were gloomy as to the efficacy of monetary policy given the potential rise in government expenditure, steel allocation was again considered although it was conceded that this was a 'fearsome subject' and building control was envisaged.[16] Also considered were import controls and exchange controls where the suggestion surfaced that the country should 'take a really big step backwards from convertibility'.[17] The memorandum concluded that:

> . . . we are not in at all a happy position to bear any great degree of extra strain on our resources. Our resources are still dangerously low, and are certain to fall pretty sharply this month . . . Our imports have remained extremely high and there is a serious possibility that the Suez crisis—whatever its outcome—may result in some movement of the terms of trade against us.[18]

Further, the Treasury was depressed at the lack of support for Britain's economic sanctions from the USA. This was epitomised by a penned note by Macmillan at the foot of a Treasury memo concerning Economic Pressure on Egypt: 'I had a talk with Dulles last night. It was not at all successful.'[19] A few days later the Cabinet was being informed that Dulles was proving unforthcoming, reluctant and doubtful on American support for British actions.[20] Thus even at this early stage—well over two months before the landings—signs were not propitious.

The Treasury now began to voice deep concern at the prospect of independent British action. Bridges wrote to Macmillan on 7 September setting out two alternative scenarios. Firstly, that Britain acted in accordance with UN wishes and overt support from the USA, Commonwealth and other countries. The second envisaged Britain and France with (prophetically) one or two others and the UN, USA, Commonwealth and other countries opposed. Bridges commented that:

> . . . unless we can secure at least US support and a fairly unified Commonwealth, then it is not possible to predict either the exact timing or the magnitude of the strains which are likely to come upon our currency. At the worst, however, the strains might be so great that, whatever precautionary measures were taken we should be unable to maintain the value of the currency . . . if we do get overt US support and support from elsewhere, including the Commonwealth, our general feeling is that our action would be regarded by world opinion as something likely to strengthen sterling. In these circumstances the broad line of our policy should be to allow things to go on as normally as possible so as to show that we have confidence both in a satisfactory and quick outcome of any military action, and in the capacity of our economy and our currency to face any strains that might come upon it. Any unusual action on our part would be likely to cast doubt on both.

What this points to therefore is the vital necessity from the point of view of our currency and our economy of ensuring that we do not go it alone, and that we have the maximum US support.[21]

This memorandum is again annotated by Macmillan and once again it is a clear recognition of American reluctance to support Britain. 'Yes: this is just the trouble the US are being very difficult.'[22]

Remarkably enough the Chancellor of the Exchequer went to the Cabinet on the 11 September, 4 days after receiving the Treasury's memo and one day after annotating the memo—in other words fully briefed as to the developing and potential economic difficulties and absolutely convinced of the American's reluctance to support Britain's position. Macmillan argued that the issue should be brought to a head.

This was of great importance from the point of view of the national economy. If we could achieve a quick and satisfactory settlement of this issue, confidence in sterling would be restored; but if a settlement was long delayed the cost and the uncertainty would undermine our financial position. He therefore hoped that Parliament would be persuaded to give the Government a mandate to take all necessary steps, including the use of force to secure a satisfactory settlement of this problem.[23]

On no account could this be regarded as Macmillan conveying the Treasury's views to Cabinet—indeed in many respects it conveyed the opposite of what the Treasury had conveyed to him. The Treasury's absolute essential requirement for success—the support of at least the USA—was not and would not be forthcoming and yet Macmillan's advice to Cabinet was that the military operation should proceed.

By 21 September Sir Leslie Rowan was reporting to Macmillan the loss of $550million from the reserves in a period of two months and he warned that even if the situation were quickly and peacefully resolved it was unlikely that sterling would be in a safe position. Rowan reported that the reserves were near what he termed the watershed mark of $2billion—this had been for some time in Treasury and Bank of England minds the standard minimum level for gold and dollar reserves—and he raised the prospect of claiming the waiver (payments usually would be $180million—with the waiver $40million). He was gloomy with regard to the terms of trade and went so far as to raise the potential prospect of devaluation. He concluded that unless Britain could gain clear guarantees from the Americans as to future policy: 'sterling will be in the greatest danger and our other resources—IMF, dollar securities, etc—will not do much to put off the day'.[24] Rowan was also acknowledging the fact that the composition of the reserves was in itself important in the sense that to the extent that dollars rather than gold were in the reserves, the reserves were less usable and more vulnerable than they might initially appear. Once again this was cryptically annotated by Macmillan: 'this is gloomy, but very likely correct.'[25]

By late September the Treasury was contemplating what actions were open to it should the drain on the reserves continue. Among the possible options—considered with the Bank of England—were the breaking up of the transferable account area and a reversion to a bilateral system of payments, the depreciation of sterling either through devaluation or by letting the rate float and the possibility of approaching the IMF for a fund drawing and claiming the Waiver under the US Loan Agreement. Most of these options were considered to be as problematic as the problem they were seeking to solve.[26] Picking up on this discussion the Chief Economic Advisor, Sir Robert Hall, remarked that 'sterling could hardly remain a currency in which people would hold substantial balances if we had another devaluation so soon after 1949'[27] and there was general agreement that parity should be held as long as it was possible.

Throughout October the military situation developed with the British and French Governments now colluding with Israel on a plan to invade Egypt and secure the Canal. On 25 October with military plans at an advanced stage the Cabinet minutes noted that 'military action would cause offence to the US Government.'[28] The Treasury continued to report bleakly to Macmillan and continued to urge that at least tacit American sympathy was essential if Britain's position were not to become catastrophic. Rowan estimated a loss of $80million for October and calculated that the reserves would fall below $2,000million by the end of the year, what he termed 'a rather crucial dividing line'.[29] The Treasury and the Bank were split as to whether an approach should be made to the IMF—the Treasury favouring an early approach on the grounds that this would not appear as if the country has been forced to go to the fund while Cobbold at the Bank argued that this would be construed as a sign of weakness. Both however were united in the view that without reasonable Anglo-American relations either an approach to the IMF or a potential claim on the waiver would be more difficult than they would otherwise be.[30]

By 26 October Macmillan was informing the Cabinet of how grave the economic situation was. He presented them with the stark choice of mobilizing all the nations financial resources in order to maintain the sterling-dollar rate or to float the exchanges. The latter course he believed would end sterling's role as an international currency and destroy the Sterling Area. Macmillan told the Cabinet that he expected the loss of gold and dollars in the month of November to be as high as $300million and that the consequent shock to international confidence would be severe. He continued to believe that there was a 'reasonable chance' that if the existing parity were maintained then dire consequences could be avoided. While he conceded that a formal approach to the Americans was out of the question he argued that informal links should be maintained: 'in order gradually to enlist their support for the loans which we should have to raise both by exercising our drawing right in the IMF and by pledging out own dollar securities in the American market'.[31] Remarkably the Cabinet was not disconcerted by Macmillan and it took refuge in the view that American public opinion was more sympathetic to Britain's actions than was American political opinion. There was certainly no suggestion that Macmillan had changed his view as to the use of force despite the deteriorating economic situation and the total absence of American support. The war plan remained on.

On 29 October Israel attacked Egypt and on 30 October the British and French ultimatums were issued and the task force sailed from Malta. On the same day Macmillan met his senior officials and the Governor of the Bank of England. Macmillan laid down that the policy was 'to remain firm and see the affair through'[32] while the Governor reported that sterling was already under pressure. Two days later it was becoming very difficult to remain firm and see through. $50million had been lost in 48 hours and the Treasury estimated that if the Canal were to be closed and pipelines cut the country would face a shortage of oil amounting to 25 per cent of total supplies with the cost of obtaining alternative supplies amounting to between $500million and $700million per year.[33] The Treasury now began to contemplate emergency action under three heads:

(a) Steps to supplement the reserves (IMF drawing, use of Treasury owned dollar securities, waiver, etc);
(b) Controls, (import licensing, restriction on dealings in commodity markets);
(c) Exchange rate policy.[34]

Despite extensive discussion however the Treasury believed they had reached 'a somewhat negative set of conclusions'. They believed that to meet the capital outflow the right course was to borrow from the IMF. They also felt that the country would be affected by both increased expenditure on alternative oil sources and shortfall in oil supplies leading to a fall in industrial output, which would result in added strain on the balance of payments and an intensification of inflationary pressure. The memo concluded:

> To meet this, further action in the fiscal and monetary fields may be required. A return to import controls cannot be excluded. It should not however be undertaken as a temporary measure but only as a definite and lasting change of policy.[35]

So much for remaining firm.

By 4 November Egypt had blocked the Canal; on the following day paratroopers landed at Port Said and Nutting and Boyle resigned. On 6 November Macmillan telephoned Washington seeking assistance and was told that it would only be forthcoming if a ceasefire was arranged before midnight, then and only then would the US support a British approach to the

IMF and consider other forms of assistance.[36] Macmillan now counselled that the operation must be terminated—the initial advocate of force who had counselled firmness and seeing the issue through had now collapsed over the very issues on which his officials had had him well briefed for over two months.

By the 7 November the Treasury was posing questions to government as to whether it was more important to hold the reserves without regard to the use of sterling or whether the rate and the sterling system were the priority and the reserves secondary.[37] $85million had been lost in one week and the Treasury continued to contemplate a drawing from the IMF, the sale of Treasury-owned dollar securities, credit from the EXIM Bank and the rationing of oil.[38] To facilitate the first of these the Foreign Office sought the likely reaction in the US to a request for standby arrangements of $236million on the gold tranche and $325million on the first credit tranche.[39] The reply was negative. 'There is at present no possibility of aid, which in any event would not be available until after further Congressional action, and I think we must take it that there is no possibility of an EXIM Bank Loan'.[40]

To the Governor of the Bank of England more radical treatment was necessary. He termed sterling 'a major casualty of recent events' and argued that three simultaneous steps should be taken: the borrowing of three tranches from the IMF, the mobilization of Treasury securities and the raising of money on them from New York banks and arrangements about the waiver.[41] None of these objectives could be achieved however until relations with the US improved and the Treasury calculated that the drain on reserves could not continue at the current rate and sterling be held at its present value. The Treasury argued that:

> If we can hold the present position until relations with the United States become more friendly, it will then be possible to make a very broad approach to them for assistance, on the grounds that it is a major interest of the United States and the whole world that the sterling system should be firmly maintained.[42]

To meet this 'crash action' might be necessary but the Treasury was prepared to insist that all practicable steps in the spheres of policy—with the withdrawal of troops from Egypt as the priority—to facilitate the opening of conversation with the US at the highest level be taken.[43]

By 16 November the drain on reserves was nearly $200million and the anticipated deficit for the month was expected to be over $300million and the Treasury thought that it was unlikely that any large scheme supporting sterling could be arranged by the end of the month.[44] The Bank of England remained opposed to going to the IMF unless American support could be secured and was also against selling US securities and called for the Government to move towards an overall budget surplus for 1957–8.[45] Cobbold called for the Government to give priority to stability of the currency and take any action necessary to maintain it. If this were not done a 'catastrophic course' would be followed with a floating pound, the likelihood of the break up of the sterling area, the dissolution of the Commonwealth, the collapse of the EPU, a reduction in the volume of trade and currency instability at home leading to severe inflation.[46] With this view and the suggested course of action Macmillan agreed and undertook to report this to Cabinet.

The Treasury now began to work through the various options as future policy. They again considered the measures which would have to be taken should Anglo-American relations remain broken: devaluation, blocking the balances, exchange guarantees and bilateralism were all considered. These were however considered as desperate measures and a package of IMF drawing and stand-by, borrowing against securities, the waiver and an EXIM Bank loan were thought to be the best measure. It was realized that the Americans would seek a quid pro quo for this and the Treasury argued that sterling convertibility would be a sufficient plum for the Americans.[47] The Treasury also began to formulate how best the approach to the Americans should be made. The suggested line was that the dangers for world trade and the sterling area were grave if America continued to take a detached attitude and they posed the question that there was a danger that: 'the Suez affair may touch off a crisis which would do irreparable harm not merely to sterling but to the whole fabric of trade and payments in the free world'.[48] Indeed Macmillan's message to the American Treasury was less subtle containing the phrases: '. . . it would be tragic — and a major victory for the Communists — if we were to allow what has happened to result in an economic disaster for the free world'.[49]

By 22 November the position had again deteriorated, $48million being lost in two days with New York in a state of near panic over sterling and the markets being described as sluggish to miserable, Cobbold reported to Makins that the City were 'beginning to fret about the situation generally'.[50] The Treasury again began to consider 'crash action' and once again attempted to galvanize ministers declaring that:

> If we are to have any real chance of succeeding in our crash action, or better still of avoiding the necessity for it, the first essential is the re-establishment of relations with the United States. It is quite clear that there is a conflict between economic and political considerations, and that the longer political considerations are allowed to prevail the greater danger there is to the whole fabric of our currency.[51]

Both external and internal courses of action were summarized and externally the Treasury envisaged: borrowing from the IMF, borrowing against dollar securities, the waiver, reduction of forces in Germany, lowering the gold ratio in EPU, an oil loan, a gold loan from the EPU, reduction of foreign commitments, import cuts, special emergency import tax and the closing of commodity markets; internally: increased direct and indirect taxation, bank rate, government expenditure, control of building and hire purchase control.[52] It began to look increasingly as if these measures would be needed as on 23 November a further $20million was lost.[53]

On 26 and 27 November the first pieces of relatively good news came from Washington. On 26 November the Embassy in Washington telegraphed that George Humphrey was stating that the US Treasury were 'profoundly shocked' by the losses in Britain and that the Americans were prepared to act as soon as 'HMG has shown in a way which the world could accept that we were conforming to rather than defying the UN.'[54] Once the political situation allowed the US would support drawing on the gold and first credit tranches and a loan from the EXIM bank.[55] Although this was welcome news no action from the Americans was forthcoming and the Treasury continued to anticipate the use of crash action or emergency measures and by 30 November the full extent of the economic difficulties was known. The loss on reserves for November was $279million—the real loss of $401million being covered up by forward sales and sales of short-term US securities—and December would open with a deficit of $285million because of payments on loans, the EPU and other losses. The reserves stood at $1,965million and by the end of the year were calculated to be not far from the lowest post-war level of $1,340million in September 1949 when devaluation had been the result.[56] It was these figures which finally convinced the Cabinet—and Macmillan—that total withdrawal from Egypt was the only option if any form of American economic assistance was to be forthcoming.

The British decision to withdraw—under severe pressure from America—eased the situation with respect to American support for the British economy. As early as 1 December 'informal' discussions had begun in the US on Britain's approach to the IMF, the EXIM Bank and the waiver,[57] with a formal letter claiming the waiver drafted by 1 December.[58] By 2 December the Americans were still stressing 'that any financial support was subject to agreement on the political front' and that undertakings must be given to withdraw all troops by a certain date—if this were done Britain could look forward to 'massive support', although the scale of this was rendered questionable with the Americans taking the view that if Britain took a third tranche from the IMF it 'would open the flood gates in the Fund and expose it to the risk of a really serious run' and that 'the United States cash position was really tight and the money market very touchy'.[59] American attitudes drew from the Minister of Education Sir David Eccles the view that: 'the best prospect for England now is the formation of a balance of power inside the free world i.e. The leadership of Western Europe'. At the end of the War, Eccles argued, this had not been possible as the Americans were the only 'financial victors', time and a big shock had been needed to bring Britain and 'the other vanquished' together. The shock was that 'The USG has unjustly hesitated between the Afro-Asians and its own committed Allies' and Eccles was willing to discuss whether the 'European fugitives from the American camp should form into a stronger sterling area'.[60] There is no record of whether this was given serious consideration.

By 5 December the application for standby credit has been made. The timing of this had been set by Paranagua the Brazilian Executive Director of the IMF who told the British to 'get your money before Dulles can see any of your ministers otherwise he will try to do a trade policy against cash.[61] So lacking in confidence in the Americans were the Treasury that they continued to hold in readiness a full programme of crash action and emergency measures.[62] By 9 December the position had eased considerably and Washington was reporting to London that 'funds will be available from the EXIM Bank' and 'We now look certain of getting $1,300m from the International Monetary Fund. Another $700m would give us the formidable total of $2billion.'[63]

By 21 December Macmillan was able to tell the Prime Minister that EXIM Bank had authorized a line of credit of $500million to Britain (interest was at 4½ per cent against sums drawn, credit was available for one year with repayments to be in semi-annual payments over four and a half years—the loan was to be used to recover dollars spent on dollar products and services).[64]

Cobbold drew stringent conclusions from the after-effects of Suez claiming that it had laid bare to the public weaknesses of which the Bank and Treasury had long been aware of. The economy, he maintained, had been moved towards uneasy equilibrium but the basic problems had been left untouched and adequate confidence in the currency had been maintained by a slender margin. The aftermath of Suez was the time to launch 'a radical attack on some of the fundamentals' and Cobbold believed that:

> The fundamental trouble is that the economy and the public purse have been over-extended for many years, partly as a result of the war and partly because of the many commitments, social, military and political, which we have since undertaken (most of them doubtless justifiable on their own merits but adding up to a total bigger than we could afford).[65]

He concluded that 'dramatic, far-reaching and convincing measures were needed and that there was no point in trying to 'keep up with the Jones" in political and military affairs which would destroy the country's economic strength.[66] The Government view was that 'Mr Governor rather likes making our blood run cold' although they did concede that one of the main lessons of Suez was that economically Britain was no longer strong enough to 'go it alone' in international affairs if disapproved of by world (which meant US) opinion. In terms of radical measures the Government could only suggest checking public expenditure although it saw this as raising 'acute political difficulties'.[67] The Prime Minister raised the issue of the 'confidence factor' and asked whether there was any way of easing the burden on sterling to which Macmillan replied:

> There is no way of avoiding the dangers to sterling which come from our being bankers to the sterling area. We have inherited an old family business which used to be very profitable and sound. The trouble is that the liabilities are four times the assets. In the old days a business of this kind, like Coutt's or Cox's Bank would have been sold to one of the big five. The trouble is I do not know who is to buy the sterling area banking system. I tried it out on Humphrey but he was not taking it. So we must either carry on the business with all its risks, or wind it up and pay 5s in the £.[68]

The issues of confidence and strain on sterling would have to be borne.

By late December the full rescue package was in place and Eden's position tenuous. But, only two days before his resignation he could not resist ammending a memorandum by Macmillan on the 'State of the Economy' with the introduction: 'I do not think that the events of Suez can be reckoned as a tactical defeat.'[69] Not surprisingly the rest of his ammendment failed to mention the economy. The 'fall-out' from the Suez operation continued well into 1957. In March with Macmillan Prime Minister and Thorneycroft, Chancellor, the Treasury was reporting the loss of $30million in one week, the pound weakening against the dollar, a loss of $38million in the month from the reserves and the country facing a run similar to that which developed during Suez. The Treasury concluded that: 'our assets are . . . quite inadequate to our liabilities' and that with second line reserves through the IMF and EXIM Bank mobilized some £200million of the total £640-million had been used: 'once we start using these, people will begin to ask what we do when these are used up.'[70] Suez had had the effect of weakening the major influence upon sterling in the world economy—confidence. Here too, however, as with their advice on Suez the Treasury was ahead of the game. In an analysis of the management of sterling conducted in February 1956 the Treasury argued that the value of sterling in current use depended entirely upon exchange markets and the policies of the British monetary authorities in which conditions ' "confidence" had become of greater importance than in the past'.[71] In the past however the authorities had been able to rely implicitly upon the confidence of the British public in the pound sterling with the economy and sterling able to sustain violent shocks to this inherent confidence. The War, the Cold War and the course of post-war economic history has caused a loss of this domestic confidence. While this was partly the case the Treasury pointed out that pre-war sterling had been managed on an anti-depression theory and that consequently the management structure was provisional and impermanent—it was a monetary structure technically designed to assist in refloating a deflated economy and this was an inheritance of an anti-depression mentalitity based on assumptions which were no longer relevant. The Treasury argued that it would: 'take years of prudent and cautious management before the confidence of the British public in the paper pound or British Government securities is restored.' Emphasis had to be placed primarily on restoring confidence abroad and bringing about a growth in reserves, full sterling convertibility was an inevitable concomitant of international responsibility and 'any major setback would not only cause a collapse of the sterling system but would also affect the Commonwealth'.[72] Suez was nearly that.

There can be little doubt that Treasury advice over Suez was accurate and that had it been accepted, a political and economic (and perhaps military?) [73] fiasco could have been avoided. What continues to fascinate is the role played by Harold Macmillan in the affair. Did Macmillan deliberately mislead the Prime Minister and Cabinet over the Treasury's warnings? The answer would seem to be that he did. Very few people saw the Treasury papers and Sir Guy Millard, Eden's Downing Street private secretary who handled the paperwork concerning Suez for the Prime Minister has said that: 'I'm not sure Eden saw the Treasury warnings. I didn't see them. Macmillan saw them, but he was a hawk.'[74] Even such Treasury papers as reached the Cabinet (or even the Inner Cabinet) would have been presented by Macmillan and it would have been easy for him to have obscured their implications. Perhaps it is too Machiavellian to see Macmillan's role in Suez as a bid to oust Eden but it was Macmillan who became Prime Minister in 1957.

Notes

1. Quoted in *Contemporary Record* **1** (Spring 1987), p. 2.
2. CAB 128/30 17th Conclusions, Minute 4, Egypt 28 February 1956.
3. Ibid; 37th Conclusions, Minute 8, Egypt 17 May 1956.
4. Ibid; 40th Conclusions, Minute 7, Egypt 7 June 1956.
5. Ibid; 50th Conclusions, Minute 3, Egypt 17 July 1956.
6. Ibid; 54th Conclusions, Minute 7, Egypt 27 July 1956.
7. Ibid; of Britain's total trade in 1955, 32 per cent went via the Suez canal.
8. Ibid.
9. T236/4635; Suez Canal Company; financial and economic measures taken by the UK and other governments against Egypt following the expropriation of the Suez Canal Co, by the Egyptian Government; unsigned memo, 27 July 1956.
10. Ibid; Telegram; FO to Washington 28 July 1956.
11. Ibid; memo, from Sir L. Rowan to Chancellor of the Exchequer, 28 July 1956.
12. Ibid; Use of sterling balances; Memo from Sir L. Rowan to Chancellor of the Exchequer, 6 August 1956.
13. CAB 128/30; op. cit; 59th Conclusions, Minutes 3, Egypt 14 August 1956.
14. T236/4188; Measures to Protect Sterling; Sir E. Bridges to Chancellor of the Exchequer, 8 August 1956.
15. Ibid.
16. Ibid; Memo from Mr Binning to Sir E. Bridges, 13 August 1956.
17. Ibid.

18. Ibid.
19. Ibid; Economic pressure on Egypt. Penned note by H. Macmillan, 19 May 1956.
20. CAB 128/30; 60th Conclusions, Minute 1, Egypt 21 August 1956.
21. T236/4188, cop. cit; Sir E. Bridges to Chancellor of the Exchequer, 7 September 1956.
22. Ibid; Penned note by H. Macmillan, 10 September 1956.
23. CAB 128/30, op. cit; 64th Conclusions, Minute 4, Suez Canal, 11 September 1956.
24. T236/4188, op. cit; sterling memo from Sir L. Rowan to Chancellor of the Exchequer, 21 September 1956.
25. Ibid; Penned note by H. Macmillan, 21 September 1956.
26. Ibid; Possible action if drain continues. Memo by Sir D. Ricketts. 29 September 1956. Floating, for example, was only a remote possibility, indeed so remote as to be almost an impossibility. Since ROBOT in 1952 even mild contemplation of floating had encountered European hostility, and in the summer of 1955 the then Chancellor, Butler, had discounted it as a possibility at the annual IMF meeting in Istanbul. I am indebted to Professor L.S. Pressnell for this observation.
27. Ibid; Memo by Sir R. Hall 2 October 1956.
28. CAB 128/30, op. cit; 74th Conclusions, Minute 1, Suez Canal, 25 October 1956.
29. T236/4188; The Reserves, IMF (a standby or drawing) and the waiver. Sir L. Rowan to Sir R. Makins 26 October 1956.
30. Ibid.
31. CAB 128/30; 85th Conclusions, Minutes 5, Economic Situation, 26 October 1956.
32. T236/4188; note for the Record, Sir L. Rowan, 31 October 1956.
33. Ibid; Emergency Action, Memo by Sir D. Ricketts, 2 November 1956.
34. Ibid.
35. Ibid.
36. R.R. James, (1986: 573).
37. T236/4189; measures to protect sterling, the foreign exchange market; Memo by Sir G. Bolton, 7 November 1956.
38. Ibid; note of meeting at 11 Downing Street, 7 November 1956.
39. Ibid; FO to Washington 8 November 1956.
40. Ibid; Washington to FO 9 November 1956.
41. Ibid; memo, from Sir R. Makins to Chancellor of the Exchequer, 9 November 1956.
42. Ibid; note of meeting held in Sir L. Rowan's room 12 November 1956.
43. Ibid; sterling, Memo from Sir L. Rowan to Sir R. Makins, 13 November 1956.
44. Ibid; sterling, Memo from Sir R. Makins to Chancellor of the Exchequer, 16 November 1956.
45. Ibid; memo from C.F. Cobbold to Sir R. Makins and the Chancellor of the Exchequer, 16 November 1956.
46. Ibid; note of a meeting at the Treasury, 19 November 1956.
47. Ibid; Treasury minute 20 November 1956.
48. Ibid; draft telegram to Washington, 21 November 1956.
49. Ibid; redraft 21 November 1956.
50. T236/4190; measures to protect sterling, memo from Sir R. Makins to Chancellor of the Exchequer, 22 November 1956.

51. Ibid; Crash action, memo from Sir L. Rowan to Sir R. Makins, 22 November 1956.
52. Ibid.
53. Ibid; memo from Sir R. Makins to Sir L. Rowan and Chancellor of the Exchequer, 23 November 1956.
54. FO 371/120816; UK financial situation resulting from the Suez Crisis, Washington to FO 26 November 1956 and Washington to FO, 27 November 1956.
55. Ibid; Washington to FO, 27 November 1956.
56. T236/4190, op. cit; Reserves, Sir L. Rowan to Sir R. Makins 30 November 1956 and Sir R. Makins to Chancellor of the Exchequer, 30 November 1956.
57. Ibid; Washington to FO, 1 November 1956.
58. Ibid; FO to Washington 1 December 1956.
59. Ibid; Washington to FO, 3 December 1956.
60. Ibid; Sterling, Sir D. Eccles to Chancellor of the Exchequer, 3 December 1956.
61. FO 371/120816, op. cit; Washington to FO, 6 December 1956.
62. T236/4190, op. cit; Policy if we do not succeed in holding the rate for sterling. Sir L. Rowan to Sir R. Makins, 6 December 1956.
63. PREM 11/1826; Washington to FO, 8 December 1956.
64. PREM 11/1818; 1956 financial policy, letter from the Chancellor of the Exchequer to the Prime Minister, 21 December 1956.
65. PREM 11/1826; op. cit; letter from the Governor of the Bank of England to the Chancellor of the Exchequer, 20 December 1956.
66. Ibid.
67. Ibid; letter from Prime Minister to Chancellor of the Exchequer, 28 December 1956.
68. Ibid; letter from Chancellor of the Exchequer to Prime Minister, 31 December 1956.
69. Ibid; note by the Prime Minister circulated to Cabinet, 7 January 1957.
70. PREM 11/1822; Chancellor of the Exchequer (Thorneycroft) to the Prime Minister (Macmillan), 19 March 1957.
71. T236/3936; The management of sterling, Treasury memo, 7 February 1956.
72. Ibid.
73. A. Gorst and W. Scott Lucas, 'Suez 1956: Strategy and the Diplomatic Processes', *Journal of Strategic Studies*, December, 1988.
74. Quoted in *Contemporary Record* vol. 1, no. 1, (Spring, 1987), p. 5.

References

Brittan, S. (1964), *The Treasury Under the Tories*, London, Harmondsworth, Penguin.
Eden, Sir A. (1960), *Full circle*, London, Cassell.
Howard, A. (1987), *RAB: The Life of R.A. Butler*, London, Cape.
James, R.R. (1986), *Anthony Eden*, London, Macmillan.

11 Neustadt revisited: a new look at Suez and the Anglo–American 'alliance'

W. Scott Lucas

In 1970, Professor Richard Neustadt of Harvard University, in his book *Alliance Politics*, attempted to define the mechanics of the Anglo-American alliance. Neutstadt (1970) was intrigued by the apparent breakdowns of the alliance during the Suez crisis of 1956 and the Skybolt missile project in 1962. Using information he gathered about the two crises and bureaucratic models of government devised by Allison (1971) and others, Neustadt proposed a framework for the Anglo-American alliance which would explain its day-to-day behaviour and the reasons why it failed in certain situations.

With the release of many British and American documents on the Suez crisis, Neustadt's approach must be re-evaluated. It is questionable whether an Anglo-American 'alliance' over Middle Eastern affairs existed in 1956. Even if it did, its apparent breakdown during the Suez crisis was not due to the failures of the actors and mechanisms of Neustadt's model but to countries and events that lay beyond any Washington–London axis. Britain's decision to join Israel and France in an invasion of Egypt, bitterly opposed by the US, was taken because of Middle Eastern developments involving France, Israel, Iraq, and Jordan. It had little or nothing to do with Anglo-American relations. Neustadt's bipolar model is intrinsically unable to explain the multilateral dimensions of the Suez affair.

The model and Suez

Neustadt's central thesis is:

> that relationships between allies are something like relationships between two great American departments. These are relationships of vast machines with different histories, routines, preoccupations, prospects. Each machine is worked by men with different personalities, skills, drives, responsibilities. Each set of men, quite naturally, would rather do his work in independence of the other set. If one government would influence the actions of another, it must find means to convince

enough men and the right men on the other side that what it wants is what they need for their own purposes, in their own jobs, comporting with their own internally inspired hopes and fears, so that they will pursue it for themselves in their own bargaining arena.

(Neustadt, 1970: ix–x)

Each machine is 'a complex array of mutually dependent, institutionalized "positions," linked to each other by lines of procedures or "action channels".' Each position is occupied by a person whose actions are influenced by his personal and political interests as well as the interests of his government. The governing of the country is a 'game' carried out by 'players' for 'stakes' derived from their interests (Neustadt, 1970: 76).

Crises in the Anglo-American alliance arise from subtle breakdowns in the action channels between positions in the two governments. Neustadt identifies four aspects of the British and American systems leading to these breakdowns: (1) political accountability to Congress or Parliament or to the public; (2) standard operating procedures; (3) job-to-job relationships; and (4) on-the-job perspectives (Neustadt, 1970: 79). He summarizes:

> Players on the one side failed to understand the stakes of players on the other. They failed to do so because they misread the interests which the other men pursued. They misread interests because they misunderstood, to some degree, the precise nature of the game in which the others were engaged: its positions, or its channels, or its history.

Efforts to understand the interests of an ally or the nature of its political channels and positions are hindered by the domestic experiences and interests of a player. Neustadt explains:

> Positions are defined at home: nothing from outside the game can enter save as it impinges on those definitions. Men grow up at home. Comprehension of their work and of their interests and each other has been shaped by a long learning on home grounds . . . Men are booed and booted out at home or cheered and reelected or promoted there. Whatever the effects on them of happenings abroad, these cannot be made manifest in their careers except at home.

(Neustadt, 1970: 115)

In his evaluation of Suez, Neustadt asks two questions: why British Prime Minister Anthony Eden thought the Americans would not oppose military operations against Egypt, especially when it involved British collusion with France and Israel without the knowledge of the US, and, conversely, why the Americans did not make clear to Eden their opposition to force. He answers both through his model. Eden, he suspects, had a 'muddled perception' of American attitudes and action channels. Neustadt claims that Eden relied heavily on the assessment of his Chancellor of the Exchequer, Harold Macmillan, who had visited the United States in late September, that 'Ike would lay doggo' and not oppose military operations against Egypt. More-over, Eden overestimated the effect of the Jewish vote upon US President Dwight Eisenhower, thinking that the President would not oppose an Israeli attack upon Egypt in an election year. Finally, Eden did not realize the division in the US Administration between US Secretary of State John Foster Dulles, who wanted to curb Nasser's power in the Middle East, and Treasury Secretary George Humphrey, who, because of the cost to the American budget, opposed any expenditure supporting British economic pressure upon Egypt. Because of these muddled perceptions, the Prime Minister discounted Eisenhower's opposition to force, as expressed in the President's letters, but feared that Dulles would continue using diplomatic manoeuvres to postpone military measures. According to Neustadt, Eden imposed the diplomatic 'blackout' upon the Americans, not because he perceived American opposition to force, but because he thought that Eisenhower, if told of the collusion, would send Dulles to Britain to counsel a further delay in action.

On the American side, Neustadt asserts that Dulles had his own 'muddled perceptions', overestimating the effect of domestic opposition in Britain to force, particularly that of the Labour Party and the press, and underestimated Macmillan's influence upon Eden. Eisenhower, because of his fondness for Macmillan, was loath to express American opposition to force during the Chancellor's visit to the US. Throughout October, the Americans could not issue an ultimatum against military action because, with the lapse in Anglo-American 'action channels,' they did not foresee the collusion between Britain, France, and Israel (Neustadt, 1970: 81–106).

The flaws in the model

In the case of Suez, Neustadt's model suffers from two flaws. First, he assumes that an Anglo-American 'alliance' existed in 1956, without defining the nature or the extent of this alliance. The vague assertion of 'formal pledges, long-standing institutional arrangements, history, language, acquaintance, shared external interests, and felt need' as a basis for alliance leads to an equally vague conclusion:

> We conceived we needed Britain in our business, for our purposes, while Whitehall took the obverse as matter of course. . . . Throughout the modern history of peacetime friendship among major powers, there is nothing comparable, save the Austro-German linkage in the generation before World War I.
>
> (Neustadt, 1970: 3–4)

Neustadt never establishes how this general assumption applies to specific areas of British and American policy, notably policy towards the Middle East. His assertion that Anglo-American co-ordination of policy began in the summer of 1954 with the final negotiations for an Anglo-Egyptian treaty over the Suez Canal Base is misleading in two respects. Firstly, his starting date for the alliance is arbitrary and inaccurate. High-level Anglo-American political and military discussions over post-war Middle Eastern policy dated from 1947. The first public declaration of an Anglo-American policy in the Middle East came with the Tripartite Declaration of 1950 (Louis, 1984; McGhee, 1983). Secondly and more importantly, British policy over the Middle East differed in its interests from American policy. While the US looked upon the Middle East in Cold War terms, seeing it as a link in a global network to counter Soviet expansion, British objectives stemmed from their political and economic involvement in the region, which had evolved since the late nineteenth century.

Until 1953, while the US accepted that they had a part to play in the Middle East, they also accepted British predominance in the region. Britain assumed the military responsibility for the area, with their bases in Egypt, Jordan and Iraq, and they took the political lead in regional initiatives such as the Middle Eastern Defence Organization. Only in Saudi Arabia, where the US had oil interests and rights to the Dhahran Air Force Base, did the Americans assume the role of the leading Western power.

The US attitude changed with the accession to power of the Eisenhower administration. US Secretary of State John Foster Dulles, following a month-long tour of the Middle East in May 1953, concluded that the British role in such matters as Middle Eastern defence and Anglo-Egyptian discussions was hindering, rather than serving, Western interests. While Britain and Egypt were arguing over the Suez Canal Base, Arab countries could not be united to fight with the West in the Cold War against the Soviet Union. Dulles advocated a new, independent American policy in the area: the Middle Eastern Defence Organization would be abandoned and the US would strengthen the 'Northern Tier' of Turkey, Iraq, Iran and Pakistan. Furthermore, the US would no longer unconditionally back the British in their negotiations with Egypt (Lucas, 1989).

Throughout 1953–4, the Americans pursued the Northern Tier policy by encouraging Turkey and Pakistan to sign a defence agreement and by funding extensive programmes of military aid to Iraq and Pakistan. The Americans became mediators in the Anglo-Egyptian negotiations, secretly furnishing Egypt with proposals drafted by the State Department and then urging the British to accept them. After the Anglo-Egyptian treaty was signed in October 1954, the US covertly attempted to arrange military aid for Egypt.[1]

The divergence between British and American policies was demonstrated by the reactions of the two countries to the military pact between Turkey and Iraq, signed in February 1955. The Foreign Office saw the pact as an 'umbrella' for revision of the Anglo-Iraqi treaty for military co-operation and facilities, and Foreign Secretary Eden attempted to bring Britain into the pact. When the British acceded on 5 April, turning the Turkish-Iraqi arrangement into the Baghdad Pact, they expected the US to follow suit. The Americans, who saw an Arab-Israeli settlement as a precondition for any comprehensive system of Middle Eastern defence linking Egypt and Israel with the Northern Tier, hesitated. They believed that the Pact would turn Nasser, who opposed Anglo-Iraqi leadership of the Arab world, against the West, ruining any chances of improved Egyptian-Israeli relations. Moreover, to make accession acceptable to the Congress, the State Department would have to guarantee Israel's borders against Arab attack, a unilateral step that the British firmly opposed.

The US was most irritated by the December 1955 mission of the British Chief of the Imperial General Staff, General Sir Gerald Templer, to obtain Jordanian accession to the Pact. The Americans had impressed upon the British the folly of bringing another Arab state into the Pact, since the move risked the complete alienation of Nasser from the West and, consequently, the failure of secret Anglo-American efforts for an Egyptian–Israeli peace settlement. When Templer's mission ended in widespread riots that threatened to topple King Hussein, Eisenhower wrote, 'The British have never had any sense in thje Middle East. . . . [I am] a little afraid of the results of the Baghdad Pact.'[2]

Thus, by 1956, British and American policies in the Middle East rested on different bases. Washington believed that no unified defence of the Middle East, including the Northern Tier and the 'defence in depth' of Syria, Lebanon, Egypt and Jordan, was possible without the prerequisite of an Arab–Israeli settlement. The aim of US policy was to create the conditions which would bring about such an agreement. In contrast, the primary objective of the British was to maintain their influence in Iraq and Jordan, both of whom had treaties with the UK, and to extend that influence to Syria and the Lebanon. The Baghdad Pact had become the vehicle for that task.

This does not mean that the divergent policies had no common aims. In March 1956, the US and Britain, for different reasons, concluded that Nasser had to be removed from power. When Eisenhower's emissary, Robert Anderson, failed in his top-secret mission to bring the Egyptians and Israelis closer to peace, the Americans were persuaded that no settlement was possible with Nasser as Egypt's leader. The removal of British General Sir John Bagot Glubb from the command of Jordan's army, the Arab Legion, convinced Eden and his colleagues that Nasser sought to destroy the British position in Jordan and Libya and to topple British-backed regimes in Iraq and the Persian Gulf. This coincidence of British and American aims led to Anglo-American planning to reduce Nasser's influence in the Middle East, a temporary but conditional 'alliance' of interests.[3]

Neustadt's second error is to treat the events of Suez solely as the product of Anglo-American relations, ignoring all other causes. He even acknowledges this mistake, writing, 'Reality is not bilateral,' but then explains that he will leave such considerations to specialists on France or Israel (Neustadt, 1970: 3). Unfortunately, this bilateral emphasis turns Neustadt's study into speculation removed from reality, for the Suez crisis developed not only because of British and American actions but also those of other countries. American hesitation to back military action against Nasser was due, in part, to the opposition of Saudi Arabia to the use of force and to the need to protect plans for covert action against Syria. The collusion which led to the invasion of Egypt did not originate with the British but with the French. The Americans were deceived not only by a British black-out but also by conflict on the Israeli–Jordanian frontier caused by the proposed movement of Iraqi troops into Jordan.[4]

The successful operation of the Anglo-American 'alliance' was conditional upon a convergence of aims in the Middle East, as well as the methods to achieve those aims. It could never be isolated from the actions of countries in the region nor those of other countries with interests in the area. It is impossible, therefore, to sustain Neustadt's central assumption of alliance functioning in any circumstances, let alone those of Suez, as an exogenous or fixed variable. The multilateral nature of international relations undermines the construction of Neustadt's model. If a 'player' in the British machine is linked to his counterpart in Washington by 'action channels,' he is also in communication with players in other machines throughout the world. Furthermore, each player interacts within his machine with other players who maintain such external links.

Far from being the stable bureaucratic world that Neustadt envisages, 'alliance' politics operates in a fluid environment, where a change in any of numerous variables outside the control of the policymaker, limits the efficacy of the 'action channels'. For example, the information which a player in London receives from sources outside the 'alliance' can only correspond with the information available to his counterpart in Washington if there is a complete and constant exchange of that information. This condition can never be met. Even if one player were willing to transmit all information he received and even if his 'machine', military and intelligence agencies included, were willing to allow full transmission, no technology can instantaneously communicate the material. Nor can it communicate all the impressions and ideas that a player draws from the information which he gathers. Furthermore, a player's interpretation of the information, based on subjective factors which may not be acknowledged by the player himself or which may elude definition, cannot be expressed completely on paper.

Two cases from Suez illustrate this point. The first involves secret American talks with the Saudis during the crisis. The US had important interests in Saudi Arabia, notably its rights to the Dhahran Air Base and the concession granted to the Arabian-American Oil Company (ARAMCO). American action or its support of British military action against Egypt could alienate the Saudis and, thus, jeopardize these interests.

London recognized the American interests but it was unaware of American attempts during the Suez crisis to reconcile the US relationship with Saudi Arabia with its position towards Egypt. In late August, Eisenhower sent Robert Anderson, his special emissary to the Middle East, on a secret mission to King Saud. Anderson pressured the Saudis to accept Western efforts to regain control of the Suez Canal, warning, 'It might become necessary for us to ensure that our allies are self-sufficient and free from threats of blackmail.' The envoy even hinted that the US would turn to nuclear energy to free itself from dependence on Saudi oil if Saud backed Egypt. The Saudis were unmoved. They insisted that nuclear energy was not a feasible alternative to oil and contended that the US should be using its diplomatic leverage against Israel in the Arab–Israeli dispute instead of threatening Egypt.

Anderson then travelled to Cairo to ascertain Nasser's position over international control of the Canal. He concluded that Egypt would 'not agree to the establishment of international supervision of the Canal,' although it 'would agree to the institution of a pact in which freedom of navigation in the Canal would be guaranteed,' and it 'might agree' to a consultative commission including representatives of the countries using the Canal. (Eveland, 1980: 209–12).[5]

Anderson's report influenced American policy in two ways. First, it established a significant deterrent, in the form of Saudi opposition, to American support of Anglo-French military action. Second, it indicated to the State Department that Egypt might be willing to reach a negotiated settlement which would take into account the rights and interests of maritime countries. Using this information, Dulles designed his plans for a Suez Canal Users Association. Since the British were not told of Anderson's mission, 'players' in Whitehall were unaware of an important external influence upon American policy that pushed the US towards conciliation with Egypt and away from force.

The second example, even more significant in the development of the Suez crisis, of the shortcomings of Neustadt's bipolar approach was the limited information given to the United States of the relationship between Britain, France, and Israel. Throughout the crisis, Britain and France did not inform the US of the progress of military plans for the bombing and invasion of Egypt. Although Lloyd and French Foreign Minister Christian Pineau met regularly with Dulles, political details of the Anglo-French discussions were withheld from the Americans. The US were never told, for example, of the Anglo-French plan to send extra amounts of shipping through the Canal in mid-September. Britain and France, believing that Egyptians could not handle the additional traffic and transit would be blocked, planned to use the resulting chaos as a pretext for military intervention.[6]

By itself, the Anglo-French collaboration did not lead to an attack upon Egypt, as the US was able to use diplomatic devices to delay military action. The French, however, were also conferring with the Israelis, talks which were withheld from the British until mid-October. France and Israel had forged close scientific, diplomatic, and military links in the 1950s, and Paris, without informing Washington or London, began large-scale shipments of tanks and jets to Tel Aviv in 1955.[7]

In May 1956, Israeli officials, with the support of Prime Minister David Ben-Gurion, met officials in the French Ministry of Defence and proposed 'massive deliveries of arms to Israel and preparations for joint action against Egypt'. The ensuing discussions culminated on 22 June when Israeli Chief of Staff Moshe Dayan and the Director-General of the Israeli Ministry of Defence, Shimon Peres, conferred with French representatives from the military, the Ministry of Defence, and the intelligence agency SDECE, to consider 'ways of containing Nasser and perhaps even causing his downfall'. They agreed to 'massive French arms deliveries to Israel; exchange of intelligence information and close cooperation in intelligence; and planning practical operations up to, and including, war'. The French arranged for delivery of 72 Mystere IV jet fighters and 200 AMX tanks to the Israelis.

Immediately after Nasser's nationalization of the Suez Canal, Israel provided the French with detailed information about the capabilities of Israeli ports and airfields and an assessment of the strength and deployment of Egyptian forces. On 7 August, the French Minister of Defence, Maurice Bourges-Manoury, received Peres' assurance that the Israelis, if necessary, would attack Egypt in concert with French, and military leaders of both sides began discussions to this end in early September. Plans for the joint attack were confirmed on 30 September and 1 October in talks between Dayan and the Israeli Foreign Minister, Golda Meir, and Pineau and Bourges-Manoury. The operation was tentatively set for 20 October.[8]

To summarize, the attitude of the French, in their contacts with the British, was determined by their collaboration with Israel. British officials, unaware of the Franco-Israeli planning, were designing a policy based on incomplete information. Anglo-American discussion consequently took place in isolation from the talks between Paris and Tel Aviv.

One may argue that both of the above objections to Neustadt's model could be mitigated by the high-level 'action channels' of the Anglo-American 'alliance'. Even if British and American officials at lower levels were working with insufficient or misleading information, Dulles and British Foreign Secretary Selwyn Lloyd or Eisenhower and Eden could forge a common policy to overcome any differences. Neustadt contends, for example, that the British deferred, despite their doubts about American attitudes, to Dulles' conference-making in August and September 1956 and that Dulles, faced with the *fait accompli* of the Anglo-French move to the Security Council of the United Nations in late September, reluctantly agreed.

According to Neustadt, it was only when misunderstandings crept into the highest level of the 'alliance' that the British and Americans split over Suez. Macmillan's assessment, made after his meetings with Dulles and

Eisenhower, that the Americans would not oppose an Anglo-French military operation led to Eden's decision to attack Egypt with the French and the Israelis. Dulles' reluctance to boycott the Suez Canal or to withhold Canal dues from the Egyptians, eventually convinced the British that economic pressure upon Egypt, by itself, would not bring a satisfactory outcome. This in turn undermined Washington's ability to prevent the British from resorting to military action. It is only by defining the causes of the Anglo-American rift as problems within the 'action channels,' rather than events outside of them, that Neustadt can sustain the argument that the breakdown of the 'alliance' was due to shortcomings on the part of the 'players'.

The error in this scenario is the assumption that high-level contacts are immune to the objections to Neustadt's model. He assumes that Foreign Secretaries, Presidents, and Prime Ministers, in times of crisis, put the maintenance of the 'alliance' above all other interests. They consider events in third countries only in relation to Anglo-American co-operation.

Dulles and Eisenhower, however, had abandoned the concept of a predetermined Anglo-American 'alliance' in the Middle East in 1953 and decided that American objectives would be pursued irrespective of the British attitude toward them. The maintenance of the alliance now depended upon British acceptance of American policies, including the US commitment to Saudi Arabia, its opposition to a British military presence in Egypt, and its rejection of membership in the Baghdad Pact.

Likewise, Eden did not believe in unqualified deference to Washington's foreign policy. As Foreign Secretary, he had risked public disputes with the US over Indochina in 1954 and Taiwan in 1955, and only British Prime Minister Winston Churchill prevented an open break between Eden and the Americans over Guatemala in June 1954. In October 1955, Eden warned:

> Our interests in the Middle East were greater than those of the U.S. because of our dependence on Middle Eastern oil and our experience in the area was greater than theirs. We should not, therefore, allow ourselves to be restricted overmuch by reluctance to act without full American concurrence and support. We should form our own policy in the light of our interests in the area and get the Americans to support it to the extent we could induce them to do so. Our policy should be based on the need to help our acknowledged friends and allies, such as Iraq and the Trucial States, on whom our oil depended.[9]

Neustadt insists, despite these differences in outlook between Dulles, Eisenhower and Eden, that the Anglo-American rift was caused by a high-level misunderstanding, rather than circumstances in other countries that affected their attitudes toward the Anglo-American 'alliance'. This claim rests upon the contention that the Prime Minister agreed to the operation against Egypt because he believed that the Americans, for the sake of the 'alliance' would not oppose the invasion. It is true that Macmillan misrepresented the American position to 'ginger' Eden into the use of force. He reported to Eden that 'Eisenhower is really determined to bring Nasser down' and that the President accepted that 'Britain must win or the whole structure of our economy would collapse'; however, the cable sent by Macmillan to the Foreign Office painted a different picture. He admitted that, in the half-hour discussion with Eisenhower, nothing very specific emerged. Although Macmillan formed the impression that 'the President understands our problems about Nasser', he added that Eisenhower, 'in the same position now as we were in May 1955 [before a general election]', would not make an unconditional commitment of American support for British action. British Ambassador Roger Makins, who was present at the meeting, has no recollection of a discussion of British force against Egypt; according to him, the conversation was a general one between two old friends from World War II and avoided details of policy. Eisenhower, reporting the meeting to Dulles, did not mention the issue of force; indeed, he noted that Macmillan was 'far less bitter' than he had been in previous weeks and that the Chancellor 'rather thought the Users Association is a good thing' since it might keep the Canal open 'and think through to a solution'.[10]

The most damaging evidence against Neustadt's thesis that the Prime Minister expected American backing for an Anglo-French invasion of Egypt is Eden's willingness to reach a negotiated settlement in early October, even after Macmillan's return from the United States. If the Prime Minister accepted the Chancellor's report, then his attitude against Nasser should have hardened; however, as late as 14 October, Eden, influenced by the Foreign Office, was suggesting further talks between Britain, France, and Egypt towards a solution in which representatives of the maritime nations would co-operate with the Egyptians on a commission supervising the operation of the Canal.

Eden's agreement to collude with France and Israel was not the result of an Anglo-American misunderstanding but the reaction to the influence of countries and events outside the scope of Neustadt's model. While factors acknowledged by Neustadt, such as right-wing pressure in the Cabinet and Parliament upon Eden, the frustration of the British military at repeated postponement of the invasion, and scepticism over Dulles' conference-making and the Users Association, reinforced Eden's decision, they were secondary to the influences of Franco-Israeli planning, the border conflict between Israel and Jordan, and London's policy to defend British interests in the Middle East through an Iraqi–Jordanian axis. Notably, it was the opinion of French Foreign Secretary Christian Pineau, not Macmillan, that the US would accept an Anglo-French invasion before 6 November, that strengthened the Prime Minister's commitment to collusion. The priority of maintaining the Anglo-American 'alliance' had been superseded by external factors.[11]

This was illustrated by the decision of the British Cabinet on 25 October to sanction Anglo-French intervention 'in the event of an Israeli attack upon

Egypt'. It was acknowledged that Britain's 'action would cause offence to the U.S. Government and might do lasting damage to Anglo-American relations. There was no prospect of securing the support or approval of the U.S. Government'. This consideration was secondary, however, to the conclusion that 'a crisis in the Middle East could not now be long delayed. If . . . force might ultimately have to be used, would it not be used more effectively and with more limited damage if we acted promptly now when an Anglo-French operation was already mounted?'[12]

A reevaluation of Suez

Given these objections to Neustadt's model, his conclusions about the crisis and the Anglo-American 'alliance' must be reassessed in light of recently-released documents.

In general, Neustadt's analysis of British and American policy in the early stages of the Suez crisis is upheld by the evidence. Initial reactions toward Nasser's nationalization of the Suez Canal Company differed. Eden sought Nasser's removal by force; the US, because of Eisenhower's belief that Nasser's nationalization was legal and the fear of negative reaction in the United States and the Arab world to the use of force, counselled caution. At this juncture, Neustadt correctly assesses that the 'allies' reconciled their differences through high-level discussions. The British, French, and Americans agreed to an international conference of the main users of the Suez Canal in mid-August. When London indicated in late August that it would take the dispute to the Security Council of the United Nations, Dulles, anxious to avoid Britain's manipulation of the proceedings to provide a pretext for military action, designed the Suez Canal Users Association and sought a second international conference to approve the arrangements. Britain, unable to create a political justification for the invasion of Egypt, agreed to the plan. In turn, when the British and French, without consulting Dulles, decided in late September to appeal to the Security Council, Dulles did not oppose them but conferred with Lloyd and Pineau about the forthcoming discussions in the United Nations.

If anything, Neustadt underestimates the amount of Anglo-American collaboration that took place in August and September. With hindsight, Dulles' conference-making could be seen as a delaying tactic, designed to play for time and make the use of force unattractive to the British, but London did not oppose the Secretary's manoeuvres at the time. The idea for the first London Conference of maritime nations was tabled by British officials as well as American representatives. Dulles' proposals in early September for a Users Association were welcomed by Eden and Cabinet ministers as 'ingenious'. Provided the organization had the power to withhold dues from the Egyptians, thus pressuring Nasser to agree to international control of the Canal, Britain was prepared to agree to its establishment. Even when Dulles, upset at the supposedly 'provocative' tone of Eden's announcement of the proposal for a Users Association, undermined the plan by saying 'we do not intend to shoot our way through [the Canal]' if the Egyptians prevented passage, the British saw the Association as a viable instrument, provided that dues were withheld from Egypt.[13]

Neustadt's assumption of an 'alliance', however, obscures the reason for this apparent co-operation between Britain and the US. London's decision to collaborate with Washington was forced upon them by necessity, rather than the priority of maintaining the Anglo-American 'alliance'. The original constraint upon the British reaction to the nationalization of the Suez Canal Company was Britain's lack of military resources in the Middle East. This had been caused by redeployment of troops from 1953 to 1956, notably the evacuation of forces from the Suez Canal Zone Base. Britain could not mount an immediate response to Nasser, as it would take six weeks to acquire the necessary equipment and to mobilize and prepare the task force. For this reason alone, no military action could be taken against Egypt before 15 September. (Gorst and Lucas, 1988)

Ironically, by agreeing to Dulles' diplomatic initiatives while military preparations were made, Britain appeared to commit herself by mid-September 1956 to the pursuit of a negotiated settlement. To resort to the use of force, she had to present world opinion with a pretext based on Egyptian actions. Operations PILEUP and CONVOY were devised in mid-September to create this pretext by breaking down the flow of traffic through the Canal, blaming the collapse on Egypt, and then using the British Navy to ensure the passage of ships. The plans failed when the Egyptian Canal Authority was able to maintain the pre-nationalization rate of transit.[14]

Up to this point, Neustadt's model and his interpretation of Anglo-American relations, while misleading in its analysis, does not lead to a misleading account of the events of the crisis. Neustadt, however, makes a serious mistake when he assumes that the appeal made by Britain and France to the United Nations Security Council in early October was only one more attempt to establish a pretext for force in the eyes of American opinion. He links the assumption to the incorrect assertion that the Cabinet had approved collusion with Israel on 3 October to prove that Eden had accepted Macmillan's assessment of US support for the use of force and that the Anglo-American 'alliance' was beginning to collapse through misunderstandings.

In fact, Britain was ready to enter negotiations with Egypt for a peaceful settlement. Foreign Secretary Selwyn Lloyd told Cabinet ministers that it would be impossible to reject all proposals for genuine negotiations at the UN and that the 18-Power proposals for international control of the Canal, devised in August at the first London Conference, might have to be modified. Ministers considered a proposal by Indian Foreign Minister Krishna Menon for a co-operative arrangement between SCUA and Egypt. Eden told French Prime Minister Guy Mollet and Foreign Minister Christian Pineau that 'we cannot refuse to negotiate under the UN' and he overruled his Private Secretary's recommendation that 'introduction of a new [Egyptian] regime must not be long delayed'. When Egypt, Britain, and France started private negotiations, mediated by UN Secretary-General Dag Hammarskjold on 9 October, Eden endorsed Lloyd's effort to achieve a settlement. Told of Pineau's resistance to the negotiations, the Prime Minister cabled Lloyd, 'I know you will do your best to keep the French in line'. Dulles was also keeping a close eye on the situation. He had told Lloyd on 5 October, 'There must be some international participation in the operation of the Canal. . . . Every possible effort must be made to secure this objective by peaceful means and . . . the use of force would be a desperate remedy.'[15]

Neustadt's narrative is sabotaged by his misinterpretation of the events of early October. Ironically, it could be argued that the alleged Anglo-American 'alliance' had not broken down but had worked to avert an international crisis. It appeared in mid-October that Anglo-American collaboration, initially forced upon the British by military weakness, had helped prevent the transformation of the Suez crisis into war. Dulles and Eisenhower believed that their pressure upon Britain to refrain from military action had paid dividends. The President said on television on 12 October, 'It looks like here is a very great crisis behind us.'[16]

Neustadt, misled by incomplete or inaccurate information and limited by the narrow scope of his model, fails to recognize that any breakdown in the Anglo-American 'alliance', and indeed the whole mystery of the Suez collusion, lay in the events of 14 October. At 1.20p.m., Eden had cabled Lloyd. The Prime Minister approved of the final Anglo-French resolution, passed by the Security Council by a 9–2 vote but vetoed by the Soviet Union, which called for Egypt, the UK, and France to negotiate an arrangement for operation of the Canal based on the 'Six Principles' adopted earlier by the Security Council. He then asked:

> Should not we and the French now approach the Egyptians and ask them whether they are prepared to meet and discuss in confidence with us on the basis of the second half of the resolution which the Russians vetoed? If they say yes, then it is for consideration whether we and the French meet them somewhere, e.g. Geneva. If they say no, then they will be in defiance of the view of nine members of the Security Council and a new situation will arise.

Eden suggested meeting Pineau and Mollet on 16 October to discuss the matter. The Prime Minister, who had been told by the British military that an invasion of Egypt could not be launched until Spring 1957 if it did not occur before the end of October, had reconciled himself to a negotiated settlement.[17]

At 3p.m., however, Acting Foreign Minister Albert Gazier and General Maurice Challe, on Mollet's orders, arrived at Chequers to ask Eden about the British reaction to an Israeli attack upon Egypt. Eden 'could scarcely contain his glee' when Gazier assured him that the 1950 Tripartite Declaration, signed by France, the US, and Britain to halt any aggression by Israel against the Arab States or vice-versa, did not apply to Egypt, since Nasser had condemned the Declaration earlier in the year. The Prime Minister said, 'So that lets us off the hook. We have no obligation, it seems, to stop the Israelis attacking the Egyptians'. Challe then unveiled the plan for Israel to attack Egypt and for the British and French to land in the Canal Zone to 'separate' the combatants. Eden, visibly excited by the proposal, told the French that he would discuss the matter with Mollet on 16 October. Within two hours, negotiations with the Egyptians had been abandoned for collusion.[18]

The story of the Challe–Gazier mission raises two vital questions: first, why the French approached Eden on 14 October with the plot for collusion and, second, why Eden so quickly jettisoned negotiation in favour of an ill-conceived plan that fooled no-one and aroused the indignation of the US and the United Nations. Here, the shortcomings of Neustadt's model are exposed, for the catalyst of the collusion was not the Anglo-American 'alliance' but events in Jordan.

Most historians of Suez have overlooked the extraordinary situation which had developed on the Israel–Jordan and Jordan–Iraq borders in September and October 1956, a situation which put British bombers on alert to attack Israeli airfields and almost initiated the dissolution of Jordan. In mid-September, King Hussein, on a state visit to his cousin, King Feisal II of Iraq, suggested to Iraqi Prime Minister Nuri es-Sa'id that the Iraqis send a full army division into Jordan to defend it against a possible attack by Israel. Nuri was receptive to the idea but would agree only if Britain promised that it would defend Jordan against Israeli aggression under the 1948 Anglo-Jordanian Treaty. Three days later, the British Ambassador to Iraq, Michael Wright, confirmed, at a meeting with King Feisal, Iraqi Crown Prince Abdul Illah, Nuri and the Jordanian Foreign Minister, that Britain would defend Jordan with bombers, fighters, and ships, but not ground troops, to Jordan if Israel attacked.[19]

Meanwhile, Britain sought American support for this proposal. Initially, the State Department was cool to the idea because it feared Israel would oppose the deployment of Iraqi troops in Jordan, but Dulles told the British Ambassador to Washington, Sir Roger Makins, on 3 October that the Iraqi–Jordanian links were 'most encouraging . . . particularly as an opportunity to strike a blow at Nasser's prestige'. Assistant Secretary of State William Rountree explained that the Israeli Ambassador to the US, Abba Eban, had communicated the view of the Israeli Government that this was a good opportunity to split Jordan and Eqypt. Given advance notice of the deployment of a limited number of Iraqi troops without heavy equipment, at a distance from the Israeli border, Israel would raise no objections. Dulles authorized the US Ambassador to Israel, Edward Lawson, to approach Israeli Prime Minister David Ben-Gurion with the plan.[20]

On 6 October, Ben-Gurion requested further information on the size of the Iraqi force and an assurance that the troops would not be deployed near Israel. Lawson warned the State Department that the previous acceptance of Eban might be misleading, as it was based on information from Nuri that he would despatch only a token force of several hundred troops. The Counsellor of the US Embassy said, 'In the back of his mind, Mr. Ben-Gurion does not view with any happiness the prospect of a large force in Jordan'. The Foreign Office, however, downplayed Lawson's pessimism, since Iraq now planned to station only one battalion inside Jordan, keeping it far from Israel.[21]

At this point, diplomatic confusion caused an important delay. The State Department, under the impression that the Iraqi deployment was imminent, told Lawson to make no further approach to Israel before the British acted. The deployment had been delayed, however, by a dispute between the Iraqis and the Jordanians over command of the Iraqi forces. The British Chargé d'Affaires in Tel Aviv, Peter Westlake, asked the Foreign Office on 9 October if, in light of David Ben-Gurion's worries and the possibility of Israeli reprisals on the Jordanian frontier, Lawson could pass details of the Iraqi movement to Ben-Gurion. The Foreign Office replied on 10 October that Westlake's idea was sound but Nuri would have to be consulted.[22]

Events had overtaken the British. At 11.55p.m. on 10 October, 'very heavy Israeli artillery and mortar fire' started on a 12-mile front between the Jordanian villages of Qalqilya and Tul Karra. The US Army Attaché in Tel Aviv estimated that a full division of the Israeli Defence Force participated in the action, which killed 70 Jordanians and injured more than 40.[23]

This was the first time an Israeli force of such strength had been used for a 'reprisal' raid. The official Israeli justification for the raids, the murder of two Israeli farm labourers on 9 October and Hussein's release of the suspected killers of five Israeli workers in a 4 October attack, was a flimsy excuse. Hussein had released the alleged murderers for lack of evidence, a judgement accepted by British representatives and UN observers. The organization of the strike and its size suggest a deeper political motive than simple retaliation against Jordanian *fedayeen*. Israel had given fair warning to the French, through its Ambassador in Paris and to the Americans, through Meir, that its patience with the Iraqis and the Jordanians was running out. On 9 October, Meir told Lawson that Israel's conditional agreement to the Iraqi troop move had been withdrawn because of a statement by Nuri, published in *The Times* two days earlier, that Israel should accept a frontier settlement based on borders set by the United Nations in 1947. Such a settlement would involve cession of territory under Israeli control. Meir added, 'Mr. Ben-Gurion's assurances were in abeyance until an assurance could be given that Iraqi troop movements were not connected with an Iraqi–British programme of forcing territorial concessions on Israel.'[24]

It is possible that the Israeli attack was a prelude to an attempt to annex part of Jordan, notably the land on the west bank of the Jordan River. The US, after a high-level meeting including Eisenhower, set out a memorandum of policy accepting the partition of Jordan between Israel and Iraq after Eban told Dulles on the morning of 15 October that '[we] think Jordan is breaking up, and it is a question of grabbing the pieces'. The *Jerusalem Post*, recognized as the voice of the Israeli Government, had argued on 14 October, 'From the British point of view, the bringing of Iraqi troops into Jordan is an insurance that the rapidly disintegrating puppet state she had set up will not fall to the Egyptians when its inevitable end comes about, but to a member of the British [camp]'. On the same day, a 'reliable informant' told the British Consulate in Jerusalem that the Israeli Cabinet had taken a 'very grave decision unanimously. . . . The Cabinet was influenced by the information that she had obtained from Her Majesty's Chargé [Westlake] about the number of Iraqi troops and their length of stay in Jordan'. Another informant added that 'Israel intended to take part of the West Bank from Ramallah to Nablus and the north.'[25]

It is equally possible that the Israelis planned Qalqilya to scare the French into an approach to the British, who had refused to collaborate with Israel over action against Nasser. Paris knew that an Israeli invasion of Jordan might precipitate a war between Israel and Britain because of the 1948 Anglo-Jordanian Treaty. Anglo-French and Franco-Israeli plans to topple Nasser would be suspended. To prevent this, Mollet ordered Gazier and Challe to travel to London to see Eden on 14 October.

It is notable that Gazier opened the talks with Eden with a discussion of the situation in Jordan. He said France was 'extremely anxious' about hostile Israeli reactions to the Iraqi move. Adding that Britain was playing with fire, as the Israelis were 'highly nervous', Gazier asked if Eden wished to provoke the situation. The Prime Minister, cutting off the objections of Anthony Nutting, the Minister of State at the Foreign Office, said he would ask Nuri to suspend the deployment temporarily.

Only after Gazier had received this assurance did he ask Eden about the British reaction to an Israeli attack on Egypt, prompting the Prime Minister to abandon negotiations with the Egyptians. Less than 48 hours after the meeting with the French, the Prime Minister issued orders for the Iraqi troop move to be suspended indefinitely, told Lloyd that there was no future in talks with Egypt, and went with the Foreign Secretary to Paris for discussions with Mollet and Pineau. It was at this point that the Anglo-American 'alliance' was circumvented, as France, Britain, and Israel eventually agreed on 24 October to a tripartite attack against Egypt. Five days later, Israeli troops launched the Suez war with their invasion of the Sinai Peninsula.[26]

Conclusions

The main objections to the application of Neustadt's model of alliance politics to Suez are, first, that any 'alliance' of British and American policies in the Middle East was conditional upon the temporary convergence of differing British and American interests in the area and, second, that decisions of policymakers such as Eden were shaped not only by Anglo-American relations but also by regional matters in the Middle East and by the influence of other countries, notably France and Israel. Both rest upon an inescapable flaw: the bipolar model is a 'closed' model, for it can only work if it can exclude the influence of other countries upon the interests, policies, and actions of the two systems analysed by the model.

If one assumes that a policymaker is motivated by self-interest and that he evaluates his options on the basis of that interest, given available information, then Neustadt's central thesis of 'alliance' as the interaction of machines with self-interested 'players' in London and Washington is a tautology. Likewise, Neustadt's four common 'aspects' of the British and American systems are merely definitions of the elements which exist in any bureaucratic government with legislative and executive components directly or indirectly responsible to the public. By restricting his model to include only these elements and only the British and American systems, Neustadt can create an artificial scenario of 'alliance'. Any breakdown in Anglo-American relations has to be due to the failure of policymakers to perceive the influence upon and positions of other policymakers or the failure to communicate information about those influences and positions, since all other possibilities lie outside of Neustadt's framework.

Such a model isolates the systems in London and Washington from the effects of other systems. It assumes that the motive of 'self-interest' is defined for players within each of the systems and that it takes no account of influences or events outside the Anglo-American 'action channels'. To defend this assumption, Neustadt asserts that the maintenance of 'alliance' is above all other political considerations, so it is the overriding self-interest of each official to preserve Anglo-American ties.

Unfortunately for the model, this condition is not necessarily true. 'Alliance' is not an objective term. It is conditioned upon the interests of the two governments, i.e. the interests of the 'players', in question. If both are served by allied action or policy, all is well; if not, the 'alliance' exists only in name.

An 'alliance' is much easier to sustain given a common threat to the two governments, as in World War II, a situation where one country has substantial interests but the other does not, or dependence of one country upon the other for goods or financial aid. Where none of the above conditions exists, 'alliance' can no longer be confined to a bipolar model. Either country may shape its policy and reach its interests through independent action or accords with other governments. In these cases, the actions of third, fourth, or fifth governments, not considered by Neustadt's model, may set the interests and thus the policies of the 'allied' governments against each other.

Such was the case with Suez in 1956. Both the US and Britain had substantial interests, which did not coincide, in the Middle East. Given the common threat of Nasser, the two countries had agreed in March 1956 to a plan of action which would isolate the Egyptian leader. This conditional 'alliance' almost dissolved after Nasser's nationalization of the Suez Canal. Eden wished to use military force to topple Nasser, but the Americans, believing the Canal issue was an unsuitable pretext for overt action and concerned about its relations with Arab states, preferred to continue with the long-term covert effort.

The 'alliance' was maintained only by the coincidence that Britain did not have the military strength to launch an immediate attack upon Egypt. Instead, there was a constant interchange of views and plans between Dulles and Lloyd, supplemented by the correspondence between Eisenhower and Eden. The Prime Minister, anxious to retain American diplomatic and financial support while Britain was readying its forces, agreed to the American call for a peaceful settlement. Ironically, when Britain and France were finally prepared for an assault, Eden could not renounce the diplomatic measures and had to postpone military action. By mid-October, he faced a situation where he either attacked Egypt or abandoned the Anglo-French plans for a quick strike against Cairo.

Although Eden was probably advised by Macmillan, that British oil supplies and the pound sterling could withstand the invasion of Egypt and that the Americans would not oppose force, he was unwilling, on that information alone, to risk the use of force without a further incentive for action. That incentive was provided, not by an Anglo-American misunderstanding, but by the French, who revealed their collusion with the Israelis after the Israeli–Jordanian border crisis threatened to erupt into war.

Neustadt's model of alliance politics establishes a framework for the actors and mechanisms of a static two-nation system. It cannot adequately evaluate the operation of an 'alliance' in a crisis situation nor can it serve as a predictive mdoel for the current conduct of international relations in a multilateral world. If Neustadt has traced some of the patterns of relations between Washington and London, he ignores many others caused by 'regional' influences and events that lie outside his Anglo-American axis. By doing so, he blinds himself to the circumstances that may again arise to trouble the Anglo-American relationship.

Notes

[PRO refers to documents found in the Public Record Office, Kew, Surrey, United Kingdom. DDE refers to documents found in the Dwight D. Eisenhower Presidential Library, Abilene, Kansas, USA.]

1. See W.S. Lucas, 'The Path to Suez: Britain and the Struggle for the Middle East', in A. Deighton (ed), *Britain and the First Cold War*, Harmondsworth, Macmillan, 1989. For US policy regarding the Turkish-Pakistani Agreement and military aid to Iraq and Pakistan, see *Foreign Relations of the United States (FRUS)*, 1952–4, vol IX, 419–97, and vol XI, 1830–45.

    For US relations with Egypt and the Anglo-Egyptian negotiations, see *FRUS*, 1952–4, vol IX, 2072ff.

    For covert US attempts to provide military aid to Egypt, see W. Eveland, *Ropes of Sand: America's Failure in the Middle East*, London, W.W. Norton, 1980, 91ff; M. Copeland, *The Game of Nations*, London, Weidenfeld and Nicolson, 1969, 123ff. Both accounts are verified by unpublished US documents.

2. For Anglo-American relations over the Baghdad Pact, see PRO, FO371/115484-115533 (V1073 series of 1955).

    For the British attempt to bring Jordan into the Pact, see PRO, FO371/115652-115659 (VJ1051 series of 1955).

3. Throughout 1955 and early 1956, an Anglo-American effort to bring an Arab–Israeli settlement, the first step being an Egyptian–Israeli peace treaty, was co-ordinated between London and Washington. The project was codenamed 'ALPHA'. See PRO, FO371/115864-115887 (VR1076 series of 1955).

    Anglo-American discussions, launched in March 1956, on a comprehensive Middle Eastern policy included measures to isolate Nasser in the region and finally remove him from power. The project was codenamed 'OMEGA'. References to the discussion are not in a central file available to the public but are scattered throughout documents in the PRO. The most concise description of the measures and objectives of OMEGA is in a 28 March 1956 memorandum, later adopted as US Government policy, by John Foster Dulles. See DDE, Ann Whitman Series, DDE Diaries Subseries, Box 13, March 1956 Diary.

4. For information on the plot against Syria, see A. Gorst and W.S. Lucas, 'The other "collusion": Anglo-American intervention in Syria, 1955–1956,' *Intelligence and National Security*, (1989).

5. DDE, Ann Whitman Series, Dulles-Herter Subseries, John Foster Dulles, Box 5, August 1956 (1), Dulles note to Eisenhower, 31 August 1956.

6. References to the Anglo–French discussions are scattered throughout PRO documents. The decision not to inform the US of Anglo-French military planning is in PRO, PREM11/1176. Operations PILEUP and CONVOY, designed to block the Suez Canal through an overload of traffic and use the British Navy to escort Western shipping through the Canal, are in PRO, CAB134/1216, Egypt Committee (56) 28th and 29th meetings, 14 and 17 September.

7. Extensive Israeli accounts of the Franco-Israeli ties are in M. Bar-Zohar, *Ben-Gurion*, London, Barker, 1978, and M. Dayan, *Story of My Life*, London,

Weidenfeld and Nicolson, 1976. The most complete French account is in A. Thomas, *Comment Israel Fut Sauve*, Paris, A. Michel, 1978.

8. Bar-Zohar, 227–32; Dayan, 149–54 and 158–64; Thomas, 112–14 and 145–54.

9. PRO, CAB128/29, C.M.34(55).

10. Macmillan report to Eden, 26 September 1956, PRO, PREM11/1102; PRO, PREM11/1102, Washington to Foreign Office, Cable 2000, 25 September 1956; author's interview with Lord Sherfield (Roger Makins), April 1987; DDE, Ann Whitman Series, DDE Diaries, Box 18, September 1956 phone calls, Dulles call to Eisenhower, 25 September 1956.

11. See footnotes 18–16.

12. PRO, CAB128/30, C.M.74(56).

13. PRO, CAB134/1216, Egypt Committee (56) 26th Meeting, 10 September; PRO, FO371/119191-119208 (JE14216 series of 1956); PRO, PREM11/1121.

14. PRO, CAB134/1216, Egypt Committee (56) 28th and 29th Meetings, 14 and 17 September 1956.

15. PRO, CAB134/1216, Egypt Committee (56) 34th and 35th Meetings, 10 and 17 October 1956; PRO, PREM11/1102, Bishop to Prime Minister draft minute and Prime Minister's revision, 26 September 1956; PRO, PREM11/1102, Foreign Office to New York, Cable 1125, 11 October 1956.

16. *New York Times*, 13 October 1956.

17. PRO, PREM11/1102, Foreign Office to New York, Cable 1198, 14 October 1956.

18. The best version of the 14 October meeting, verified by separate accounts and unpublished documents, is in Anthony Nutting, *No End of a Lesson*, London, Constable, 1967, 90ff.

19. PRO, FO371/121486/VJ10393/60, Baghdad to Foreign Office, Cable 1048, 15 September 1956; PRO, FO371/121486/VJ10393/69G, Baghdad to Foreign Office, Cable 1097, 27 September 1956, and Foreign Office to Baghdad, Cables 1948 and 1949, 28 September 1956; PRO/121486/VJ10393/72G, Baghdad to Foreign Office, Cable 1110, 29 September 1956.

20 PRO, FO371/121487/VJ10393/82, Washington to Foreign Office, Cable 2053, 3 October 1956.

21. PRO, FO371/121487/VJ10393/101, Tel Aviv to Foreign Office, Cable 467, 6 October 1956.

22. PRO, FO371/121487/VJ10393/109, Tel Aviv to Foreign Office, Cable 471, 9 October 1956, and Foreign Office to Baghdad, Cable 2077, 10 October 1956.

23. United States National Archives, Washington, DC, Records of the Joint Chiefs of Staff, Record Group 218, Geographical File 1954–56, Box 11A, EMMEA (11-19-47), S. 45, Collins memorandum to Radford, 11 October 1956.

24. PRO, FO371/121780/VR1091/297, Washington to Foreign Office, Cable 2096, 10 October 1956; PRO, FO371/121780/VR1091/296, Paris to Foreign Office, Cable 360, 10 October 1956.

25. PRO, FO371/121780/VR1091/321, Tel Aviv to Foreign Office, Cable 491, 14 October 1956; PRO, FO371/121780/VR1091/320, Jerusalem to Foreign Office, Cable 385, 15 October 1956; DDE, John Foster Dulles Series, Telephone Calls Subseries, Box 15, 1 October to 29 December 1956, John Foster Dulles call to Allen Dulles, 15 October 1956; DDE, Ann Whitman Series, Dulles-Herter

Subseries, John Foster Dulles, Box 2, October 1956 (2), 'U.S. Opportunities in the Middle East,' undated.

26. Footnote 19; PRO, FO371/121488/VJ10393/134G, Foreign Office to Baghdad, Cable 2152, 14 October 1956.

References

Allison, G. (1971), *Essence of Decision*, Boston, Little and Brown.

Bar-Zohar, M. (1978), *Ben-Gurion*, London, Barker.

Copeland, M. (1969), *The Game of Nations*, London, Weidenfeld and Nicolson.

Dayan, M. (1976), *Story of My Life*, London, Weidenfeld and Nicolson.

Deighton, A. (1989), *Brtain and the First Cold War*, London, Macmillan.

Eveland, W. (1980), *Ropes of Sand: America's Failure in the Middle East*, London, W.W. Norton.

Gorst, A. and Lucas, W.S. (1988), 'Suez 1956: Strategy and the Diplomatic Process', *Journal of Strategic Studies*, December 1988.

Louis, W. (1984), *The British Empire in the Middle East, 1945–1951*, Oxford University Press.

Lucas, W.S. (1989), 'The Path to Suez: Britain and the Struggle for the Middle East' in A. Deighton (ed), *Britain and the First Cold War*, Harmondsworth, Macmillan.

McGhee, G. (1983), *Envoy to the Middle World: Adventures in Diplomacy*, New York, Harper and Row.

Neustadt, R. (1970), *Alliance Politics*, New York, Columbia University Press.

Nutting, A. (1967), *No End of a Lesson*, London, Constable.

Thomas, A. (1978), *Comment Israel fut Sauve*, Paris, A. Michel.

US Department of State. *Foreign Relations of the United States*, Washington, Government Printing Office, various dates.

12 Brothers in arms: Anglo–American defence co-operation in 1957

G. Wyn Rees

This paper aims to explore the nature of the defence relationship between Great Britain and the United States in 1957, from the perspective of the British Chiefs of Staff (COS). This year was of particular importance because it marked both a quantitative as well as qualitative change in the co-operation between the two countries. Yet 1957 would not have appeared at the time to be an auspicious year for such an improvement, as relations between the two countries had reached a very low ebb by the end of the preceding year. The Suez operation of 1956 had caused a deep rift between Britain and the United States and raised a question mark over the trustworthiness of America as an ally. In addition to this, the year began with Britain reducing her forces, both conventional and nuclear, in order to achieve financial savings. The Sandys review 'Defence: Outline of Future Policy'[1] seemed to decrease the likelihood of closer defence co-operation with the United States as it led to cuts throughout the spectrum of British military capabilities. Despite this background, however, by the end of 1957 co-operation was flourishing between the two countries. The first significant steps were taken at the Bermuda Conference in March and then further advances followed from the Washington Conference in October. Britain had secured the sort of special relationship in the defence field that she had long sought with the United States and this relationship was to deepen still further in later years.

In order to understand why Britain was so eager to secure co-operation with the United States, it is necessary to investigate the perceived threats to the country's security at this time. The Chiefs of Staff Committee was the body with the task of assessing this threat and passing recommendations to the politicians. From an understanding of the threat, it will be possible to appreciate the importance of the United States to military planning and outline the means by which the Chiefs sought to establish co-operation with their trans-Atlantic cousins.

The nature of the threat

To the Chiefs of Staff in 1957, security was not a concept limited to the territorial defence of the United Kingdom but rather a global defence concept that extended to major overseas interests. The only direct military threat to the home base was posed by the Soviet Union and it was believed to be necessary to participate in a collective security arrangement, the North Atlantic Treaty Organisation, to counteract this threat. Outside Europe, Britain had colonial and Commonwealth interests which were likely targets for aggression sponsored either by the Soviet Union or one of her satellites. There were also many states, not directly within the British sphere of interest but nevertheless favourable to the West, which the Chiefs of Staff did not wish to be taken over by hostile neighbours. To protect these overseas interests, Britain contributed to a number of alliance systems that opposed Communist infiltration or outside aggression. The South East Asia Treaty Organisation was seen to resist principally a Chinese threat in the Far East whilst the Baghdad Pact resisted Soviet hostility in the Middle East. The ANZAM Treaty, in which Australia, New Zealand and Britain were pledged to the defence of Malaya, was an example of one of the extraordinary commitments that Britain maintained outside the main alliance systems, and contributed to the feeling, amongst defence planners, that Britain held a special status. The Chiefs of Staff therefore identified a variety of threats to a wide spectrum of British interests.

These threats existed at two different levels. The first level was total war, which would be fought against the Soviet Union and would be global in its coverage. The chiefs foresaw that such a conflict would inevitably involve the use of nuclear weapons. Even if the Soviets did not employ nuclear weapons in the first place, the West would be forced to attack Soviet cities with such weapons in order to offset the enemy's superiority in conventional forces. Britain herself would be highly vulnerable to devastation by hydrogen weapons due to her small size and concentrated population and the chances of recovery from such an attack would be small. Britain contributed forces to NATO under the assumption that a war in which NATO was involved would be global and that nuclear weapons would be used. As a Chiefs of Staff paper stated in 1957: 'There is no conception in NATO of graduated deterrence, of war limited in weapons used, or of war limited in aims or by boundaries'.[2] The threat of total war to Britain's overseas interests was accorded a lower priority as the principal damage would be done to the UK itself and the chances of being able to reinforce distant theatres after nuclear bombardment, were judged to be small.

Below the level of total war, the Chiefs recognized that wars could occur in geographically circumscribed areas due to outside aggression or internal disintegration. Such limited wars threatened all Britain's overseas interests and the Chiefs feared that if one state in a region was to become a victim, then a whole series of other states could fall in rapid succession. The key to preventing such an occurrence was for the West to promise support to the underdeveloped world to give them confidence to resist intimidation. Such support would also be valuable for territories attempting to combat internal subversion that might be sponsored by the Soviet Union, China or a proxy state. The fear was that Communism would feed, like a disease, upon internal weakness and therefore regimes had to be supported with whatever aid was necessary to prevent their collapse. The Chiefs recognized that Britain might have to fight a limited war overseas, with or without the assistance of allies. The Suez experience had demonstrated the difficulty of conducting large scale operations at long distances from the UK as well as the growing sophistication of potential opponents who might receive military equipment from the Soviet Union.

In order to combat these levels of threat, the Chiefs of Staff developed a concept of defence that was based upon three tiers.[3] At the top would be an Allied deterrent force that would dissuade the Soviet Union from embarking upon total war. As no credible defence was possible from nuclear bombardment, the British believed that only the threat of retaliation could deter attack. This retaliation would have to be overwhelming in capability and directed at the sources of power within the Soviet Union, to ensure that the costs to the aggressor would clearly outweigh any possible gains. In the unlikely event of such a war breaking out, conventional forces in NATO and the other alliance systems would provide a token level of resistance whilst awaiting the impact of thermonuclear retaliation against the Soviet heartland. The Chiefs felt it necessary for Britain to contribute to the main Allied deterrent, the bulk of which was provided by the United States.

The second and third tiers of defence were those forces committed to the defence of overseas areas. The second tier was made up of mobile forces based in the United Kingdom that could be transported rapidly overseas. This capability would be employed in limited wars as a sort of fire brigade that could be deployed to a state in an emergency, to resist outside aggression and strengthen the indigenous forces. These were also the forces that Britain pledged to the support of the major alliances, SEATO, the Baghdad Pact and ANZAM. The third tier was made up of small garrisons that Britain maintained in her colonies. These garrisons were not considered to be large enough to cope with major external threats but were thought to be important in maintaining the cohesion of small states and demonstrating Britain's intention to aid them if attacked. Such forces would form the first line of defence against subversion and could hold the situation whilst reinforcements were transported from the United Kingdom.

In the face of such a variety of threats to interests that were defined globally, the Chiefs of Staff recognized that Britain could not combat these threats alone. Britain lacked the resources to fund a global defence policy as well as the manpower to carry it out. In the White Paper of April 1957, the

Defence Minister made it clear that Britain was allocating too large a percentage of her national wealth to defence and major economies of spending would have to be made.[4] Within the tiers of defence concept put forward by the Chiefs, none of the three tiers could adequately be met by British forces alone and it was acknowledged that the help of allies would have to be sought in the event of an emergency. In attempting to deter global war, the Chiefs were of the opinion that the emerging British nuclear force was not sufficient in itself but could only act as part of an allied force. Similarly, British forces were spread thinly around the world in states that were vulnerable to attack by hostile neighbours; the ability to reinforce areas with UK reserves might be limited by the lack of transport aircraft or over flying rights. With insufficient resources available to Britain, the Chiefs of Staff looked to the United States for assistance.

An unequal partnership

It is not difficult to understand why the British turned to the United States to help solve their problems. The United States, of all Britain's allies, was the country endowed with the military and economic strength to underpin Britain's defence effort. America was the foremost nuclear power in the world, the backbone of the Western Alliance and possessed a capability to project military power overseas. It was therefore vital in the eyes of the Chiefs of Staff to develop defence co-operation with the United States in order to influence American policy in line with British interests. The British looked back with nostalgia to the years of the Second World War when defence co-operation between the two countries had been at its height and Churchill and Roosevelt had maintained a very close personal friendship. Yet Suez had shattered the basic assumption that British and American interests would always be identical and ended the confidence of the Chiefs in relying on American support. By putting pressure on sterling in international currency markets and temporarily blocking the passage of loans, the Americans exposed the economic weakness of the United Kingdom. The Chiefs emerged from the Suez debacle with a determination not to seek greater independence, as might have been expected, but rather to seek closer co-operation with their Atlantic partner in order to avoid such a split ever recurring. They realised how dependent future overseas operations would be upon American support and resolved to tie Britain more closely to the United States. The relationship would have to be nurtured in future and Britain would have to prove she had something special to contribute.[5]

The Chiefs of Staff were clear about the types of military co-operation they desired from the United States in 1957. As a global power, they believed Britain could offer the United States the ability to consider strategy on a worldwide basis. As Sir William Dickson, Chairman of the Chiefs of Staff Committee, declared:

We and the Americans were the only two powers with global interests and this aspect ought to be stressed as a reason for discussing defence matters with the Americans outside Treaty alliances.[6]

The Chiefs also believed that Britain's status as a nuclear power and her sharing of membership of all the major alliances with the United States, conferred upon this country the right to special consultations. If necessary these consultations might be conducted in secret, outside alliance forums, between representatives of the British and American governments only. The Chiefs wished for joint planning to be undertaken between the two countries, the co-ordination of offensive operations and information from the Americans on their contingency plans for less important theatres of war. The British thought that through consultation with their American colleagues, the Joint Chiefs of Staff, British interests could be placed upon the US agenda. This might help to prevent aberrations in American policy that would be prejudicial to European interests, such as a change in the American commitment to keep forces on the continent. With American scientists pressing forward on the development of inter-continental ballistic missiles (ICBMs), it could not be taken for granted that forces would be maintained in Western Europe in the future.[7]

The desire for close co-operation with the United States raised deeper and more fundamental questions for the United Kingdom. The Chiefs had to ask themselves what sort of a relationship would be the result if these policies reached fruition; would Britain become interdependent with the US in military policy and, if so, would all Britain's interests be catered for satisfactorily, by such an arrangement? The Chiefs never fully resolved these issues in 1957 because the Americans refused to enter into a genuinely co-operative relationship until towards the end of the year. The Americans were not prepared, at first, to grant the British such a special status in defence planning, preferring instead to deal with countries through the collective security organizations. They distrusted British colonial policy and feared that collaboration would ultimately lead to American forces propping up British overseas interests. It was not until the time of the Washington Conference in October 1957, that the British felt that the situation had changed sufficiently for them to discuss the issue of a joint defence policy between the two countries.[8]

Problems experienced by the Chiefs of Staff in securing co-operation with the United States brought home the realization that such a policy objective had certain costs as well as benefits. Britain would have to be prepared to follow the American lead in areas of the world where American interests did not necessarily coincide with those of the British. This might prove particularly problematical in relation to overseas dependencies and Commonwealth interests that Britain regarded as special responsibilities of her own. There was also room for disagreement between the respective Services of the two countries over the likely course of a future war. Elements within the American Armed Services believed that a war in which NATO was involved would not necessarily escalate to the use of thermonuclear weapons and there was a possibility of keeping such a war limited in intensity.[9] Furthermore, the US Navy pressed the view that even if global war did occur, the nuclear phase might be of prolonged duration[10] and NATO might have to fight on after this phase with conventional weapons. This was a contradiction of the British position. The Chiefs maintained that a war against the Soviet Union would inevitably be nuclear and that this phase would be short, intense and decisive. Such debates as were provoked by the American view, encouraged the Services in Britain to press their own sectional interests to gain resources for additional roles and missions. There were thus a number of ways in which co-operation with the United States could prove costly to Britain.

As areas of interest could still diverge in future and because the Americans demonstrated reluctance to co-operate, the Chiefs had to decide whether a capability to act independently was essential. The United States did not need Britain as much as Britain needed her and it could therefore be seen as dangerous to rely solely upon the American's goodwill. In the belief system of the Chiefs of Staff, the essence of military power was to offer options to decision-makers and they disliked the prospect of limiting Britain's flexibility in any regard. Even Prime Minister Harold Macmillan, who was the warmest advocate of co-operation with the United States, held the view that a minimum nuclear capability should be retained and conventional forces must be able to intervene on an independent basis in one of the colonial territories. It was difficult to forecast how American policies might change in the future and therefore the nucleus of an independent conventional and nuclear force was considered prudent. This was not thought to be incompatible with efforts to gain the maximum amount of co-operation with the United States.

The Chiefs of Staff can therefore be seen to be clear about what they wanted from the United States; namely full defence co-operation and joint planning. However, they were not clear about the means by which they could achieve these aims for, owing to the disparity in resources between the two countries, Britain was in a weak negotiating position with the United States. The Chiefs also failed to think through the implications of their policy objectives; for instance, the extent to which foreign policy interests would have to be harmonized before Britain could relinquish her ability to act independently with military forces. As co-operation between the two countries did begin to deepen, policymakers had to face up to these sorts of issues. Nowhere was this more apparent than in the nuclear relationship that blossomed towards the end of 1957.

Nuclear defence co-operation

The Chiefs of Staff accorded the highest priority to obtaining nuclear co-operation with the United States. This area became the locomotive for the whole of the defence relationship for the British believed that if they could establish co-operation here, then other areas of exchange would naturally fall into place. This was because nuclear weapons were regarded as the most important weapons in a state's armoury and they comprised the foundation of the Western deterrent against the Soviet Union. In the Defence White Paper of 1957 it was acknowledged that there could be no defence against nuclear bombardment and therefore the only strategy that would deter aggression would be a strategy based on the threat to retaliate with nuclear weapons. Britain was a firm advocate of the strategy of 'Massive Retaliation' that had been adopted by the United States in 1954. In fact, the British re-think of strategy in 1952, embodied in the Global Strategy Paper, had probably helped to influence American thinking in this regard.

There was no doubt in British minds as to why co-operation with the US in nuclear matters would be of great benefit to this country. The Americans were the foremost nuclear power in the world in 1957, with the Strategic Air Command providing the backbone of the Allied deterrent. She was also far ahead of all other states in the technology of fabricating nuclear devices, stockpiling weapons and the sophistication of delivery vehicles. The United States had been the sole provider of the nuclear deterrent until 1955 when the first VALIANTS of RAF Bomber Command entered operational service. Co-operation between the two countries could secure substantial benefits to the UK such as the provision of information about weapon designs and the loan of bombs until the British indigenous programme could satisfy the requirements of the full V-bomber force.[11] The Chiefs also wished to purchase tactical nuclear weapons, such as the CORPORAL missile, from the United States as it was not anticipated that Britain could develop such weapons by herself before the early 1960s. For Britain, with her extensive interests overseas, American nuclear forces could provide the basis of the deterrent against the Soviet Union in the Middle East and Asia, as well as in Western Europe.

The key objective for the British was to gain influence in the planning process for the employment of American nuclear forces. After all, to influence the Americans was to influence NATO as the United States was the most powerful member of the Alliance. The Chiefs of Staff did not wish to see the Americans plan independently for the use of their airpower in wartime and desired a voice for British officials in the formulation of targeting policy. The British felt that the Americans were less experienced in the art of using force for political ends and sought to obtain an ability to restrain American zeal. The experience of Korea was still vivid in British minds, when Prime Minister Clement Attlee had rushed to Washington in

December 1950, to forestall the feared use of atomic weapons against China. The Chiefs were also eager to co-ordinate the strategic offensive between the two countries to prevent the omission or duplication of targets. There would be targets within the Soviet Union that it would be urgent for Britain to destroy, particularly submarine bases and airfields that might be used by the Soviet Union to strike this country. As the United States would not necessarily share the same priorities in their targeting programme, it was imperative for the British to find out the precise nature of the American plans. As an Air Ministry Note for the preceding year had recognized:

> It has been calculated that there are many hundreds of targets to attack, and the Americans will not necessarily be most interested in those targets which most closely affect the UK capacity to survive.[12]

The Chiefs of Staff had pressed the idea of integrated nuclear planning upon their American colleagues for many years before 1957.[13] The Joint Planning Staff had recommended to the COS in July 1955, that a unified military authority should be established to manage the British and American nuclear forces, according this country an equal status in the planning and targeting of the nuclear strike. The British were prepared to conduct such co-operation on a covert basis outside the perimeters of the major alliances. However, until the latter part of 1957 the US rejected such attempts to integrate strategic planning. The McMahon Act of 1946 limited the co-operation that could be undertaken in the field of nuclear energy and the Joint Committee on Atomic Energy (JCAE) maintained supervision over the transference of sensitive information abroad. Many Congressmen and senior military officers in the United States were opposed to granting Britain a preferential nuclear relationship for it appeared to offer little benefit to the US yet threatened to place relationships with other allies at risk (Botti 1987: 80–203). The British came to see the repeal of the McMahon Act as a top priority, almost a symbol of American good faith towards Britain. President Eisenhower, a well known friend of Britain, had made an attempt to improve the level of co-operation in August 1954 by passing the Atomic Energy Act. This authorized the release of intelligence on the nuclear capabilities of the USSR and on information for training allies in the use of atomic weapons but fell short of providing Britain with data on American targeting or the circumstances under which weapons would be used. Britain was therefore to be found at the outset of 1957 striving to broaden the level of co-operation with the Americans.

In order to improve co-operation, the Chiefs of Staff adopted policies that were designed to convince the Americans that it was in their own best interests to treat Britain preferentially. These policies included the acceptance of American Intermediate Range Ballistic Missiles (IRBMs) on UK soil and the contribution of a British nuclear force to the overall Allied deterrent. The acceptance of US Air Force THOR missiles in the United Kingdom was a policy designed to demonstrate that Britain was a trustworthy ally of the United States and was willing to provide additional real estate to that which was already enjoyed by American aircraft that were forward based in Europe. Such bases were vital for THOR whose limited range precluded its being stationed in the United States. In March 1957 Eisenhower met Macmillan at Bermuda and forged the outline of an agreement for the basing of 60 missiles in the United Kingdom under a dual-key arrangement. Britain thereby maximized her links with the US and provided a veto over the use of these systems, earning a place for herself in American eyes as a special partner. As Rosencrance and Dawson have argued, the best way to ensure consultation by a partner is to make that consultation necessary (Rosencrance and Dawson, 1966: 41).

The second strand of COS policy was to build an indigenous force within Britain which would play a role in the nuclear offensive against the Soviet Union. This was based upon the belief that only when Britain could offer a meaningful contribution to the Allied force would the United States be willing to share its nuclear secrets with its ally. Lawrence Martin comments:

> Nuclear forces were thought to increase positive influence over the U.S. by undertaking a share in the task of deterrence and demonstrating technological skill.
>
> (Martin, 1962: 27)

Yet to argue that the V-Bomber force could buy Britain influence in Washington was to assume that it was possible to gauge the size of force that the Americans would consider worthwhile. It also assumed Britain would have the resources to fund such a force. Harold Macmillan in his previous job as Chancellor had argued on financial grounds that the V-force should be no larger than the minimum required to convince the Americans of Britain's 'sincerity' as allies.[14] In the event, a debate ensued between the Air Ministry and the Ministry of Defence over the proposed size of the British strategic nuclear force and the issue was finally resolved by economic criteria. The completion of the Sandys Review led to a force of 184 aircraft being decided upon as the figure for the British deterrent (Navias, 1988).

Therein lay a deeper question for the British Chiefs of Staff: to what extent should Britain rely upon the United States for the Western deterrent? If, for instance, the V-bomber force was merely a ticket to gaining influence in Washington, then a strong case could be made that once this influence had been established, it would be possible for Britain to relinquish its independent capability. After all, the resources saved in this way could be put towards much-needed conventional forces. In October 1957 Sir Gerald Templer, Chief of the Imperial General Staff, discussed the possibility of giving up the deterrent due to the pressing resource constraints that Britain faced.[15] Britain was by this time an important target for Soviet nuclear forces by virtue of American nuclear bases alone. Writers such as James Cable have argued that Britain was moving inexorably into a dependency relationship with the United States and the logical conclusion of British policy was to rely totally upon American nuclear protection (Cable, 1983).

Yet the COS never believed that the securing of co-operation with the United States would obviate the requirement for an independent national capability. The Chiefs held the view that Britain must retain the ability to produce her own independent force, that the US should not be the sole provider of the Allied deterrent. In the opinion of the RAF, a deterrent force was the symbol of supreme military power and an instrument that provided Britain with a measure of independence from its allies.[16] With the explosion of Britain's first hydrogen bomb in May 1957, there was a psychological benefit for British statesmen in knowing that they shared the ultimate weapon with the US. Although the Chiefs never regarded the British deterrent as sufficient in its own right, it was nevertheless a powerful force that could act as a last line of insurance if the Americans failed to honour their pledge to the Alliance in an emergency. When Charles Wilson, the US Defence Secretary discussed his country's intention to deploy IRBMs to the UK,[17] the British did not cancel the development of their own ballistic missile, BLUE STREAK. Rather, they concluded that the cancellation of BLUE STREAK would preclude the UK from acquiring ballistic missile technology and it was therefore necesary to continue with the national project until Britain could replace the THORS with her own IRBMs. As Duncan Sandys made clear in his speeches, American intentions could change in the future and in such an issue of national survival, nothing could be left to chance. In a House of Commons speech of April 1957 he declared:

> It is just as well to make certain that an appreciable element of nuclear power will, in all circumstances, remain on this side of the Atlantic, so that no one might be tempted to think that a major attack could be made against Western Europe without the risk of nuclear retaliation.[18]

The cruel irony for the British was that to maintain a national force, the high cost and rapid technological change in the field of nuclear weapons pushed Britain towards seeking assistance from the United States. The Americans had already covered much of the ground that the British were hoping to explore in 1957 and with their vastly greater resources, could offer savings in time and money to the British research and development programme. Of particular concern to the Chiefs was the choice of a successor system to the V-bombers and since 1954, Britain had been developing a supersonic aircraft as well as a ballistic missile to provide insurance against a gap developing in the deterrent force. The Sandys Review led to the termination of the aircraft project, the AVRO 730 on financial grounds, and reliance was placed upon BLUE STREAK alone, to replace the V-force in the 1960s. In depending upon a single system, the Chiefs were eager to gain technological assistance with this project from American companies as well as financial aid from the Eisenhower administration. As usual, the British had little to offer in return for assistance with their national programmes, other than to claim that the resources saved would be spent elsewhere in the defence of the Western hemisphere. Britain was therefore to be found pressing for co-operation in the midst of her national effort, apparently reinforcing the point that any independent project would require aid from the resources of a superpower in order to prevent its obsolescence before it entered operational service.

The watershed in nuclear co-operation came with the launch by the Soviet Union in October 1957 of the Sputnik satellite. This caused profound disquiet in the United States where it was felt that American cities would now be vulnerable to missile attack and that America had lost its technological lead to the adversary. The US now welcomed co-operation with Britain for its own sake and Eisenhower met Macmillan in Washington to forge a new basis for the relationship. As T. Botti comments on this fundamental change:

> The British were now convinced that the Americans were serious about repealing the remaining McMahon Act restrictions against nuclear co-operation and about building a genuine collective defence against the Soviet threat (Botti, 1987: 201).

A committee was set up under Sir Edwin Plowden to discuss the subject of nuclear collaboration with the Americans and Macmillan believed that co-operation would flow from the agreement as well as putting an end to the wasteful duplication of effort between the two countries.[19] A 'Declaration of Common Purpose' was the immediate result of the Washington Conference and, much to the satisfaction of British officials, was followed in 1958 by the repeal of the McMahon Act. In place of this came legislation that positively discriminated in favour of the British by sanctioning nuclear co-operation with countries who had achieved substantial progress already. The Chiefs could now feel that their arguments in the past for co-operation had been vindicated by events.

By the close of 1957, the Chiefs had gained the level of co-operation with the United States for which they had long sought. This satisfied the threat from global war with the Soviet Union as the British were now enjoying an interdependent relationship with the United States in which they shared in privileged information about all aspects of the American nuclear programme. In November 1957, for example, a team from Strategic Air Command visited Bomber Command in High Wycombe to co-ordinate stategic targeting whilst in December the Americans offered to let Britain purchase a nuclear submarine reactor for their own DREADNOUGHT programme. Britain benefited disproportionately from the relationship in terms of the prestige she gained from this special status with the US, the technology secured for the British nuclear effort and the information extracted on the American strategic plan. In turn, Britain had tied herself further into American policy and limited her own room for independent manoeuvre. Whether Britain would follow such a closely aligned policy in the sphere of conventional forces, as it did in nuclear forces, is the subject of the next section.

Overseas interests and alliance cohesion

The avoidance of global war against the Soviet Union was not the only objective of the policies of the Chiefs of Staff, although it may have been the most important. Below the level of global war, the Chiefs identified a spectrum of threats to Britain's overseas interests that would demand a capacity to respond in the event of limited aggression. There had always been a feeling amongst military planners that the colonies and Commonwealth gave Britain special responsibilities in countering the spread of Communism throughout the world and supporting states, predisposed towards the West, from falling victim to take-over from external threats. The Chiefs believed that it was necessary for Britain to take an active role in the various alliances that had been established NATO, SEATO and the Baghdad Pact for these would provide the backbone of viable defence systems in their respective areas. These alliances would also serve to maintain the cohesion of the pro-Western states against threats of subversion and internal fragmentation.

The policy goal of the Chiefs of Staff was to secure support and leadership from the United States; support of British overseas policy and leadership of the main alliances. America alone possessed the material resources necessary to conduct a global defence policy whereas Britain lacked both the manpower and the economic strength. This weakness on the British part was exacerbated further in 1957 when the Defence Review announced the end of National Service by 1962. The Army was to be reduced to only 165,000 men which was regarded by many, including Sir Gerald Templer,[20] as insufficient to fulfil the commitments that Sandys chose not to cut. Furthermore, cuts were effected in other areas of conventional forces. The surface strength of the Navy was reduced with forces focused around four carrier groups that would maintain the ability to intervene out of the NATO area. The Royal Air Force also suffered cuts in its new aircraft programmes and the size of Fighter Command. As a Joint Planning Staff paper made clear in February, UK contributions to the major alliances were being 'considerably reduced',[21] and renewed emphasis was being placed upon strategic mobility and air transportability. The White Paper made this thinking quite explicit, stating that wars could now be expected to be fought in concert with allies and not independently and that British strength lay in her partnership with friends.[22] In effect, the Chiefs were acknowledging that a large scale conflict would be beyond the resources of a country such as Britain unless she enjoyed the full support of the United States.

In seeking American leadership of the major alliances, the British Chiefs were implicitly stating that UK interests were sufficiently close to that of their partners to rest under the American aegis. This was all the more remarkable considering it came so soon after the Suez affair. The Americans, however, resisted pressure to take a leading role in the alliances and refused to enter into a special planning relationship with their British counterparts. The US Joint Chiefs of Staff were unwilling to be seen to support British colonial policy and desired to give the United Kingdom no special status among its alliance partners. The British pressed for covert discussions outside the regular alliance channels on the grounds that Britain alone shared common membership of all the major alliance systems with the United States. The COS were critical of this American attitude, accusing them of enjoying a free ride at the expense of allies, resting in the stability that resulted from the alliances but avoiding the contributions. The Americans only appeared to welcome co-operation in areas where Britain enjoyed preponderant influence, such as the Middle East, and refused co-operation where they were the dominant force.[23] In 1954 for example, the Americans had encouraged the formation of the Baghdad Pact but drawn back from joining themselves. The COS were eager to secure greater American commitment, men and money to the alliances and gain agreement for US personnel to take over leadership positions in these organizations. In May 1957, the British requested that an American military representative should become the Chief of Staff of the Baghdad Pact.

Apart from the greater cohesion and political benefits that would result from American leadership, the Chiefs believed that there were two important military considerations. Firstly, American nuclear forces would be available to the alliances to deter both limited conflicts as well as escalation to global war. The 1956 White Paper on defence had recognized that nuclear weapons might be necessary in limited wars to defeat overwhelming enemy conventional forces and reduce disparities to manageable levels.[24] As the British were reducing their conventional forces overseas, the potential value of American nuclear forces-in-theatre had increased and the US could offer a tactical nuclear capability in such an area as the Middle East, long before British forces would be available. This was especially important in areas where it would be difficult to reinforce in wartime, where nuclear weapons were the only realistic option against major levels of aggression. Furthermore, nuclear forces provided by the United States would have an important role to play in deterring escalation to global war. The Soviet Union and China would be unlikely to intervene in a regional conflict if US forces were deployed as this might precipitate American nuclear strikes against their homelands. Such an over-arching American deterrent would act as a powerful guarantee of the security of many of the lesser members of SEATO and the Baghdad Pact as well as of NATO.

The second military consideration was the provision of US conventional forces to the alliances. The Chiefs of Staff wanted American forces to provide the core contributions that would help to deter both limited wars and internal subversion. The chiefs recognized that without American assistance, British forces would be critically overstretched and the viability of SEATO and the Baghdad Pact would be uncertain. Britain's contribution to these alliances was largely hypothetical, forces that would be transported to that theatre in wartime rather than forces in-being. The Chiefs privately acknowledged that there would be little likelihood of reinforcing distant theatres in global war because the manpower would not be available. However, the presence of American forces would bridge this credibility gap, would psychologically reassure allies and allow Britain to concentrate her attentions in particular areas. The British were eager to secure from the Americans details of their contingency plans so that the two countries could avoid duplication of effort. The Americans, however, were reluctant to discuss contingency planning with the British and proved unwilling to be tied to formal operational plans. They preferred instead to retain their flexibility, to act as they considered appropriate in any possible emergency. The Chiefs came to suspect that their counterparts did not have detailed plans to discuss with the British and that to seek to be taken into the American confidence, was illusory.[25]

Although the COS struggled to achieve closer co-operation with the United States there was no altering the fact that Britain maintained certain obligations and commitments that would remain outside the alliances she shared with the Americans. For example, Britain had an obligation to the defence of Malaya through the ANZAM alliance which was a unique commitment between Britain, Australia and New Zealand. As ANZAM was a part of the SEATO area, there was a perpetual tension between Britain and the United States over this subsidiary treaty; the Americans regarding it with disapproval as a carry-over from Britain's imperial past. In the words of a Chiefs of Staff report:

> There was anxiety lest support of ANZAM should interfere with the priority need to obtain under SEATO the support in Asian defence of the United States, whose attitude to ANZAM has always been lukewarm.[26]

The Chiefs attempted to get such obligations recognized by all allies as a contribution to the collective defence effort of deterring Communist expansion. Nevertheless, there continued to be a tension in such cases between Britain's national priorities and her alliance efforts. There were also differences between Britain and the United States over their attitudes to various countries which further complicated co-operation. The US Joint Chiefs of Staff, for instance, viewed China as the major threat in the Far East, a power under direction from Moscow. The British, on the other hand, had a more realistic perception of China, acknowledging it as a potential threat but viewing it as independent from Soviet control. In a number of different areas, British and American strategic plans and perceptions were at variance with one another.

These divergences of interest proved to be particularly troublesome, when, from October 1957 onwards, co-operation between Britain and the United States began to broaden and flourish. This was a direct result of the 'powerful psychological shock'[27] experienced in the US over the Sputnik launch and mirrored the closer nuclear collaboration that was being established between the two countries. From this point onwards, the Americans appeared willing to take on the mantle of leadership in SEATO and the Baghdad Pact and proved amenable to discussions on closer co-operation and joint planning. The Chiefs of Staff were eager to capitalize upon this new American zeal and proposed that force between the two nations might be balanced collectively rather than nationally. This would allow for role specialization between the respective armed services and tie the two countries together in an interdependent relationship. Sir Richard Powell, Permanent Secretary at the Ministry of defence, outlined the thinking behind this policy: 'Unless we and the Americans set a lead in establishing forces which were not balanced nationally, nobody else (in the alliances) would.'[28] Yet because of divergent interests the Chiefs could never advocate the sacrifice of an independent capability to project force. If Britain wished to maintain her special commitments, she had to retain a national ability to act that was not interdependent with the United States. This remained a tension in British policy—the degree of trust one could enjoy in the US against the need to be able to act alone—for a considerable period of time after 1957.

While acknowledging that differences between the two countries would remain, it is difficult not to be impressed by the success of the British Chiefs of Staff in securing so many of their objectives by the close of 1957. With insufficient national resources to meet the threats that were identified to overseas interests, the British had achieved a level of interdependence with the United States that satisfied these requirements. The Americans had originally resisted British pressures to assume the leadership of SEATO and the Baghdad Pact and had opposed the granting of a special status to Britain itself in joint planning. This attitude was later reversed and the British came to enjoy a disproportionately large degree of influence. That this was attained at the very time when Britain was reducing her conventional forces overseas and the ability of her armed services to act globally, was indeed a reflection of the skills of British diplomacy.

Conclusion

The year 1957 marked a watershed in Anglo-American relations and upon this foundation, a military alliance characterized by co-operation and reciprocity, was developed. Despite the events of the previous year, a number of factors brought Britain and the United States together, including the desire of President Eisenhower to repair the relationship and the launching of a satellite by the Soviet Union. These events were largely outside British control but the contribution made on this side of the Atlantic to the deepening of co-operation was not negligible. After all, Britain's independent efforts in the field of nuclear weapons made, in the words of the 1958 White Paper, co-ordination 'necessary',[29] as she had amassed a substantial deterrent force of her own. Nuclear weapons were to remain the driving force behind continued co-operation particularly in such fields as procurement and targeting. With US THOR missiles shortly to be deployed on national territory, the British were demonstrating their willingness to undertake sacrifices on behalf of this relationship. Similarly, in the conventional field, the Chiefs had argued that Britain alone shared the burden of the three main global alliances with the US and she therefore deserved to enjoy a special intimacy with the Americans. Britain's efforts had indeed been considerable and they deserved recognition.

By the end of the year the British Chiefs of Staff had secured most of what they wanted from the United States. The 'Declaration of Common Purpose' that emerged from the Washington Conference in October promised Britain a special status above all America's allies. In the following year, the United States repealed the McMahon Act to enable privileged access by Britain to America's nuclear programme and the United States acceded to British requests to play a greater role in the three main alliance systems. The COS could now regard the threats to British interests with a measure of equanimity from the level of global war to the lowest level of subversion. This form of interdependence with a more powerful ally could give Britain confidence in her own security at a time when she was reducing the proportion of national resources devoted to defence. With the abolition of National Service and the reductions by Sandys in all forms of conventional forces, Britain was less able to maintain her commitments around the world and would therefore need American help more than ever before.

There was, however, a price to pay for this interdependence. By tying herself to the United States, Britain was limiting her capacity for independent action. In limited wars, the Chiefs had to accept that they could not undertake major operations without assistance; a situation made more sensitive by the continuation of different interests between Britain and the United States. There was also the realization that influence was a two-edged sword, for the United States would now have a voice in British planning. Changes, for instance, in future British force levels would have to be justified to American colleagues. In the nuclear field, Britain was moving closer towards a dependency relationship with the United States in the production of nuclear delivery systems. Already by the end of 1957, Britain was placing reliance upon a single ballistic missile system that would supersede the

V-bomber force and this required technological information from across the Atlantic. Later in 1960, Britain was to take the decision to depend upon an American missile, SKYBOLT, with all the attendant dangers of reliance upon a foreign country. But this line of argument presumes there was an alternative for Britain by seeking to pursue its defence interests independently. In reality, faced with a situation in which resources were contracting and commitments remained undiminished, it is plain to see why the Chiefs of Staff considered this new-found co-operation with the United States to be in Britain's interest.

Notes

1. Command 124, 'Defence: outline of future policy', HMSO, London, 1957.
2. DEFE 5/80 COS 57 (280) 19/12/57, 'Minimum essential forces required for period until 1963'.
3. DEFE 4/96 JP(57) 28 Final 22/3/57, 'CPX 7' p. 4.
4. Command 124, 'Defence: outline of future policy', HMSO, London, 1957 p. 2.
5. DEFE 6/45 JP(57) Note 12 21/10/57, 'Common defence policy for the UK/US', p. 2.
6. DEFE 4/101 COS(57) 81st Meeting 21/10/57, 'Anglo-US defence policy', p. 3.
7. FO 371/129309 17/4/57, 'Sandys speech to House of Commons'.
8. DEFE 4/101 COS(57) 81st Meeting 21/10/57, 'Anglo-US defence policy', p. 2.
9. DEFE 4/101 JP(57) 135th Meeting 6/11/57, 'NATO Minimum force studies'.
10. DEFE 4/96. COS(57) 24th Meeting 28/3/57, 'Overall strategic concept'.
11. For further details about the size of Britain's nuclear armoury at this time see: J. Simpson *The Independent Nuclear State: The United States, Britain and the Military Atom*, Macmillan, London, 1983, p. 110.
12. DEFE 5/70. COS(56) 276, 'The size of the deterrent', p. 2.
13. DEFE 4/94. COS(57) 3rd Meeting 8/1/57, 'Co-ordination of USAF and RAF nuclear strike plans'.
14. AIR 8/2046, Chancellor of the Exchequer letter to Minister of Defence 24/11/56.
15. DEFE 4/101 COS(57) 81st Meeting 21/10/58, 'Anglo-US defence policy', p. 4.
16. AIR 8/2046, 29/11/56, Letter from VCAS to CAS.
17. FO371/129306, Record of a meeting held at the Pentagon, 28/1/57.
18. FO 371/129309 17/4/57, Sandys speech to House of Commons, p. 8.
19. Macmillan, H. '*Riding the Storm 1956–1959*', Macmillan, London, 1971, p. 323.
20. AIR 8/2046 4/12/56, Minutes of discussion between the Minister of Defence and the Chiefs of Staff.
21. DEFE 6/45, JP(57) Note 2. 1/2/57, 'Long term defence policy', p. 10.
22. Command 124, 'Defence: outline of future policy', HMSO, London, 1957, p. 2.
23. DEFE 5/60 COS(55) 213 30/8/55, 'Exchange of military information with the US', par. 9.
24. Command 9691, 'Statement on defence, 1956', HMSO, London, 1956, p. 4. 'Equally we have to be prepared for the outbreak of localised conflicts on a scale short of global war. In such limited wars the possible use of nuclear weapons cannot be excluded'.

25. DEFE 6/33 JP(55) Note 20, 11/10/55, 'Anglo-American strategic policy', p. 2.
26. DEFE 5/78 COS (57) 219 12/11/57, 'The future of ANZAM', p. 2.
27. DEFE 4/100 COS (57) 77th Meeting 8/10/57, 'Earth satellite', p. 1.
28. DEFE 4/101 COS (57) 81st Meeting 21/10/57, 'Anglo/US defence policy', p. 2.
29. Command 363 'Britain's contribution to peace and security', HMSO, London, 1958.

References

Botti, T. (1987), *The Long Wait. The Forging of the Anglo-American Nuclear Alliance 1945–1958*, New York, Greenwood Press.

Cable, J. (1983), 'Interdependence: a drug of addiction?', *International Affairs*, 59, Summer 1983.

Martin, L. (1962), 'The market for strategic ideas in Britain', *American Political Science Review*, March 1962.

Navias, M. (1988), 'Strengthening the deterrent? the British medium bomber force debate 1955–1956', *Strategic Studies*, 11(2).

Rosencrance, R. and Dawson R. (1966), 'Theory and reality in the Anglo-American alliance', *World Politics*, 19, October 1966.

13 The state of the literature on post-war British history

Peter Catterall

It is now over 40 years since the end of the Second World War. 1945 no longer constitutes an insuperable barrier beyond which the writing and teaching of history must not venture. Nor should it, for the period since has been one of tremendous change. This is indeed the case in almost all departments of post-war British history. It is perhaps particularly true of Britain's role and status in world affairs. Britain has ceased to be one of the Big Three and become part of the European Twelve. The historiography of the period may disagree on those fruitful grounds of controversy, the when, how, and why of the ebbing of Britain's power, but there is no dispute over its dramatic nature.

Changes in British society, the history as it is experienced by the ordinary citizen, have however been scarcely less dramatic. New problems, such as race relations, have appeared. The character of education and mass communication has been transformed. No less significant has been the great increase in the affluence of the average citizen, despite the slow growth of Britain's economy. Post-war rationing has been replaced by a credit-card society, increased leisure, mass tourism and second homes in Marbella, with all the accompanying implications for the survival of Britain's class system.[1]

The very environment we inhabit has meanwhile been radically altered. The skyscrapers that jostle round St Paul's, the re-developed centres of provincial cities, the motorways that snake across the countryside and in the countryside itself, the torn up hedgerows and the retirement villas, all bear silent witness to the processes of change. No less eloquent are the vanished features of the landscape, such as the mills and pithead gantries that once dominated the south Lancashire skyline. It is these changes that form the backdrop to Britain's current situation and the current decisons that will shape the future, and it is these changes that the literature of post-war history must observe and reflect.

Interest in the post-war era has been stimulated in recent years by the apparent challenge to the post-war consensus mounted by the Thatcher government over the past decade. Objectives born in the light of the social and economic problems of the inter-war years—such as full employment or regional development—seem to have been abandoned. Emphasis has instead been placed on controlling the trade unions, privatizing state industries, and encouraging private enterprise and profit. This programme is founded upon the government's reading of the causes of Britain's relative economic decline. Of all the problems which the post-war historian has to address this is the most fundamental, and it has inspired a steadily growing body of literature since the 1960s. Although there remains much dispute over the course and chronology of this decline,[2] and of the success of the Thatcher experiment to combat it, this is nevertheless a clear instance of the importance of contemporary historical discussion to current politics.

The novel features of the Thatcher government have meanwhile also attracted considerable attention. In the process the break it has supposedly made with the past has stimulated increasing interest in themes such as the post-war consensus or the post-war practice of Cabinet government. It would be wrong to conclude however that interest in the history of the post-war period is a recent phenomenon. The fact that there is still reluctance to teach the period, both in schools and universities, does not mean that there has not been much written about it.

The proliferation of academic journals since the war has helped to ensure an abundance of post-war historiography. This is not so much because the number of historical journals has increased at roughly the same rate as academic periodicals in general. Historical journals, with the exception principally of the *Journal of Imperial and Commonwealth History*, the *Journal of Contemporary History*, *Albion*, and the *Journal of British Studies* have in the main only recently begun to carry articles on the post-war period. However, useful articles can also be found in a number of journals which are not principally historical in flavour. Politics journals, such as *Parliamentary Affairs*, or the *Political Quarterly* often contain material of interest. So do journals such as *New Community* which is concerned with race relations, or the *British Journal of Industrial Relations*.

The gradual appearance of such specialist journals has reflected the growth in recent years of academic departments concerned with such subjects as industrial relations or social policy. Some of these fields are therefore already reasonably well served by bibliographies. There is however as yet no good historical bibliography for the period. *Historical Abstracts*, published by ABC–Clio Information Services, gives good coverage of articles. Both the Royal Historical Society's *Annual Bibliography of British and Irish History* and the Institute of Historical Research's *Writings on British History* (still not beyond work published in 1973–4) are general in scope and very selective when it comes to post-war material. The Historical Association's *Annual Bibliography of Historical Literature* is often more informative but is broader in scope and variable in quality. In view of these deficiencies it is not surprising that it is not so much the lack of literature, as the lack of general awareness of it that is the main problem. This is something which the Institute of Contemporary British History's forthcoming *Bibliography of British History 1945–1987* should do much to remedy.

The gradual appearance of the official documents at the Public Record Office under the thirty-year rule is meanwhile encouraging an increasing number of substantial monographs on the early part of the post-war period. These include major studies of the Attlee government by Kenneth Morgan and Henry Pelling.[3] Much of the existing literature was however written without the benefit of access to these files. Not all historiographical endeavour, whatever some historians may think, is however dependent upon the good offices of the PRO. There are other sources that can be drawn upon in the interim, such as parliamentary papers, official statistics, or replies to parliamentary questions, all of which can and have been put to good effect. Some Committee and Royal Commission reports are also very useful not just as primary sources but also because of the assessment of the historical background and current situation they provide and because of the original research they sometimes generate. The research conducted for the Royal Commission on the Distribution of Income and Wealth between 1974 and 1979 is a case in point.

The published findings of government research units and the research conducted on the government's behalf by university departments also provide useful raw material. An example is the three-volume *Investigation of Difficult to Let Housing* published by the Department of the Environment's Housing Development Directorate in 1980–1.[4] The government has also encouraged the writing of a number of historical studies. The official peacetime series has admittedly been somewhat disappointing (Gooch, 1988: 43). It has produced major and detailed monographs but it has rarely done so in advance of the release of the relevant documents. There are however other studies of the development and outcome of policies, such as the histories of various New Towns that appeared in the 1970s, that escape this objection.[5] A number of the other New Town histories were specially commissioned by the various Development Corporations.[6] Much of the rest of the literature on subjects such as the New Towns or housing has focused upon social and economic developments unlikely to be elucidated by the release of the public records. Certainly the papers released so far do not seem to have required any major reappraisal of the existing historiography of the New Towns programme.

It is the question of how far the development of the New Towns, and the resulting migration of population from the city centres, has contributed to the current problems of the inner cities, rather than the release of documents, that has led to some revision of the previously received view of this programme in recent years.[7] The problems of the inner cities, which have replaced New Towns on the government agenda since the late 1960s, have meanwhile attracted increasing attention. There are already a number of studies of the development of government policy on this issue. While it is conceivable that the eventual release of the records will lead to the supersession of these works as histories of policy-formulation, the expression the best of these give to the environment to which it was addressed and the contemporary perception of government intervention will remain of permanent value.

The formulation and expression of urban policy is to a large extent conducted within the public domain. There are however other areas of recent history which are clearly affected by lack of access to the records. The release of the records has for instance led to considerable reassessment of the post-war development of economic policy. Keynesianism has been under attack not only in contemporary politics but in contemporary historiography and the conventional wisdom that there was a 'Keynesian Revolution' in Whitehall during and after the Second World War has been somewhat modified.[8]

No area of historiography is however as affected by lack of access to the public records as diplomatic history. Recently released British diplomatic papers have led to a flood of studies which have not only served to illuminate the strategic considerations behind the British position in the Middle East in the years before Suez, but also the British contribution to the development of the Cold War. The historiography of the post-war confrontation between East and West was for a longtime dominated by American scholars who minimized the British role. It is only since the release of the papers that the British part in important preliminaries to Cold War, such as the creation of the joint British-American zone in Germany, or the background to NATO has been increasingly appreciated and reassessed.[9]

Even in the area of diplomatic and defence history however the release of the records does not always lead to this kind of new insight. For instance the recent release of papers relating to the Suez crisis has not substantially amended the picture which had already emerged from memoirs and other accounts (Seldon, 1988: 4). These early accounts, often based on a particular branch of oral history known as discreet information, retain their value. Clearly the extent to which the thirty-year rule handicaps the writing of post-war history should not be exaggerated. As Keith Middlemas (1986: 2) has pointed out:

> As far as documentation is concerned the gap can partly be made good from the archives which are, in any case, necessary to complement government papers and offset the various sorts of administrative bias they contain. Beyond that lies the whole area of oral history, the immensely valuable but still underused memories of participants and those recently retired from politics, business, civil service or the labour or financial sectors . . .

Oral history can not only flesh out the rather dry picture that emerges from the papers. It should be remembered that much business is now transacted on the telephone and is in danger of passing unrecorded. Record-keeping anyway is often less thorough than historians would wish. The early tapping of memories is an important way of remedying these defects.

The development of oral archives in recent years means that in some areas of post-war history the written record can now be supplemented by the collected memories of the great and the good. A good example is the Oxford Development Records Project at Rhodes House, Oxford, the objects of which include the taping and transcribing of interviews with people connected with the Colonial Service. Few areas of elite oral history have however been approached so systematically. There has been a considerable amount of work undertaken by institutions such as the Open University Media Library. However extensive, systematically compiled oral archives remain largely the province of those working in special areas such as colonial or military history. The collections of the National Sound Archives and the BBC in no way form an oral equivalent of the Public Record Office. Lack of funding has thus far prevented the Institute of Contemporary British History from fulfilling its ambition of remedying this deficiency.

Many local oral history collections leave much to be desired. Too frequently they offer little of interest on the post-war era for even the most parochial of contemporary historians. Nor are they always well organized. Some local oral history projects supported either by institutions of higher education or by local authorities are however substantial undertakings with clearly defined areas of interest and classification systems. A number of these are of considerable value not only for local historians but also for those wishing to investigate particular areas of contemporary history. There is, for example, quite a lot of useful material on immigration at the Bradford Heritage Recording Unit.

There are a number of other historical genres which have either appeared or flourished in the post-war era. It is not impossible to find 'instant' histories of particular events, such as the General Strike,[10] from the inter-war period, but these have certainly become much more common since the war. Some of these betray journalistic origins. At the very least however these accounts convey something of the contemporary reaction to the Aberfan disaster or the Profumo Affair.[11] In the murky area of political and financial scandals instant histories indeed remain in many cases the only literature on the subject. However, despite the substantial monographs that have begun to appear on British policy in Palestine since the release of the official papers,[12] even so slight a narrative as Arthur Koestler's 1949 publication retains some value as an account of the atmosphere at the end of the mandate.[13] It might of course be necessary to treat even the most scrupulous works of this kind as, at best, provisional, to be checked as and when possible against diaries, memoirs and documentary sources (Barnes, 1988: 45–6). Lawrence Freedman's comments on the long-term value of the many instant histories of the Falklands war (1987: 34–5):

> When the PRO opens its 'Falkland files' it will not be simply a question of comparing the new version of events with the old version. The files will require a knowledge of the contemporary commentary to help interpret them. The impressions of what was going on, the relationship between the key personalities, will still be recorded in the instant histories in a way which even the surviving participants will be unable to recall in 2013.

nevertheless also hold good for instant histories of economic policy making or of the negotiations to join the European Community.[14]

The other main type of instant history, accounts of industrial conflicts, pre-eminently the miners' strike of 1984–5, is in some ways even more useful. Not all industrial disputes are as scrupulously recorded at the time as the Upper Clyde Shibuilders work-in, where the taped transcripts of deliberations have since formed the basis of a substantial account.[15] In many cases the instant history is likely to remian the authoritative record. Instant histories like Raphael Samuel, Barbara Bloomfield and Guy Boanas' collection of oral testimony, diaries, and letters relating to the 1984–5 strike can in fact help to preserve the record.[16] Many are also principally insider accounts.[17] This means that caution is required in treating these accounts as history, though the nature of the bias is at least usually easy to discern. It however also means that these accounts remain most useful as sources.

Another genre that has been growing in value has been that of business history. Much that is written in this field remains of the in-house variety. A number of the works on motor and aircraft manufacturers are moreover the product of enthusiasts (this is also very much the case in most branches of transport history) more interested in design than in business history per se. Furthermore the coverage is rather patchy. There is an abundance of literature, as might be expected, on the communications industry and also on motor and aircraft manufacturing. The politically sensitive and economically powerful pharmaceuticals and tobacco industries however seem to have received scant attention, as yet, from business historians.[18] So has the consumer durables industry. There are as yet, very few histories of building societies. The weaknesses of the British electrical appliances industry, in stark contrast to those of the motor industry, have also received little attention. The lack of attention the electronics, with the exception of information technology, industry has received is even more surprising. There are few histories of major companies in this field despite the challenge of attempting to explore the important relationship between many of these companies and the Ministry of Defence. The efforts of the Business Archives Council to ensure the preservation and use of company archives,[19] the advent of the periodical *Business History*, and the growth of business history as a serious academic discipline are nevertheless all encouraging post-war trends.

So is the growing number of autobiographies, memoirs and diaries that have appeared. Although the Thatcher years have thus far proved rather unproductive in this respect[20] the post-war historian is much better served by material of this kind than those of earlier periods. The resolution of the Crossman Affair in a satisfactory manner as far as the post-war historian is concerned, has perhaps been of particular value in bringing about this happy situation. Now, well before the records are released, we have available as sources three substantial Cabinet diaries of the 1964–70 Wilson government,[21] plus Wilson's own well-used account[22] and a substantial number of ministerial memoirs.[23] These diaries certainly have their drawbacks. Reflecting the personalities and perspectives of their authors, they sometimes offer rather different versions of the same event. As diaries they are prone to reflect prejudices and omissions as well as objective facts. They are also far from being universally reliable.[24] Nevertheless they convey the atmosphere and antagonisms of the government in a way which is scrupulously avoided in consensually recorded Cabinet minutes. There is indeed no reason to suppose that these minutes are any more objective or accurate. Furthermore, defective though political diaries may be as records of events, as insights into the perspectives, activities and attitudes of the prime movers of these events they remain indispensable.

The value of many of the autobiograhies and memoirs of the post-war years is enhanced, at least within the thirty-year period, by the privileged access to the official papers enjoyed by their authors. Even after the 30 years have elapsed they can sometimes remain the only source of certain events (Barnes, 1988: 36). So far Labour politicians have perhaps been more forthcoming than their Conservative counterparts, whilst Liberals and Nationalists have been far less productive.

It is not only politicians who write useful memoirs. Civil servants, with the exceptions of diplomats and colonial administrators, may still be rather reluctant to commit themselves to print and, too often, depressingly bland when they do so. Journalists however suffer no such scruples, and their memoirs sometimes supply most useful insights into the operation of government, foreign policy, industrial relations or whatever their specialist area of interest, as well as developments in their own industry.[25] The memoirs of lawyers and judges, though far less numerous, can also help to illustrate the workings of the legal system, the background to important judicial decisions, and in the case of figures like Lord Radcliffe, the work of the many committees of inquiry on which he sat or chaired.[26] The memoirs of scientists are also of considerable value in the unravelling of science policy and nuclear weapons and energy policy[27] as well as for historians of science. Another area which is well stocked with autobiographies, mostly of dubious value, is that of sport. The armed services have produced a good number of campaign memoirs [28]. There are however relatively few autobiographies of service figures in the forces. This is also true of senior figures in, for instance, the police, the City, or in industry. There have however been relatively few memoirs by senior figures in, for instance, the police, the City or in industry.[28]

There is nevertheless a vast amount of historiographical material on the post-war era. The post-war period is in fact in some ways comparatively well covered. For instance, there is certainly far more literature on the Thatcher government, whatever its quality, than on the early nineteenth century government of Lord Liverpool, whose tenure of Prime Ministerial office Mrs Thatcher has yet to exceed.

A number of areas of post-war history are particularly well covered. There is, for instance, an enormous amount of literature on all aspects of the Troubles in Northern Ireland, from the difficulties of managing housing policies in a situation of civil unrest to the level of Irish American support, in terms of money, arms and influence, for the Republicans. There are obvious reasons for this saturation coverage. The history of the Province before 1968, if attracting less attention, has however not been neglected.

The process of decolonization has also received substantial attention. The historiography of this process has been complicated both by the need to account for the speed of change and by the differing perspectives born of the colonial legacy. Much of the material has been written by Commonwealth historians for whom independence has cast new light on the colonial past. For instance, Indian historians now often refer to the 1857 Mutiny as a war of independence. The Mau Mau emergency in Kenya is sometimes treated in similar fashion. Only gradually is both this and the similarly misleading contemporary government picture of irrational and evil thugs giving way to a more plausible account of the nature and causes of the rising and its part as the backdrop to the independence process.[29]

The other major issue, the historiography of which has been complicated by post-independence perspectives, is the partition of India. As the background to the tense and often bloody relations between India and Pakistan since 1947 it has remained an emotive issue, generating a massive amount of literature. The historiography on the subject is still littered with mutual recriminations. Pakistani historians are resentful of what they see as British hostility to the Muslims both at the time and subsequently, and criticize British historians for their treatment of Jinnah and of the partition process.[30] Indian historians on the other hand detect signs of a nefarious game of divide and quit on the part of the British, pointing to the encouragement the British gave to the Muslim League as a counterweight to the Congress during the War both as evidence and as the crucial background to the demand for a separate Muslim state.[31]

Controversy of a rather different kind surrounds one of the principal debates of post-war history, concerning Britain's withdrawal from empire and diminishing world role. The speed of the process has led to a tendency to focus on key events such as the Accra riots of 1948 or the debacle at Suez.[32] A key event which has perhaps not been sufficiently examined, is the British withdrawal from Palestine and its aftermath. It has nevertheless been argued that the Arab defeat in the 1948 war was much more a defeat for Britain, undermining the Arab goodwill on which the British position in the Middle East depended.[33]

There has perhaps however been too much emphasis on these key events and on the idea that there was something approaching a policy of decolonization, a hypothesis that can only be fully tested when the documents on the scramble out of Africa become available in a few years' time. Nor have all the conventional assumptions of the large literature on the subject always received as close a scrutiny as might have been expected. It is rightly asserted that Britain consciously strove to maintain her global status during and for the first two decades after the War,[34] a policy which is often portrayed, slightly more contentiously, as both misguided and as a major contributory factor in Britain's post-war economic decline. The question of whether it would have been feasible for Britain to relinquish her global responsibilities any quicker than was in fact the case, assuming that success in war had not obscured from the Foreign Office the dwindling strength that has been all too obvious to subsequent historians, has however received scant attention. Nor have the economics of Britain's declining ability to meet her imperial commitments always been examined in sufficient detail. Too often the role of economic difficulties in imperial decline has been assumed rather than analysed. Furthermore those studies which have been made do not always support the tenets of the conventional arguments.[35] There is a need for more work of this kind to examine the economics of Britain's post-war global commitments in greater detail.

The other area of this otherwise well covered subject which has perhaps been rather neglected is the post-independence relations of Britain with its former colonies and dependent territories, particularly those in the Caribbean and, more importantly in the Gulf.[36] The consequences of imperial withdrawal for Britain and the world have not always been properly assessed.

Cultural history is, like the end of empire, a relatively well covered area of post-war history. This is particularly true of literary history in the period. Already attempts have been made to provide historical reassessments of perhaps the major theme in this subject area, the Angry Young Men of the 1950s.[37] Cultural history in general has also been better served than any subject other than high politics by the diligence of the biographer.

The literature on developments in post-war education is also fairly comprehensive. This is partly because the large amount of post-graduate work in the field of education studies generates a regular stream of theses on almost all conceivable aspects of post-war education. The number of theses on all aspects of post-war history is in fact most encouraging.

The debate on the quality and role of education in Britain since the 1960s[38] is however as yet hardly discernable in the historiography. Apart from in the context of its role in the creation and perpetuation of an anti-industrial culture the question of whether the deficiencies of Britain's education system has been a factor in economic decline has hardly been considered.[39] The concern with vocational training in recent years and the evidence of skill shortages in British industry[40] however suggest that it should be considered in this context, not least because Britain's economic decline is without doubt the key issue in post-war historiography and any avenue which can help to explain this process should be explored. In the light of the critique represented by the 1988 Education Reform Act it is also clearly high time that the quality of post-war education was re-examined. Too much of the literature on this subject is focused on policy-making and administration rather than education's social and economic impact.

The same is true to some extent of the literature on social history in general. The focus is more often on social policy rather than on people's lifestyles, living conditions or habits. The creation of the Welfare State has been rightly emphasized as undoubtedly one of the major themes of these years. Nevertheless something of the humanizing tendency oral history has brought to our understanding of late nineteenth century social history is still needed for the post-war period. We need to put ordinary people back into history. There are general histories of the Fifties, Sixties and Seventies, often of the coffee table variety, which recapitulate the fashion and mood of those years. In all the vast literature on housing however, while there is plenty of material on the de-humanizing architecture of the 1960s there is hardly anything on something so mundane but significant, to ordinary people, as the spread of central heating. The encouragement the 1956 Clean Air Act gave to this development is not reflected in the literature on the subject,[41] which tends to focus on policy-making and environmental impact, missing out its impact on millions of homes. Suprisingly little has in fact been written on the changing character of Britain's homes.

The related, and currently very controversial subject of post-war architecture, has received rather more attention. Too much of the literature however is in the form of catalogues.[42] Relatively few of the works on the subject reflect on the issues which dominate this current debate about the quality, impact on the environment and humanity or otherwise of recent British architecture (and also of post-war town-planning). The remedying of the lack of adequate biographical treatment of important figures such as Sir Basil Spence or Erno Goldfinger, and further historical enquiry into the character of post-war architecture would help to enrich this debate.

Rationing is another neglected theme.[43] So is the development of the consumer society that has evolved since rationing ceased in the 1950s. This development has been accompanied by a growing amount of leisure and leisure facilities, and by changes in consumption habits. These changes have yet to be analysed in depth. It is now time that youth cultures, continental holidays, or changes in social attitudes were subjected to historical rather than almost exclusively sociological treatment. Other trends have received next to no attention. Despite its long past and recent dramatic growth there is no history of vegetarianism in this country. The growing concern over animal welfare, spawned in part by increasingly intensive farming methods, has been similarly neglected.

Recent governmental concern over levels of alcohol abuse has also failed to prompt the sort of interest that has been shown in drug control policies.[44] Despite similar government concern crime in general in the post-war period is yet to receive much historical attention. Such work as there is available tends to be either Home Office material or to focus particularly on violent, as opposed to other sorts of crimes.[45]

The literature on post-war religious history is similarly patchy. Although church history has not been badly covered greater consideration of other faiths is also now required.[46]

A number of themes in post-war economic history remain similarly unexplored. For instance, the interest shown in balance of payments crises has not been matched on issues such as the nature and promotion of trading relations or the fixing of tariffs.

Although there is already a considerable amount of material on recent changes in the City, its post-war success in maintaining its place in the international money markets could be more fully investigated. Despite its power, the workings of the City, like those of the Civil Service, remains an arcane and under-explored subject. Some sections of the financial world have been particularly neglected. The most important of these is accountancy. The role of the City in Britain's economic decline has rightly received considerable attention. Accountancy however has yet to be considered in this context. Its influence upon business activity, not least in comparison with the United Kingdom's competitors, the dramatic growth of the profession since the 1930s, and the disproportionate number of graduates it attracts nevertheless suggests that the time for such an investigation is over-ripe. As one commentator put it (Welsh, 1986: 167); 'That so many of our brightest young people . . . can seek no finer end than to be bookkeepers is disturbing enough, but the consequences are even more so.'

There are also other aspects of this problem of economic decline which merit further investigation. The concern about the 'Brain Drain' of scientists and technologists which led to the setting up of the Jones Committee in the 1960s, and which continues to be expressed,[47] has not been adequately reflected in the literature on economic decline. Nor has the question of whether this problem has had a serious affect on innovation, research and development in British industry been properly addressed.

The dramatic changes in working conditions in factories, shops and offices over the post-war era, particularly under the impact, in recent years of information technology, have also yet to be chronicled. Even the important developments in health and safety at work legislation in the period have received relatively little attention.[48] The same is true of the growing importance, as an earner of foreign currency, and success of the British tourist industry. The question as to how much this success is due to government-interventions, through agencies like the British Tourist Board, has been particularly overlooked. This is also largely true of Cod War, despite the considerable impact it had on the fishing industry and on the British attitude towards the concept of territorial waters.[49] The energy industries also merit further investigation. North Sea oil and gas apart, even so sensitive an issue as nuclear energy seems to have attracted less attention than might have been expected.

Although the literature on local government in the period is vast, analysis of the fire services or the water authorities meanwhile remains, to a large extent, confined to the standard textbooks on the subject. Water privatization will perhaps stimulate more interest in the latter in the next few years. Parliamentary papers meanwhile remain the best source of information on developments in the fire services.

Another gap in the literature on local government is the decline in the quality of local political life. The fiscal squeeze on local authorities under the Thatcher government and the resulting conflicts has encouraged an emphasis on central/local relations which has tended to obscure other developments. From a nineteenth century perspective however the most remarkable characteristic of modern local government is its diminished power and prestige. This decline requires more investigation. Such material as there is on the lamentably low turnout in local elections, and the general public's ignorance of the personalities and functions of local government[50] also suggests that there is need for more studies on local government's relations with local community as well as with Westminster.

The dwindling quality of the local press in the course of the twentieth century has perhaps been a major factor in this decline in local political life. The local media however hardly feature in the large literature on broadcasting and the press, except in the form of a few rather anodyne in-house histories. There are, as yet, scarcely any studies of this decline in quality and of its impact on local government and the local community, nor of the apparent failure, thus far, of the local radio services and the new free newspapers that have appeared in recent years to make good this deficiency. There is clearly still much work to be done on the history of Britain since the Second World War.

Nor is the literature on post-war history always entirely satisfactory from the historian's point of view. Much of what has been written in such areas as public order, policing or race relations, is distinctly partisan, if not polemical in flavour. Equally serious is the ahistorical method that is often adopted. The historical approach, the well documented attempt to explain what actually happened and why, has been, in much of the existing literature on certain fields of post-war history, subsumed in a theoretical framework.

Too often in political and social science texts the empirical evidence is treated as secondary to the theory. As Paul B. Rich pointed out (1988: 355) in reviewing a 'highly generalised' argument that racism in the foundry industry in the 1940s and 1950s was the result of the importation of colonial relations; this

> simply remains a general sociological hypothesis so typical of work in race relations. But it may well come to be treated as *fact* by students of race. The challenge to historians for more detailed and rigorous research in this area thus remains.

Many political science textbooks also tend to be unsatisfactory from the historian's point of view. A few may retain a certain value as snapshots of the state of government and politics in Britain. Too many however are rather bloodless creations, which describe the form but do not convey the substance. Their tendency to focus almost exclusively on developments since 1945 is also potentially misleading. The distance between the National government, which pioneered regional development policy, albeit somewhat ineffectively, and nationalized BOAC, and the Attlee government should not be exaggerated.

Electoral historians could perhaps also benefit by developing a greater appreciation of the pre-war era. This is not to denigrate work such as the excellent Nuffield series of studies on post-war general elections. The contemporaneity of these studies and their privileged access to information has ensured that they have fulfilled their intended function of providing an authoritative and durable account of each general election since 1945. This is contemporary history at its best. Research into long-term changes in electoral behaviour however seems to have been constrained by the limitations electoral historians seem to have decided the lack of adequate opinion poll data until after the Second World War places upon their work.

The principal debate in electoral history currently, focuses on partisan dealignment since the 1950s.[51] The main facet of electoral patterns since then is seen as the decline in class-based voting. There is certainly much truth in this analysis. However the idea underlying most of this literature, that there is some sort of normative class-based voting pattern that has gradually been eroded, seems misleading. The electoral history of the immediate post-war and 1950s period certainly seems to conform to some extent to this notional pattern. The fact that psephology was then in its infancy and grew up under the shadow of this pattern perhaps accounts for the continuing tendency to treat it as normative. However, viewed within a longer perspective this period appears at best as the apogee of class-based voting. It was unusual rather than typical, and was accentuated by the paucity of Liberal candidates during these years. Its nostrums led commentators of the 1960s to treat the working class Tory voter as a rather unusual phenomenon.[52] However there were large numbers of such voters in the inter-war years, and even in the 1950s the Tory working class vote remained substantial. The growth of this vote since should perhaps be compared, as far as possible, with the inter-war years as well as the 1950s. The question of whether changes in the Labour party have assisted this process by alienating working class voters also needs to be further explored. The emphasis on changes in the working class vote has meanwhile obscured the nature of the middle class vote, particularly the Labour middle class vote, which has yet to receive the attention it deserves.

The analysis of partisan dealignment has moreover perhaps been too exclusively concerned with the haemorrhage of votes from the two main parties. A discernable trend towards voting against rather than for a party does not seem to have received sufficient attention yet. Neither has the signs of increasing political apathy and the related important question of why some people do not exercise their constitutional right to vote.

Another difficulty with the literature on post-war history, particularly that on the most recent past, is that it can often prove provisional, easily overtaken by events. Even so good, if committed, a study as Philip Bagwell's account of railway policy under the Thatcher government[53] has been thus affected. The broad outline of his indictment of Conservative hostility to public transport may remain valid. The decision that the Channel Tunnel should provide a rail rather than a road link, apparently against the Prime Minister's wishes, has however necessitated a more positive attitude to the railways in the last few years.

Much of the rest of the literature on the Thatcher government or aspects of its policies may in the long-term prove to be of value only in as far as it reflects the contemporary view. Some of it nevertheless already seems to skate dangerously close to the making of myths. The notion of Thatcherism for instance, so assiduously promoted by the writers on *Marxism Today*,[54] far from giving the opposition a stick with which to beat the Government, as they seem to have mistakenly at one time believed, has flattered the Prime Minister and confirmed her self-image of unswerving pursuit of her objectives. This has tended to obscure the many changes and developments in government policy since 1979 and the cautious, even hesitant way in which the Government has often pursued its goals. Privatization for instance, has been characterized as 'the unexpected crusade' (Grimstone, 1987: 23–5). Some of the initial reactions to the Thatcher years, such as the notion that privatization, and particularly the sale of council houses, has proved a popular vote winner, may also in time seem open to doubt in much the same way that the contribution of the 'Falklands factor' to the Conservatives 1983 election triumph is already being questioned.[55]

This does not mean that history so close to events should not be attempted. Research into the historical background and development of current problems or the record of particular policies is an essential component in future decision-making. More importantly perhaps, history is the collective consciousness of a society, a record and reflection of its nature, failings, progress and aspirations. The literature on post-war history therefore makes a valuable contribution to the debate on contemporary problems and to our awareness of the nature of modern British society. The coverage has of course been variable. The historiography of a period in part reflects the interests of the authors, as well as the relative weight to be attached to various themes. The fact that there has been roughly twice as much written on the Labour party as on the Conservative party in this period seems to illustrate this point.

Nevertheless most of the themes in post-war history have been broached. Some subjects however require greater emphasis. Neglected areas, flawed analysis and inadequate scholarship remain as problems. The thirty-year rule also presents difficulties. The problems it poses are sometimes exaggerated, have little or no impact on areas such as cultural history, and fail to prevent the writing of good institutional histories using original documents such as Keith Middlemas's history of the National Economic Development Office.[56] Much of the literature, however well it maps out themes, will nevertheless have to be checked and reassessed as and when the papers fall due, as has happened in the fields of post-war economic policy and diplomatic history. Important historiographical controversies on economic decline, the end of empire or the nature of the post-war consensus need to be pursued further. There thus remains a full agenda for post-war historians, not least because they are dealing with a period of such dramatic change. It is to be hoped that continuing research will not only help to remedy gaps and deficiencies. Better awareness of the range and quality of the literature on the subject may eventually persuade schools and universities to overcome their general reluctance to teach post-war British history.

Notes

1. See Neil Kinnock's speech to the Labour party conference, *Sunday Times* 27 September 1987.
2. The main lines of argument are represented by works such as S. Pollard, *The Wasting of the British Economy. British Economic Policy 1945 to the present* (2nd ed, Croom Helm, 1984), which emphasizes failure to modernize and the negative impact of government policy, or M. Stewart, *Politics and Economic Policy in the UK since 1964. The Jekyll and Hyde Years* (Macmillan, 1977), which emphasizes adversarial politics. A. Glyn and Bob Sutcliffe, *Workers, British Capitalism and the Profits Squeeze* (Penguin, 1972), focus on the negative influence of trade union strength, while K. Williams, J. Williams and D. Thomas, *Why are the British Bad at Manufacturing?* (Routledge and Kegan Paul, 1983) take a more managerial approach. R. Bacon and W. Eltis, *Britain's Economic Problem: Too Few Producers* (Macmillan, 1978), argues that a major problem is the disproportionate size of the service sector. C. Barnett, *The Audit of War: the Illusion and Reality of Britain as a Great Nation* (Macmillan, 1986), in a famous argument focuses on the growth of welfarism. The emphasis of most of these on the wartime or post-war period is however somewhat misleading. Awareness of relative economic decline certainly

became much more acute in this period. M.W. Kirby, *The Decline of British Economic Power since 1870* (Allen and Unwin, 1981), however shows that relative economic decline dates from the late nineteenth century and that some of the structural flaws that have been identified as responsible were already present. M. Weiner, *English Culture and the Decline of the Industrial Spirit 1850–1980* (Cambridge University Press, 1981), which points to the problem of an anti-industrial culture, takes a similarly long-term view. D. Coates and J. Hillard (eds), *The Economic Decline of Modern Britain. The Debate Between Left and Right* (Wheatsheaf, 1986), usefully collects and edits all the main viewpoints on this most important issue.

3. O. Morgan, *Labour in Power 1945–51*, Oxford University Press, 1984; H. Pelling, *The Labour Governments 1945–51*, Macmillan, 1984.

4. Department of Environment, Housing Development Directorate, *An Investigation of Difficult to Let Housing*, 3v, HMSO, 1980–1.

5. W.V. Hole, I.M. Anderson and M.T. Pountney, *Washington New Town: The Early Years*, HMSO, 1979; R. Smith, *East Kilbride; The Biography of a Scottish New Town 1947–1973*, HMSO 1979; A.A. Ogilvy, *Bracknell and its Migrants. Twenty-One Years of New Town Growth*, HMSO, 1975.

6. H. and J. Parris, *Bracknell: The Making of our New Town*, Bracknell Development Corporation, 1981; J. Balchin, *First New Town. An Autobiography of the Stevenage Development Corporation 1946–1980*, Stevenage Development Corporation, 1980; F. Gibberd, B. Hyde Harvey, I. White *et al*, *Harlow: Story of a New Town*, Publications for Companies, 1980; H. Barty-King, *Expanding Northampton*, Secker and Warburg, 1985; S. Holley, *Washington: Quicker by Quango: The History of Washington New Town 1964–1983*, Publications for Companies, 1983; G. Anstis, *Redditch: Success in the Heart of England. The History of Redditch New Town 1964–85*, Publications for Companies, 1985; P. Riden, *Rebuilding a Valley. A History of Cwmbran Development Corporation*, Cwmbran Development Corporation, 1988.

7. See for instance M. Aldridge, *The British New Towns: A Programme without a Policy*, Routledge and Kegan Paul, 1979.

8. This point of view is best represented in J. Tomlinson, *British Macroeconomic Policy since 1940*, Croom Helm, 1985 and, by the same author, *Employment Policy. The Crucial Years 1939–1955*, Clarendon, 1987.

9. See for instance B. Rubin, *The Great Powers in the Middle East 1941–47: The Road to the Cold War*, Cass, 1980; R. Ovendale (ed), *The Foreign Policy of the British Labour Governments 1945–51*, Leicester University Press, 1984; E. Barker, *The British between the Superpowers 1945–1950*, Macmillan, 1983; A. Deighton 'The "Frozen Front": the Labour Government, the division of Germany and origins of the Cold War', *International Affairs* **63**(3), 1987, pp. 449–65; N. Petersen 'Who pulled whom and how much? Britain, the United States and the making of the North Atlantic Treaty', *Millenium: Journal of International Studies*, **11**(2), 1982, pp. 93–114.

10. R.W. Postgate, E. Wilkinson and J.F. Horrabin, *A Worker's History of the Great Strike*, Plebs League, 1927.

11. Tony Austin, *Aberfan*, Hutchinson, 1967; Clive Irving, Ron Hall & Jeremy Wellington, *Scandal '63: A Study of the Profumo Affair*, Heinemann, 1963. For instance: M. Jones, *Failure in Palestine: British and United States Policy after*

the Second World War, Mansell, 1986; A. Nachmani, *Great Power Discord in Palestine: The Anglo-American Committee of Inquiry into the Problems of European Jewry and Palestine 1945–1946*, Cass, 1987; A. Shlaim, *Collusion across the Jordan. King Abdullah, the Zionist Movement and the Partition of Palestine*, Clarendon, 1988.

13. A. Koestler, *Promise and Fulfilment. Palestine 1917–1949*, Macmillan, 1949.

14. See for instance: H. Brandon, *Into the Red. The Struggle for Sterling 1964–66*, Andre Deutsch, 1966; W. Davis, *Three Years Hard Labour*, Andre Deutsch, 1968 (also on attempts to maintain sterling's value); P. Jenkins, *The Battle of Downing Street*, Charles Knight, 1969 (the crisis over *In Place of Strife*); and M. Camps *Britain and the European Community 1955–63*, Princeton University Press, 1964.

15. The oral material is held at Glasgow University Archives. This has been extensively used in J. Forster and C. Woolfson, *The Politics of the UCS Work-In. Class Alliances and the Right to Work*, Lawrence and Wishart, 1986.

16. R. Samuel, B. Bloomfield and G. Boanas (eds), *The Enemy Within. Pit Villages and the Miners' Strike of 1984–5*, Routledge and Kegan Paul, 1986.

17. See for instance T. Griffiths, *The Teachers' Strike (1969–70)*, National Union of Teachers, 1970; or J. Dromey and G. Taylor, *Grunwick: The Workers' Story*, Lawrence and Wishart, 1978.

18. The best business history in this field is B.W.E. Alford, *W.D. and H.O. Wills and the Development of the UK Tobacco Industry 1786–1965*, Methuen, 1973. A history of Glaxo is in progress.

19. See for instance L. Richmond and A. Turton, *Directory of Corporate Archives*, 2nd ed. Business Archives Council, 1987.

20. The main exceptions being Peter Carrington *Reflect on Things Past. The Memoirs of Lord Carrington*, Collins, 1988; N. Tebbit *Upwardly Mobile. An Autobiography*, Weidenfeld and Nicolson, 1988; James Prior *A Balance of Power*, Hamish Hamilton, 1986.

21. J. Morgan (ed), *The Diaries of a Cabinet Minister* [Richard Crossman] 3 vols, Jonathan Cpe/Hamish Hamilton, 1975–7; Barbara Castle, *The Castle Diaries 1964–70*, Weidenfeld and Nicolson, 1984; Tony Benn, *Out of the Wilderness. Diaries 1963–67*, Hutchinson, 1987, *Office Without Power. Diaries 1968–72*, Hutchinson, 1988.

22. Harold Wilson, *A Personal Record: The Labour Government 1964–1970*, Weidenfeld and Nicolson, 1971.

23. Including Lord Longford, *The Grain of Wheat*, Collins, 1974; Michael Stewart, *Life and Labour. An Autobiography*, Sidgwick and Jackson, 1980; James Callaghan, *Time and Chance*, Collins, 1987; Douglas Jay, *Change and Fortune. A Personal Record*, Hutchinson, 1980; Richard Marsh, *Off the Rails. An Autobiography*, Weidenfeld and Nicolson, 1978; James Griffiths, *Pages From Memory*, Dent, 1969; George Thomas, *Mr Speaker*, Century, 1985; George Wigg, *George Wigg*, Michael Joseph, 1972; George Brown, *In My Way*, Gollancz, 1971.

24. See J. Morgan *et al.* 'Symposium. The Crossman Diaries Reconsidered', *Contemporary Record*, 1(2) Summer, 1987, pp 22–30, and D. Butler 'The Benn Archive', *Contemporary Record* 1(1), Spring 1987, pp 13–4.

25. See for instance T. Barman, *Diplomatic Correspondent*, Hamish Hamilton, 1968; C.L. Sulzburger, *A Long Row of Candles. Memoirs and Diaries 1934–1954*,

Macdonald, 1969; N. Davenport, *Memoirs of a City Radical*, Weidenfeld and Nicolson, 1974; G. Wyndham-Goldie, *Facing the Nation: Television and Politics 1936–1976*, Bodley Head, 1977; L. Mitchell, *Leslie Mitchell Reporting . . .*, Hutchinson, 1981; I. McDonald, *A Man of The Times*, Hamish Hamilton, 1976; L. Heren, *Growing up on 'The Times'*, Hamish Hamilton, 1978; P. Einzig, *In the Centre of Things*, Hutchinson, 1960; H. Cudlipp, *Walking on the Water*, Bodley Head, 1976; J. Cameron, *Point of Departure*, Arthur Barker, 1967; T. Hopkinson, *Of This Our Time*, Hutchinson, 1982; J. Margach, *The Abuse of Power*, W.H. Allen, 1978, and *The Anatomy of Power*, W.H. Allen, 1979.

26. See for instance: Lord Radcliffe, *Not in Feather Beds*, Hamish Hamilton, 1968; J. Pickles, *Straight From the Bench. Is Justice Just?*, Phoenix House, 1987; A. H. Smith, *Lord Goddard: My Years with the Lord Chief Justice*, Weidenfeld and Nicolson, 1959; Lord Wheatley, *One Man's Judgement*, Butterworths, 1987; Lord Denning, *The Family Story*, Butterworths, 1981, and *The Closing Chapter*, Butterworths, 1983.

27. See for instance: O. R. Frisch, *What Little I Remember*, Cambridge University Press, 1979; Sir Rudolf Peierls, *Bird of Passage. Recollections of a Physicist*, Princeton University Press, 1985; Solly Zuckerman, *Monkeys, Men and Missiles. An Autobiography 1946–1988*, Collins, 1988.

28. Notable exceptions include the Commissioners of the Metropolitan Police, Sir Robert Mark, *In the Office of Constable*, Collins, 1978, and Sir David McNee, *McNee's Law*, Collins, 1983; and the former Chairman of BL, Sir Michael Edwardes, *Back From the Brink. An Apocalyptic Experience*, Collins, 1983; Anthony Farrar-Hockley, *The Edge of the Sword*, Muller, 1954 (as Korea), Sandy Cavenagh, *Airborne to Suez*, Kimber, 1965 (Cyprus and Suez), Oliver Crawford, *The Door Marked Malaya*, Rupert Hart-Davis, 1958 (Malayan emergency), Julian Paget, *The Last Post: Aden 1964–67*, Faber, 1969 or Julian Thompson, *No Picnic*, Secker and Warburg, 1985 (the Falklands).

29. A useful recent review article is Frederick Cooper 'Mau Mau and the Discourses of Decolonisation' *Journal of African History*, **29**, 1988, pp. 313–20.

30. See for instance K.K. Aziz, *Britain and Muslim India*, Longmans, 1963; S.H. Raza (ed), *Mountbatten and Pakistan*, Quaid-i-Azam Academy, Karachi, 1982; L.A. Sherwani, *The Partition of India and Mountbatten*, Council for Pakistan Studies, 1986.

31. The best example of this thesis is A. Inder Singh, *The Origins of the Partition of India 1936–1947*, Oxford University Press, 1987.

32. See A. Low and B. Lapping 'Controversy. Did Suez Hasten the End of Empire?', *Contemporary Record*, **1**(2) Summer, 1987, pp. 31–3, and R. Holland's response in *Contemporary Record*, **1**(4), Winter 1988, p. 39.

33. See J. Kimche, *Seven Fallen Pillars. The Middle East 1945–52* 2nd ed, Secker and Warburg, 1953; J. and D. Kimche, *Both Sides of the Hill. Britain and the Palestine War*, Secker and Warburg, 1960; W.R. Louis and R.W. Stookey (eds), *The End of the Palestine Mandate*, I.B. Tauris, 1986.

34. This gave the impression of a long and determined retreat reflected in such titles as F.S. Northedge, *Descent From Power: British Foreign Policy 1945–1973*, Allen and Unwin, 1974, or C.J. Bartlett, *The Long Retreat: A Short History of British Defence Policy 1945–1970*, Macmillan, 1972. Some more recent studies have placed more stress on successful adjustment to the different requirements of the

nuclear age; see F. Gregory, M. Imber and J. Simpson (eds), *Perspectives upon British Defence Policy 1945–1970*, Department of Adult Education, University of Southampton, 1978, or A. Cyr, *British Foreign Policy and the Atlantic Area. The Techniques of Accommodation*, Macmillan, 1979.

35. See for instance D. Greenwood, *The Economics of 'The East of Suez Decision'*, Aberdeen Studies in Defence Economics 2, University of Aberdeen, 1973.

36. The nearest to a study of the latter is J. Whelan (ed) 'UK and the Gulf 1971–1981: a MEED Special Report' *Middle East Economic Digest*, December 1981.

37. See for instance R. Hewison, *In Anger. Culture in the Cold War 1945–60*, Weidenfeld and Nicolson, 1981.

38. See the various Black Papers: C.B. Cox and A.E. Dyson (eds), *Fight for Education*, Critical Quarterly Society, 1969; *Black Paper Two: The Crisis in Education*, Critical Quarterly Society, 1969; *Black Papers on Education*, Davis-Poynter, 1971; C.B. Cox and Rhodes Boyson (eds), *Black Paper 1975: The Fight for Education*, Dent, 1975; *Black Paper 1977*, Temple Smith, 1977.

39. A notable exception is S.F. Cotgrove, *Technical Education and Social Change*, Allen and Unwin, 1958. His opening remarks, 'The present state of trained scientific manpower in England is without precedent. Moreover, in spite of post-war increases in output from the universities and technical colleges, the numbers of trained technologists and technicians in England compare very unfavourably with those in other advanced industrial countries,' remain depressingly accurate. Such warnings however do not seem to have been heeded either by educational historians or, until recently, by politicians, despite the concern that has repeatedly been expressed by learned societies in science and engineering.

40. Attempts to combat this date from the 1964 Industrial Training Act. It should be pointed out that the subsequent development of training policy has been extensively analysed.

41. However see H.A. Scarrow, 'The impact of British domestic air pollution legislation', *British Journal of Political Science* 2(3), 1972, pp. 261–82.

42. Though see L. Esher, *A Broken Wave: The Rebuilding of England 1940–80*, Allen Lane, 1981.

43. Though see A. Harvie, *The Rationed Years*, Regency, 1982.

44. The standard works on drug control are P. Bean, *The Social Control of Drugs*, Martin Robertson, 1974, and N. Dorn and N. South (eds), *A Land fit for Heroin? Drug Policies, Prevention and Practice*, Macmillan, 1987. The standard work on drink remains G. Prys Williams and G. Thompson Brake, *Drink in Great Britain 1900–1979*, Edsall, 1980.

45. T. Morris, *Crime since 1945*, Blackwell, 1989.

46. Though see A. Helweg, *Sikhs in England*, 2nd ed, Oxford University Press, 1986; J. Swinney, *The Hindus in Britain*, Batsford, 1988.

47. Committee on Manpower Resources for Science and Technology, *The Brain Drain: Report of the Working Group on Migration*, (Chairman Dr F.E. Jones), Cmnd 3417, *Parliamentary Papers* xxxix, 1966–67; Science and Engineering Policy Studies Unit, *The Migration of Scientists and Engineers to and from the UK*, The Royal Society/The Fellowship of Engineers, 1987.

48. Though see P.B. Beaumont, *Safety at work and the Unions*, Croom Helm, 1983; P.W.J. Bartrip, *Workman's Compensation in Twentieth Century Britain: Law, History and Social Policy*, Gower, 1987.

49. Though see H. Jonsson, *Friends in Conflict: The Anglo-Icelandic Cod War and the Law of the Sea*, Hurst, 1982.
50. See for instance J. Gyford, *Local Politics in Britain*, Croom Helm, 1976; W.L. Miller, *Irrelevant Elections? The Quality of Local democracy in Britain*, Clarendon, 1988.
51. See for instance: M.N. Franklin, *The Decline of Class Voting in Britain. Changes in the Basis of Electoral Choice 1964–1983*, Oxford University Press, 1985; A. Heath, R. Jowell and J. Curtice, *How Britain Votes*, Pergamon, 1985; R. Rose and I. McAllister, *Voters Begin to Choose: From Closed Class to Open Elections in Britain*, Sage, 1986; B. Sarlvik and I. Crewe, *Decade of Dealignment. The Conservative Victory of 1979 and Electoral Trends in the 1970's*, Cambridge University Press, 1983.
52. See for instance: R.T. Mackenzie and M. Silver, *Angels in Marble: Working Class Conservatives in Urban England*, Heinemann Educational, 1968; E.A. Nordlinger, *The Working Class Tories*, Macgibbon and Kee, 1967.
53. P. Bagwell, *End of the Line? The Fate of British Railways Under Thatcher*, Verso, 1985.
54. See S. Hall and M. Jacques (eds), *The Politics of Thatcherism*, Lawrence and Wishart, 1983; S. Hall, *Thatcherism and the Crisis of the Left. The Hard Road to Renewal*, Verso, 1988.
55. See D. Sanders, H. Ward and D. Marsh 'Government popularity and the Falklands War: a reassessment', *British Journal of Political Science*, **17**, 1987, pp. 281–314; M.N. Franklin and L. Freedman, 'Controversy: The Falklands Factor' *Contemporary Record*, **1**(3) Autumn 1987, pp. 27–9; Helmut Norpoth, 'The Falklands War and government popularity in Britain: rally without consequence or surge without decline?' *Electoral Studies*, **6**, 1987, pp. 3–16.
56. K. Middlemas, *Industry, Unions and Government: Twenty-One Years of the National Economic Development Office*, Macmillan, 1983.

References

Barnes, J. (1988), 'Books and Journals' in A. Seldon (ed), *Contemporary History. Practice and Method*, Basil Blackwell.

Freedman, L. (1987), 'The literature on the Falklands conflict 1982', *Contemporary Record*, 1/2 Summer 1987.

Gooch, J. (1988), 'Missing Histories? The Post-War Official Histories', *Contemporary Record*, 1/4 Winter 1988.

Grimstone, G. (1987), 'Privatisation: the unexpected crusade', *Contemporary Record*, 1/1 Spring 1987.

Middlemas, K. (1986), *Power, Competition and the State. Volume I: Britain in Search of Balance 1940–61*, Macmillan.

Rich, P.B. (1988), review of K. Lunn (ed), *Race and Labour in Twentieth Century Britain*, Cass, 1986, in *History*, 73/238 June 1988.

Seldon, A. (1988), 'Interviews' in Anthony Seldon (ed), *Contemporary History. Practice and Method*, Basil Blackwell.

Welsh, F. (1986), *Uneasy City: An Insider's View of the City of London* Weidenfeld and Nicolson, 1986.

Index